Advance Praise for *Glimpses of Henderson County*

This is a treasure of local heritage, backstories, documents, portraits, little known facts, biography and hidden history. Terry Ruscin has delved into the rich soil and mountain valleys of Henderson County, as no one has before, and delivered a thrilling and memorable tour of both our past and our present.

—*Robert Morgan, author of* The Road from Gap Creek

Once more the flow of history astounds under the melodious pen of Terry Ruscin. He presents a record of eastern and north-central Henderson County, beginning in the Green River Valley to the south then north through Edneyville and Hoopers Creek and environs in between. The sanctity of family names, dates, places and events—hallowed and unique to this area—are again immortalized for the reader's pleasure. Glimpses *is a masterful book by one of our best local writer-researchers.*

—*Ann Greenleaf Wirtz, author of* The Henderson County Curb Market: A Blue Ridge Heritage Since 1924

This is still another well-written volume by Terry Ruscin depicting previously overlooked and unrecorded areas of our local history. The many great photo illustrations allow the reader to go back in time and visit the people and places of yesteryear. We are fortunate in that Terry loves and appreciates our heritage enough to devote the time and talent required to produce a history of this caliber. It is Terry's aim to separate historical facts from lore and exaggerations, which exist. Mission accomplished, Terry. Glimpses *is a must-read and will be appreciated for generations to come.*

—*V. Leon Pace, seventh-generation Henderson County native; vice-president/ office manager, Henderson County Genealogical and Historical Society, Inc.*

Terry Ruscin has created marvelous portals through time, revealing the strength and spirit of those mountain folk forever connected to Henderson County. His glimpses challenge us to look not only to the past but also within ourselves, reminding us that we have our own roles to play before the judge of history.

—*Mark de Castrique, author of* A Murder in Passing

If you think you know Henderson County, read this book. You will be amazed at what you discover. If you don't know much about Henderson County but would like to, read this book. You will be amazed at what you discover.

—*Hilliard Staton, fifth-generation Henderson County native*

GLIMPSES OF HENDERSON COUNTY NORTH CAROLINA

TERRY RUSCIN | Foreword by Hilliard Staton

THE History PRESS

Published by The History Press
Charleston, SC 29403
www.historypress.net

Cover photos by Terry Ruscin.
Unless otherwise credited, all internal photographs are by Terry Ruscin.

First published 2014
Second printing 2014

Manufactured in the United States

ISBN 978.1.62619.693.3

Library of Congress Cataloging-in-Publication Data

Ruscin, Terry, 1951-
Glimpses of Henderson County, North Carolina / Terry Ruscin.
pages cm
Includes bibliographical references and index.
ISBN 978-1-62619-693-3
1. Henderson County (N.C.)--History. 2. Henderson County (N.C.)--History, Local. 3. Historic sites--North Carolina--Henderson County. 4. Henderson County (N.C.)--Social life and customs. 5. Henderson County (N.C.)--Biography. I. Title.
F262.H47R865 2014
975. 6'92--dc23
2014028794

Notice: The information in this book is true and complete to the best of our knowledge. It is offered without guarantee on the part of the author or The History Press. The author and The History Press disclaim all liability in connection with the use of this book.

Dedicated to the memory of Louise King Howe Bailey, Arthur Farrington Baker, Donald McArthur Barber, Joseph Egerton "Jody" Barber, Kermit Edney, James Toole Fain Jr., Frank Lockwood FitzSimons, Roy "Bush" Laughter, Charles Lenoir Ray, Lucile Stepp Ray and Dorothy (Kelly) "Dot" MacDowell Wood.

CONTENTS

Contents

Contents

FOREWORD

After reading Terry Ruscin's *Hidden History of Henderson County*, published in 2013, many asked for more and eagerly awaited his next work. Well, here it is: an extensive, fast-moving collection of names, dates and places that represent a tour de force presentation—another example of meticulous research and attention to detail that illustrate Ruscin's determination to recapture the past before it altogether fades into oblivion.

This book takes in essentially the eastern half of Henderson County, running from Green River, up through Edneyville and Fruitland and then on to Hoopers Creek in words and pictures—including an entire chapter devoted to mysteries and the sinister.

If you think you know Henderson County, read this book. You will be amazed at what you discover. If you don't know much about Henderson County but would like to, read this book. You will be amazed at what you discover. I learned a great deal from it, and I grew up in Hendersonville with a grandfather who served as sheriff, mayor of Hendersonville, postmaster, judge and lifelong attorney.

If this excellent work of history leaves you thirsting for more, take heart; more volumes are planned. When they come out, I believe we will again be amazed at what we discover.

HILLIARD STATON
Fifth-generation Henderson County native

PREFACE

Historians take care of battles and big events but much of history is lost because everyday people do not write about the "little things" of other times.
—Fay Morgan (1896–1983)

In spite of its relatively modest size of 375 square miles with a comparatively youthful epoch dating back merely to 1838, Henderson County encompasses diverse geography and a complexly layered heritage, and here we probe more of its intricacies.

Since the release of *Hidden History of Henderson County, North Carolina*, many folks have asked for more—more historical gleanings of noteworthy, lesser-known facts from points in the county not covered in that earlier book. And so, accordingly, the survey resumes, canvassing Edneyville and its environs, Hoopers Creek and Green River Township. As did the previous volume, this one, too, discloses personalities that helped shape the county's character, likewise conveying a sampling of structures with stories to tell.

Moreover, *Glimpses of Henderson County* unveils examples of the region's isolated coves and hollers, as well as byways, burial grounds, country stores, rural post offices, educational facilities and houses of worship. Murders, mysteries and catastrophes figure into the mix, as do mining, milling, hospitality concerns and further commercial, industrial and agricultural pursuits that flowed and ebbed with the passage of time.

Explore the hidden history of Henderson County—the journey continues…

Note: The author obtained permissions to access and photograph historic sites and structures. The material within these pages is not intended for readers' use as a guide to the properties cited, nor does the author or his publisher condone trespassing on privately held land. Rather, enjoy an armchair tour through these passages and photographs, and please respect property owners' privacy.

ACKNOWLEDGEMENTS

Tracing the past can prove even more exhilarating in the company of trusted sounding boards and kindred history buffs. As stated in an early twentieth-century brochure, "More than twenty-five years ago it was said of Hendersonville: 'There seems to be a harmony of effort among its citizens to make the stay of strangers pleasant by furnishing them both information and entertainment.'" I couldn't agree more, feeling honored and blessed to be a protégé of people so willing to teach a transplant about their heritage. Heartfelt thanks to my friends Gayle Hamilton Stepp, V. Leon Pace, Kevin Haynes, Barbara Lackey and Susan Summerville for their generous gifts of time and knowledge and for assisting in making connections to the past. I also owe a debt of gratitude to Parker Andes, Carmen Beddingfield Armour, Robert Elias Ballard, Robert Bane, Richard Barnwell, Octavia Freeman Beddingfield, Ruth Beddingfield, Edwin and John Bell, Carroll Biddix, Nancy Dalton Bishop, Jamie Withers Brown, Virginia Youngblood Brown, Nicole Bushway, Carolina Baptist Association, Jane Cunningham Coates, Knox Crowell, Dwayne Durham, Elizabeth Freeman Enloe, George Erwin, JoAnn Fain, Wayne Fisher, Greg Flack, George Newton Fowler, the most cordial Jimmy P. and Cheryl Garren, William Penn Garren, Barbara Capps Head, the Henderson County Mineral & Lapidary Museum, David Hill, John Horton, Barbara Freeman Hunnicutt, Douglas and Gaye Hurst, Boyd "Bub" Hyder, Phalbia Ballard Ireson, Rená Durham Johnson, Steve Jones, Darrell and Marcia Kruse, Ruth Orr Lancaster, Robert Livingston, Garfield Long, Norman C. Lyda, Doris Banning Marlowe and Robert Marlowe,

Theron Maybin, Rex McCall, Reverend Bryan Melton, Robert Morgan, Arnetta Osteen Mullinax, Benny Pace, Jean Pace, Fred Pittillo, Patricia Taylor Reed, Larry Rhodes, Stan Shelley, Mabel Shipman, Mark Splawn, Reverend David Lewis Staton, Hilliard Staton, Jane and Stan Stepp, Larry Stepp, Pat Stepp, Seth Swift, James H. Toms, Jeff Tweed, Sharon Dalton Waldrup, Robert Wallace, Lyn Wilkie, Ann Greenleaf Wirtz and Reverend Phillip Youngblood. I especially appreciate the field trips, interviews and jaunts through off-the-beaten-path nooks of the county.

Local historian Jennie Jones Giles drew from her indefatigable research of the county to answer queries, assisting in sorting through the labyrinth of erroneous material, inconsistencies and the oft-told and written lore. I am most grateful—and highly recommend her history courses at Blue Ridge Community College.

Many thanks to my editor, Banks Smither; his assistants; and all the folks at The History Press for their support and vision.

A heartfelt shout out to genealogist extraordinaire Janet Goad Hill, who, with her exceptional knack, unearthed some misplaced, transient folks of Henderson County's past.

Once again, the Henderson County Genealogical and Historical Society's president, Virginia Thompson, and volunteers Bill Barnwell, Sally Berger, Helen Ingle, Jeannie Taylor Lindsey, Stella Mace, V. Leon Pace and Margaret Payne stepped up to the plate, providing assistance and tips.

Thank you kindly, one and all.

I

HOW GREEN THE GREEN RIVER VALLEY

Green River Township: Latitude 35.207, longitude -82.442, population 3,948, 55.6 square miles, 2,149 feet above sea level.

Bounded by ramparts known as the Pinnacle, Grassy, Little Rich and Grassy Top, Green River Township lies east of the Continental Divide in the southeast sector of Henderson County, north of the Greenville Watershed. By all appearances, this unfrequented corner of the county proposes for the most part a sleepy, loamy swath dotted with barns and fields, family cemeteries, nestled-away campgrounds and an occasional spire piercing the rarified air—unspoiled, arrestingly serene—but scratch the surface and its pedigree entails so much more.

Here, for the most part, life proceeds as it always has. Make a jaunt astride the entire stretch of Green River Road and its byways and sometimes encounter not another soul—unless cattle and horses indeed possess souls—yet this unpretentious territory once captured the attention of Thomas A. Edison. An illustrious duel transpired here. The regionally celebrated country doctor William Bell White Howe III (1881–1948)—aka "Old Doc," father of the beloved storyteller and columnist Louise Bailey (1915–2009)—kept a hunting cabin on a slope above Rock Creek. Bestselling author and North Carolina poet laureate Robert Ray Morgan (1944–) grew up here. And resident-farmer extraordinaire Theron Maybin (1943–) and his wife, Mary Lois Jackson Maybin (1950–), have grossed more ribbons for homegrown products than any other resident in the

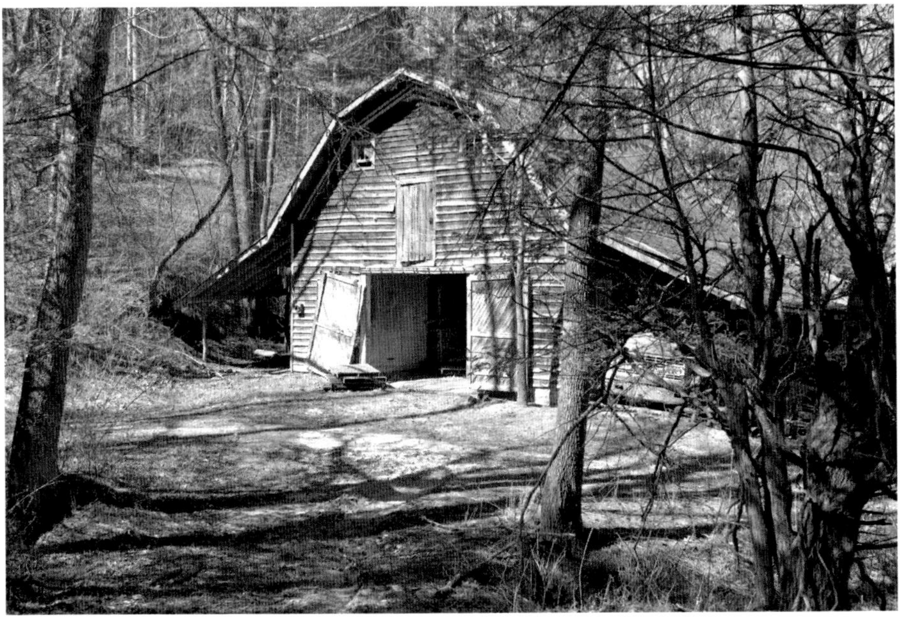

Alongside a bend of Green River Road stands the abandoned farm of Hiram Kimsey Pace (1865–1945) and Janie Heatherly Pace (1888–1963) and their bachelor son, Edwin E. Pace (1912–1997).

county, with impressive credentials renowned statewide. The Maybin family, owners of Theron Maybin and Sons farm, remains deeply rooted in the fertile soil of Green River. A descendant of early settler Matthew Maybin, Theron—considered by many to be the "mayor of Green River"—is the son of Lincoln Luther Maybin (1913–1991) and Carrie Capps Maybin (1922–2010). Carrie was the daughter of Homer Gladson "Sam" Capps (1897–1985) and Pearl Margaret "Pearlie" Levi Capps (1906–1998). The Maybins count among the members of Cedar Springs Baptist Church, located near their home and farm in Rock Creek.

William Davis (1750–1820), John Walter Staton (1768–1839), John Peter Corn (1751–1843), James Stepp (1744–1821) and Matthew Maybin (1756–1845) acquired some of the earliest land grants in the region, including thousands of acres of the Green River sector in 1787. Other early family names included Beddingfield, Capps, Freeman, Heatherly, Levi, Morgan, Osteen, Pace, Taylor and Ward.

When this territory fell within Buncombe County, Robert Murphy acquired two federal grants of 799 acres on Green River between Cabin Creek and Bob's Creek in 1814 and sold the land to Daniel Justus (1792–

after 1870) in 1823. Daniel Pace (1791–1871), the highest bidder when the Justus holdings came up for auction in 1838, acquired a large section of this acreage. Pace owned almost one square mile of land, including choice bottomland alongside the Green River extending to the base of Mount Olivet.

By virtue of soil enriched by the river and its tributaries—Rock, Bob's and Cabin Creeks—family farms have since days of old turned out superior crops. The Buncombe Turnpike once brought drovers and stages through this area, where some of the early residents operated grist- and sawmills, the John Davis family and Philip Jackson Hart operated boardinghouses and the Merideth Freemans took in occasional overnight guests. Old-timers in the area also speak of a cannery that operated during the early twentieth century near the Hart property.

A *French Broad Hustler* edition in May 1908 printed the following note:

> *P.J. Hart comes along and insists that you go home with him to dinner, and you go, of course, and you're glad of it when you sit down to that fine dinner of chicken and dumplings and corn bread and strawberries and such cake!—made by the little daughter of your host—and Mrs. Hart, hospitable and kindly, insisting that you have more.*

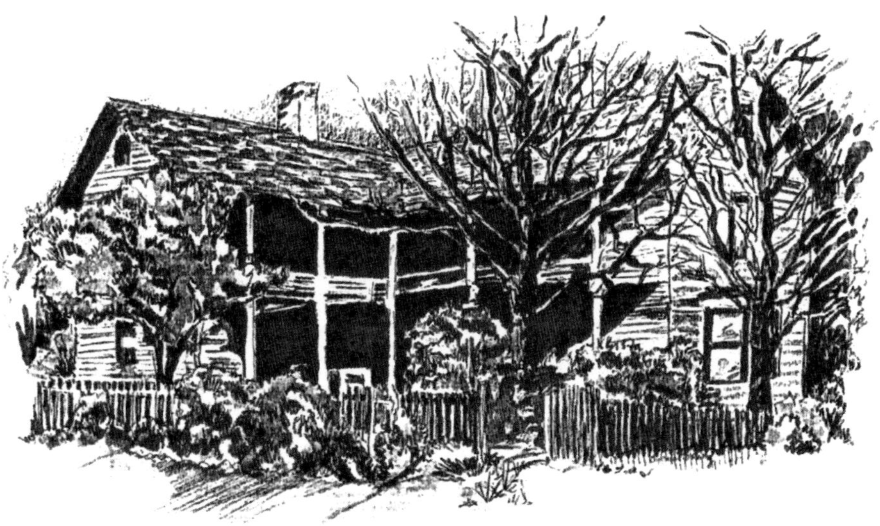

The Philip J. Hart home, inn and Splendor Post Office once stood above the intersection of Old U.S. 25 and Riverwood Drive. *Sketch by Cynthia O'Reilly, courtesy of Barbara Freeman Hunnicutt.*

Philip Jackson Hart (1845–1917)—son of John Henry Hart (1814–1875) and Mary Pace Hart (1824–1857)—first married Temfire (Temple/Tempy) E.M. Jane Ward (1851–1884), next Rachael M. Anders (1862–1892) and then Hattie Lugenia Shipman (1866–1950). With his three wives, Hart had as many as seventeen children, including those who died in infancy. Philip J. Hart bought land in Green River from Levi Jones* and more from Mary P. Corn, W.P. Revis, W.A. Smith, Edward H. Freeman, J.T. Staton, J.B. Ward and others between 1885 and 1889. Appointed postmaster at Green River in 1875, Hart also operated a general store and served as depot agent. Hart sold his store to Thomas E. Hughston (1851–1926) and relocated to Hendersonville, where he served as treasurer of school funds for the Henderson County Board of Education. He moved back to Green River in 1897 and served as postmaster in his home at Splendor, where he ran a store, tavern, hotel and government distillery. Hart died from complications of influenza. The old family place burned down, and today a ghostly pair of stone chimneys marks P.J. Hart's Green River homesite.

Vance-Carson Duel Site

On November 5, 1827, two gentlemen, as a matter of honor, settled their dispute by engaging in an unlawful act. Just north of the South Carolina line, Robert Brank Vance (1793–1827) and Samuel P. Carson (1798–1838) entered into a duel, having found a loophole in the law.† Robert Brank Vance, uncle of Governor Zebulon Baird Vance (1830–1894) from Reems Creek, Buncombe County, studied medicine at the Newton Academy and was a North Carolina congressman. Carson was a North Carolina senator and farmer from Marion. After the two men competed for a seat in the Nineteenth Congress in 1825, Carson won the election. When the two jockeyed again for a seat in the 1827 Twentieth Congress, Vance, in a smear campaign, slung mud about Carson and his father. Carson again won the seat and challenged Vance to a duel. Vance accepted, and the two men met near the North Carolina/South Carolina border adjacent to the Davis property and carried out a contest that mortally wounded Vance, who

* *Henderson County Deed Book*, 15: 536, 538.

† In 1802, the North Carolina General Assembly deemed dueling unlawful and punishable by death "without benefit of clergy…for fending, accepting or being the bearer of a challenge…for fighting a duel, where one party is killed." Vance and Carson believed they had chosen a dueling site in South Carolina.

died the following day and was buried at the Vance family burial ground in Reems Creek. Carson removed to Texas, where he was appointed secretary of state for the Republic of Texas in 1836 and died two years later in Hot Springs, Arkansas.

Before the pavement disappears down the old wagon road known as "winding stairs," North Carolina Highway Historical Marker P25 stands alongside NC Highway 225 (Old U.S. Highway 25), adjacent to Kingdom Place and the Jones Gap Tree Farm, approximately a half mile from the dueling site.

Oakland

The roadside inn and family home Oakland stood just north of the North Carolina state line, near the dueling site of Vance and Carson. "Colonel" John Davis (1780–1859) and Serepta Merritt Davis (1802–1889) built above the "winding stairs" their substantial brick home within reach of the old Indian path known as "Saluda," a wagon road that would become part of the Buncombe Turnpike by 1828. According to Buncombe County deed records,* Davis purchased 850 acres in Mud Creek from Robert Alexander

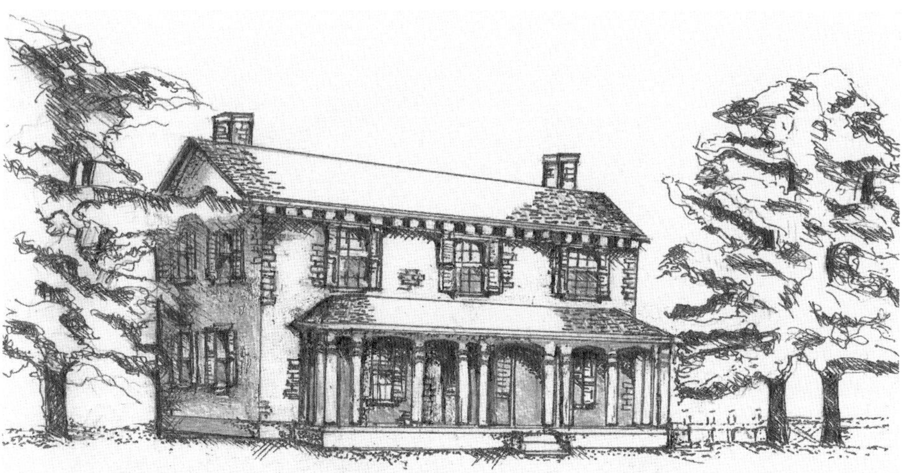

Oakland. *Sketch by Nicole Bushway.*

* *Buncombe County Deed Book* 13: 372; 16: 175; 2: 312.

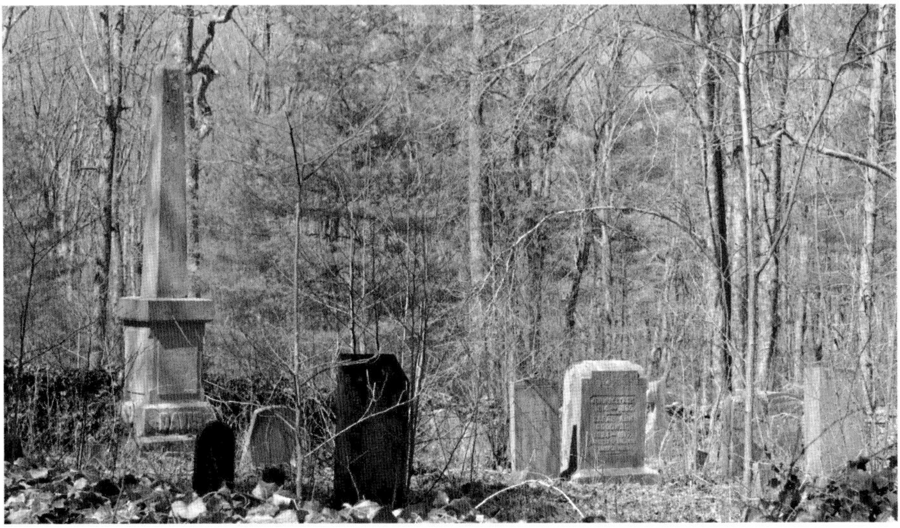

Davis Family Cemetery.

Murray (1785–1857) in 1823, 200 acres in Green River from Abraham McGuffey (1796–1848) in 1830, an undisclosed amount of acreage in Little Mud Creek from Noah Parr Corn (1802–1874) in 1837 and additional land from the State of North Carolina and from "Sheriff Buncombe."

According to legend, an on-site grove of oaks inspired the name of the Davises' home in Green River. The family opened Oakland to the traveling public, and it served as a stagecoach stop. Robert Brank Vance died in this house, which was described as having a dining room table that "groaned with its load of good things to eat, prepared by Mother Davis," and with "spacious rooms furnished with four-poster beds and snowy sheets."

John Davis, born in Virginia to parents who had emigrated from Wales, served in the U.S. Army as sergeant major in the War of 1812 under General Andrew Jackson and fought at the Battle of New Orleans. Davis removed to Tennessee and Alabama and then to Merrittsville, South Carolina, where he met his wife-to-be. He involved himself in agricultural and mercantile pursuits. His friends called him "Colonel." The couple settled in Flat Rock in 1823 on land later purchased from Davis by Charlestonian Judge Mitchell King (1783–1862) for his summer home, Argyle.* Lincoln Fullum (1792–1863) operated the mills on the Davis property and lived there in a house

* *Buncombe County Deed Books* 13: 16: 206.

that predated Argyle. Davis influenced the formation of Henderson from Buncombe County, convinced Judge King to give fifty acres for a county seat and chaired the "Road Party" for the location of the city of Hendersonville. He also became the first postmaster of Flat Rock in 1829.

Promised Land

When a group of emancipated slaves migrated from Civil War–devastated plantations in Mississippi and other parts south, arriving near the North and South Carolina line by 1868, the widowed Serepta Davis fed and housed them, offering hospitality in exchange for labor. According to sketchy and mostly undocumented accounts, these valiant freedmen also worked odd jobs for neighboring landowners and, according to legend, saved enough money to buy from Serepta and her son, William Thomas "Tom" Davis (1834–1902), 180 acres at one dollar per acre. (Henderson County deed records show no such transaction.)* They named their communal village "Happy Land"—characteristic of an African tribal village—where they constructed sheds, corncribs and their log homes, one serving also as a chapel. They farmed the soil and developed and sold crafts and a natural curative known as Happy Land liniment. Some of the men worked as teamsters, hauling products for neighboring farmers and innkeepers. Villagers shared resources through a common treasury under the jurisdiction of "King" William Montgomery and his wife, Louella Bobo Montgomery, the "queen." (William's brother Robert succeeded him as king, according to legend.) By the late 1800s, the commune had grown to nearly four hundred people, with others having joined from Kentucky, Georgia and South Carolina.

In addition to the Montgomerys, members of the kingdom included George (1839–?) and Margaret Elizabeth "Maggie" Rampley (or Rambley) Couch (1843–?), their daughter Mary Couch Russell (1892–1960), their son Ezel Couch (1872–1961) and Ezel's wife, Ella (1895–1947); Perry Williams; Harold and Hannah Whitmire and their daughters, Chaney Whitmire

---

* The only Henderson County deed record concerning Robert and Louella Montgomery and the land known as the "Kingdom" in Green River would be found in Book 15: 37, March 14, 1882, for 210 acres (in three tracts) purchased by Robert and Louella Montgomery from John H. Goodwin and his wife, Sarah A. Goodwin. Goodwin had acquired the acreage from Alfred McDowell (1815–1899). Sarah Goodwin was a daughter of John and Serepta Davis.

Greene (1868–1948) and Mary J. Whitmire Greene (1877–1948); Wiley Bennett (1837–?) and his wife, Rachel (1835–1936); Louella Montgomery's brothers Ambrose and Henry Bobo; Jerry Casey (1858–1918); Elmira Montgomery (1848–1943); Robert Montgomery's children Robert S. Jr. (1874–?), Cornelia (1872–?) and Julia Ann (1870–?); and William and Louella's children Lily, Waties and Joshua.

As time wore on, the colony disbanded as residents left for work in Flat Rock, Hendersonville and beyond, dwindling the "kingdom" until its ultimate abandonment before 1900. Henderson County confiscated the property due to lack of tax payments. Deeds and tax records refer to separate sections of the acreage as "Jerry Casey home tract," "Sarah Bennett home tract" and "home tract of Kingdom of Happy Land."

Today, telltale signs hint at former root cellars and homesites: random foundation stones, one ruined chimney of stone and the intermittent mesh of periwinkles or patch of lilies marking the footprints of homes in a once-thriving settlement. And in spite of what Sadie Smathers Patton wrote of the intact, squat log cabin on the site, this structure postdated the "kingdom," having been built in the 1930s.

Straddling the North and South Carolina line, most of the enigmatic kingdom's acreage spread within the Green River sector and seventy-five acres

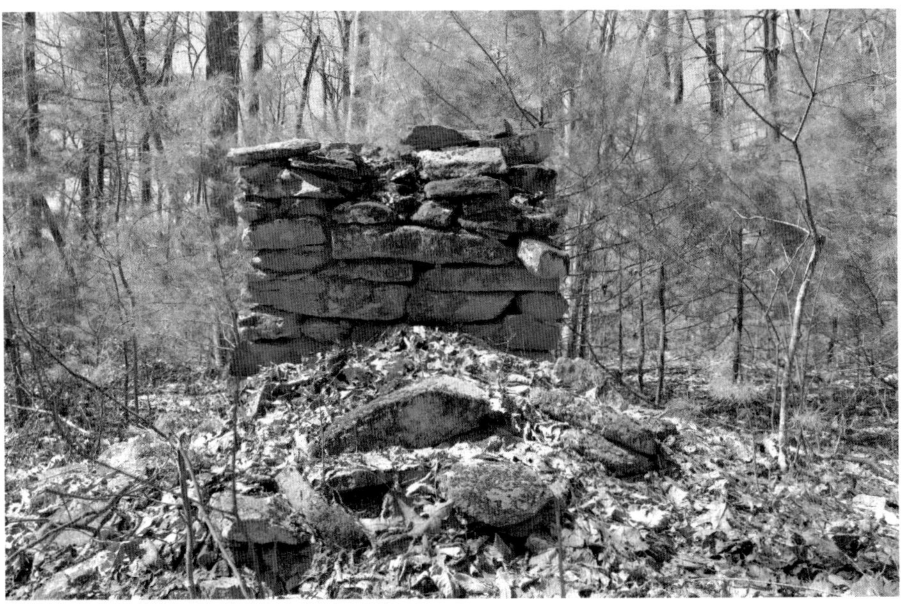

Chimney ruins of one of the log homes in the Happy Land. *Photographed with permission.*

in the Greenville Watershed district. Except for a broad pasture, the isolated scene unfolds as dense forestland crisscrossed with crystalline creeks and softened with wildflowers and *lycopodia* galore. Descendants of the J.O. Bell family, who have owned the property since 1910, attribute the paucity of architectural vestiges to the havoc wreaked by fortune seekers goaded by raconteurs' suggestions of gold coins having been stashed in the cabins' chimneys—and to Frank Durham Bell (1898–1993) having razed the derelict structures.

Briggs/Capps Mill

Traversing the wee bridge on Rock Creek Road, the passerby might catch—through the forested cove—a glimpse of gushing water but without any possible notion of the phenomenon that lies far below. Eli Capps (1868–1931), James A. Capps (1885–1963) and Homer Gladson "Sam" Capps (1897–1985) operated there a mill owned by South Carolinian Henry Briggs (1851–1940). Beneath the ruinous site, a breathtaking fifty-foot stair-stepped cascade plunges to a pool as the creek continues its surge toward the Green River. Viewing the mill's carcass, one cannot help but ponder the intrepid feat of constructing such an operation on the wall of a precipitous bank. Bulky components of iron that drove the facility, the expansive chase, the massive grinding stones and twenty-foot-tall rock pillars surely required—besides engineering acumen—the brute strength of man and beast, sheer determination and the wonders of leverage. Surveying the site of the circa 1900 mill, one wonders, too, if the miller used a catwalk to access the building from the bank. Whatever the case, the impressive ruins stand today in testimony to the mettle of our early farmers and millers.

Henry Briggs, married to Loula McBee Briggs (1856–1937), established the American Bank in Upstate South Carolina and directed other business concerns as well. He served as mayor of Greenville from 1911 to 1913, having retired from business at age fifty when told by doctors he had six months to live. Briggs built a summer home in Henderson County's Sky Valley—on land once owned by his wife's grandfather Vardry McBee (1775–1864), who owned mills in Greenville County, South Carolina, including the historic Conestee Mill and was considered the "Father of Greenville." Many years later, Briggs attributed his improved health to the "fine drinking water" in his mountain retreat. He lived until the age of eighty-eight.

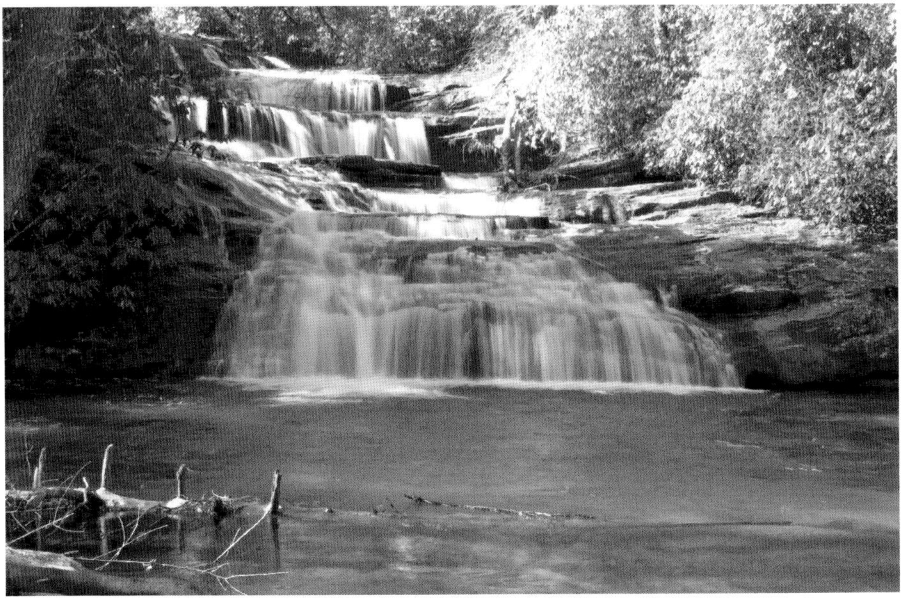

At the foot of the ruins of the Briggs/Capps mill site, Rock Creek Falls rivals Polk County's Pearson's Falls in compass and splendor. *Photographed with permission.*

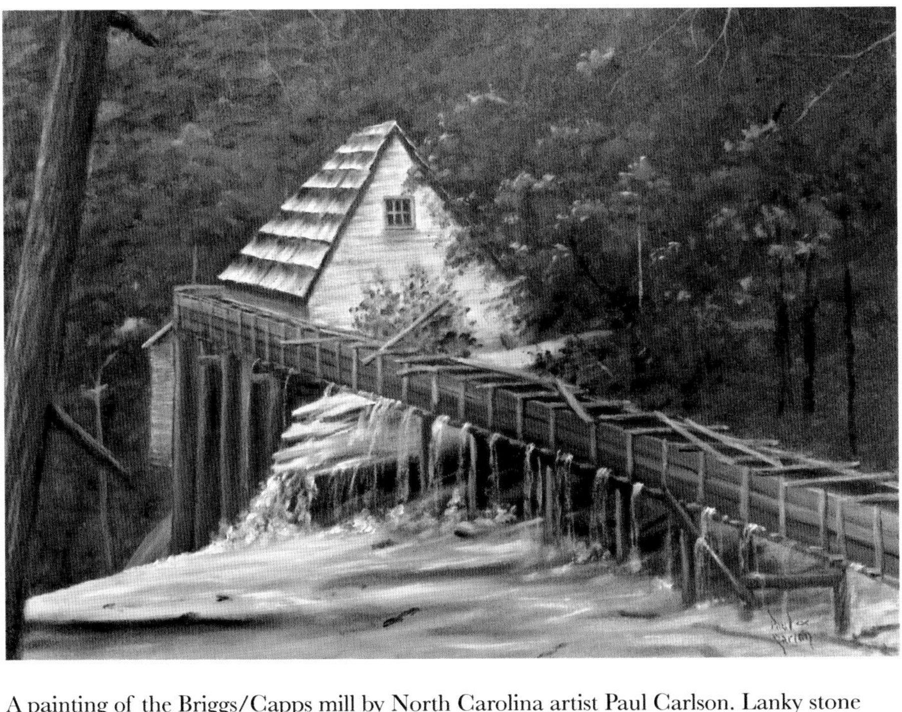

A painting of the Briggs/Capps mill by North Carolina artist Paul Carlson. Lanky stone pylons stand today in the midst of rusting milling components and rotting wooden boards. *Photographed with permission.*

The following article appeared in the *French Broad Hustler* in November 1913:

> *ZIRCONIA DOINGS*
> *The public school at Mt. Olivet closed November 18, a good number of the patrons and friends of the school were present and were highly entertained with some nice recitations by the children after which dinner was served. The nice library secured through the efforts of the teacher, Miss Eufala Ledbetter, was presented to the school. Glover Osteen has moved to his new home at Sandy Flat. E.A. Ballard has purchased a fine yoke of oxen; price paid $90. M.T. Tankersley has smallpox in his family. Corn shuckings are over and our people are looking forward to the Christmas holidays. Mr. J.F. Ballard says he made 200 bushels of fine assorted corn. T.B. Ballard butchered a large hog last week. Peter Gosnell of Tuxedo will soon be a resident of our community. Glover Osteen has purchased a fine mule for $200. J.M. Osteen is delivering nursery stock at Tuxedo now. J.W. Tankersley sold a yoke of oxen to Tom Jones; price paid $100. Columbus Anders of River Falls, S.C., was a visitor at Rev. John C. Ward's Sunday.*

The Freemans of Green River

Octavia Freeman Beddingfield (1922–) speaks proudly of her illustrious family and homeplace, as well she should. This gracious lady lives on part of the ancestral land of an early settler—her great-grandfather Merideth Malone Freeman (1800–1869) of Rutherford County, who first married Elizabeth Murray (1799–1829), next Lucinda Dugan Murray (1809–1844) and then Julia Ann Mansell Hamilton (1817–1888). Each of Merideth's fathers-in-law owned a plantation in South Carolina. Elizabeth, a cousin of Lucinda, was a granddaughter of Samuel Murray Sr. (1739–1817) and Elizabeth Rees Murray (circa 1741–1815), who owned the Murray Inn and Tavern in Murraysville (now Fletcher). Merideth had as many as fifteen children, including those who died in infancy.

Mrs. Beddingfield's genealogical research disclosed an ancestor, Edmund Freeman (1596–1682), assistant governor of the Plymouth Colony under Governor George William Bradford (1590–1657) and cofounder of the town of Sandwich, Massachusetts, on Cape Cod.

Merideth Freeman involved himself in politics, serving as justice of the peace and judge for the Flat Rock precinct (which included the entire

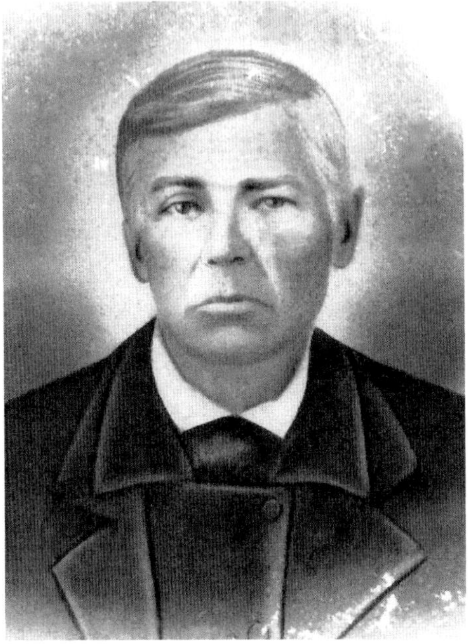

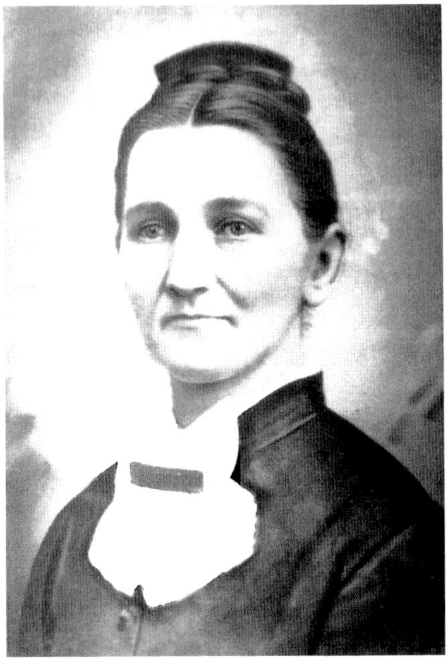

Merideth Malone Freeman and Julia Ann Mansell Hamilton Freeman. *Courtesy of Octavia Freeman Beddingfield.*

southern portion of Henderson County) and as first postmaster at Green River. Buncombe County deed records show Freeman purchasing land in Green River Cove in 1829 from David Lowry Swain (1801–1868) and from the State of North Carolina.

In the early 1830s, Merideth built his grand country home—referred to as the "Old House" by Freeman descendants—in the Green River sector of what is now Henderson County near present-day Tuxedo. The two-and-a-half-story manse featured a center hall plan with massive stone chimneys and porches garnished with elaborate balustrades of profiled boards and brackets on its first two levels. A creek named Freeman with a waterfall of the same name meandered through the 1,009-acre property, which also included a springhouse, a pond, an open-air kitchen house, a sizeable barn, an infield and fruit trees and a knitting mill at the foot of Vernon Falls. Merideth's descendants continued living in and summering at the old family place for many generations in spite of its having had no modern conveniences. The home served as a stage stop in its earlier years, and Camp Greystone kept horses in the barn in the early 1900s. Freeman descendants razed the home in the 1960s.

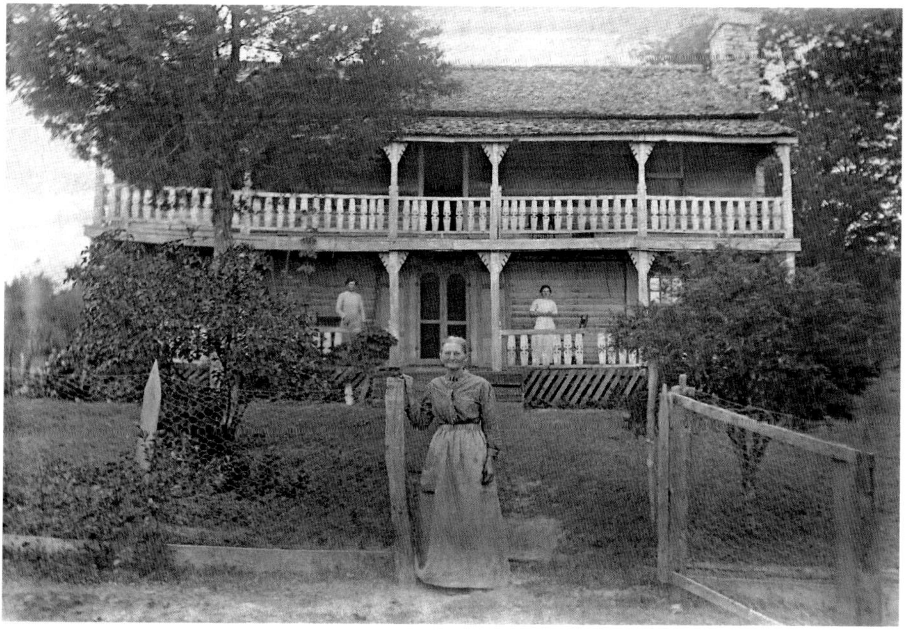

Valle de la Paix, the Merideth Freeman home, featured open-air sleeping porches in the rear of the dwelling, later enclosed. Standing at the gate is Mary Marinda "Mayme" Fuller Freeman. *Courtesy of Octavia Freeman Beddingfield.*

Although not a trace of the "Old House" remains for the sake of history, memories wrought with family visits and picnics and moments of laughter and kindness resonate in the hearts of Freeman descendants—recollections of homespun aromas, al fresco meals taken in the open-sided kitchen house during summertime, gentle breezes wafting through the wraparound porches and the giggles of children as they swayed from a grapevine swing. Family members enjoy recounting the occasion of Merideth's daughter Julia Ann Freeman (1850–1938) having secreted herself in a closet as she peered through a crack, watching Union soldiers searching her family home back in Civil War days.

Octavia Freeman Beddingfield recalled, "It was the beginning of one family home, 1,009 acres. Through the years it became a whole community. What would Merideth Freeman think if he could look through these two hundred years and see what he began?"

Merideth's sons Edward and "Mont" entertained themselves by exploring for gemstones. When they discovered minerals of commercial significance on their land in the early 1880s, the family commenced mining semiprecious zircon crystals. The Freeman mine—owned and operated by Julia Ann Freeman and her sons Edward Hamilton Freeman (1849–1920) and Vartha Montraville "Mont" Freeman (1847–1928) and son-in-law Hilliard W. Vernon (1848–1926)—counted among three mining operations in the Green River section, the others belonging to Levi Jones and John Benjamin Franklin Pace. The lion's share of activity took place at the Freeman mine, where family members and hired helpers worked in earnest sifting through open pits, mining tons of zircons and other minerals. This earned for the Freemans a tidy profit, having produced as much as twenty-six tons of zircon-rich ore in a single year, which they shipped to Thomas Edison's laboratory in New Jersey to be pulverized and the thorium content extracted. The Freeman mine stood east of Freeman Creek just north of the present town of Tuxedo; Lake Summit swallowed up most of the Jones mine site, situated to the east and south of the Freeman mine; and the Pace mine lay to the south of Green River Baptist Church and southwest of Vernon Creek.

In one of his entrepreneurial sprees, Captain Marion Columbus Toms (1843–1917) bought the Jones mine and also the title for mineral rights in the Green River Valley. At the time, zircon ore fetched $250 per ton. According to the *French Broad Hustler* in July 1909, "Capt. M.C. Toms spent yesterday at his zircon mines near Zirconia where he has a force of hands at work."

Hilliard Vernon married Merideth Freeman's eldest daughter, Julia Ann, on November 21, 1877. He became a Baptist minister, preaching for more than forty years in Henderson and neighboring counties.

Edward Hamilton Freeman, manager of the Freeman mine, frequently hosted three world-renowned scientists in his home: William Earl Hidden (1853–1918) of Providence, Rhode Island, a geologist, mineralogist and broker for Thomas Edison; Alexander Grant Ogilvie (1869–1935) of Wales and Bedford, England, an engineer; and George Letchworth English (1864–1944) of Philadelphia, Pennsylvania, a mineralogist with expertise in thorium. Freeman and his wife, Mary Marinda "Mayme" Fuller (1859–1919), would later name their sons Hidden Earl Freeman (1888–1953), Ogilvie Freeman (1897–1969) and George English Freeman (1899–1953) after their associates. The Freemans had twelve children. Besides the mining operation, Edward also operated a gristmill on his homesite flanking Vernon Creek.

Letters and telegrams between W.E. Hidden and Edward Freeman—saved by Freeman's granddaughter Octavia Freeman Beddingfield—shed interesting light on Captain M.C. Toms's involvement in the enterprise. A sample from Hidden:

As to my difficulty with Mr. Toms, I have settled it in full. I made him a proposition by letter and he drew a draft for the moment that I was always willing to pay him and so the case is settled! He did not get within one hundred dollars of the amount he claimed. He is a gentleman when he cares to be, but also he is a bluffer from "Blufftown," or I am mistaken. Why, do you know that he threatened, by letter, to attack my possessions in Alexander County, and in Burke County at Captain Mills' and he even threatened to attack the Bayne mine, so as to get what he only thought was due him by me? Why, I never heard such bluffing in all my life—did you? Really, did you?

In another letter, Hidden wrote:

If we continue to work together we will show the captain a thing or two, and between you and I the captain isn't in it! You want to be on your guard about Mr. English for he has lately been talking about me in a way that is ungentlemanly and un-business-like. When I see him again I shall give him a piece of my mind. He uses my name as a reference and then talks about me behind my back. Now you would not like such two-faced action and I think you would resent it very forcibly and at short notice.

In Hidden's frequent communications to Ed Freeman, he wrote "Friend Freeman" in each of his salutations.

In February 1915, the *French Broad Hustler* reported:

MINERAL PRODUCTION IN HENDERSON COUNTY
The North Carolina mining industry gives Henderson County prominent mention in the mining of gold, zircon, brick, limestone, etc. Zircon in commercial quantity occurs associated with pegmatite in Henderson County, about two miles west of Tuxedo. Two mines were in operation during 1911, one known as the Freeman mine, which was operated by W.E. Hidden and the other known as the Jones mine, operated by M.C. and C.F. Toms of Hendersonville. Both of these deposits have been known for many years, but the Freeman mine has not been operated for the last 24 years. The Jones mine has been operated more or less regularly since 1902, when there was again a commercial demand for zircon, this time for use in the manufacture of the glower in the Nernet lamp. The former use of zircon was in the manufacture of mantles for incandescent lights, but the zirconium was replaced by thorium, then the demand for this latter material at once created the demand for the metallic monazite.

Green River Gems

Merideth Freeman settled on land rich with veins of minerals, including monazite and zirconium silicate. Confederate general Thomas Lanier Clingman (1812–1897) discovered and mined zircons in the region of Green River in 1869 and leased acreage there for twenty-five years, yet he and others dismissed this discovery as unimportant. In this mineral-laden sector, Maybin family members also extracted lead for musket balls.

Containing trace impurities such as "rare-earth" elements thorium and uranium, zirconium silicate ($ZrSiO_4$) occurs in various locales, including the Carolinas, Virginia, Florida, Brazil, Australia, India, Ceylon and South Africa. Green River zircons qualify not as gemstones but as industrial-grade crystals. North Carolina and Florida are the only two states in North America with a recorded mineral production of zircons.

The Old North State bustled with exploration and mining activity in the late nineteenth century as mineralogists and mineral brokers arrived in eager pursuit of materials relevant to the newly invented gas

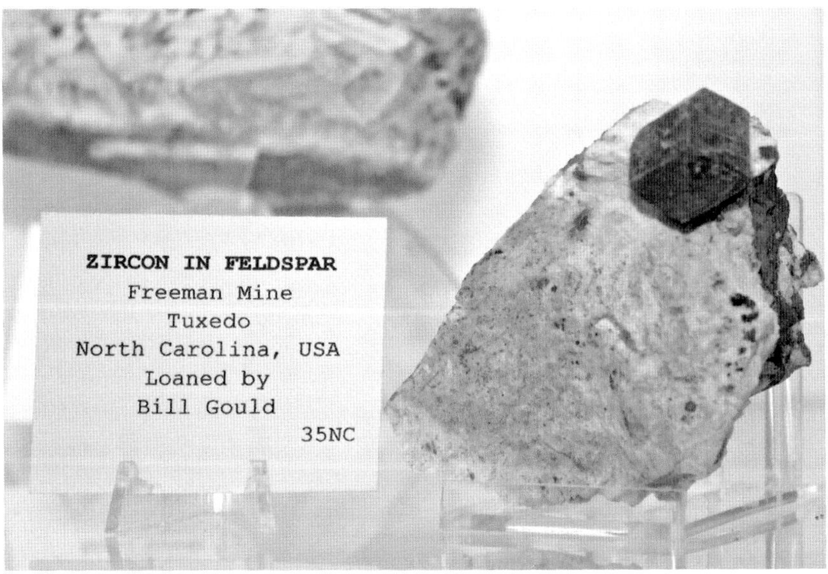

Zircon. *Photographed with permission of the Henderson County Mineral & Lapidary Museum.*

lamp. In addition to zircons, miners also discovered veins of thorium-rich monazite and traces of auerlite among the mineral wealth. Miners picked through Carolina gneiss, obtaining zircons by gathering loose pegmatite—decayed granite, an igneous rock pushed to the surface over eons of uplifting of the earth's layers and ongoing erosion. In Green River, zircon occurs in a pegmatite dike about one hundred feet wide and can be traced for more than a mile and a half. The zircon material in this dike is noted to be well crystallized, with a grayish to gray-beige coloration. Elsewhere, crystals range from colorless to yellows and blues.

Spurring the flurry of mining activity, Dr. Carl Auer Freiherr von Welsbach (1858–1929) of Vienna had announced his application of rare-earth elements to the manufacture of incandescent lamp mantles. Thomas Edison pursued the same path, having recently perfected a carbonized filament of high resistance using artificial silk fashioned from cotton thread for his incandescent light bulb. Edison was in the market for platinum (for wire filaments) and the radioactive element thorium—or, specifically, its oxide content as a component in light mantles.

In the midst of the Industrial Revolution, Austrian chemist Welsbach's announcement spiked the demand for thorium and cerium. With locations in Columbus, Ohio, and Riverton, Camden and Gloucester City, New Jersey, the Welsbach Lighting Company—which experimented with alternative light sources—sent agents to European and American mining sites in search of commercially viable quantities of rare-earth elements. Welsbach, as did Edison, sought materials to develop more durable mantles for incandescent light bulbs.

Thomas Alva Edison (1847–1931) dispatched noted mineralogist William Earl Hidden in 1879 to the Carolinas in pursuit of platinum deposits, hence immortalizing the region's mining industry in the late nineteenth and early twentieth centuries. Hidden brokered material for Edison and others and rediscovered a gemstone to be named for him—a variation of spodumene, which had already been discovered by a man named Lackey in Alexander County, North Carolina. Hiddenite can occur in emerald deposits and ranges in color from clear or light yellow to yellowish green, vivid yellow and emerald green. Deposits of hiddenites occur also in Brazil, China and Madagascar. Where W.E. Hidden rediscovered the material in Alexander County, officials later named a town Hiddenite in honor of the discoverer. When Hidden

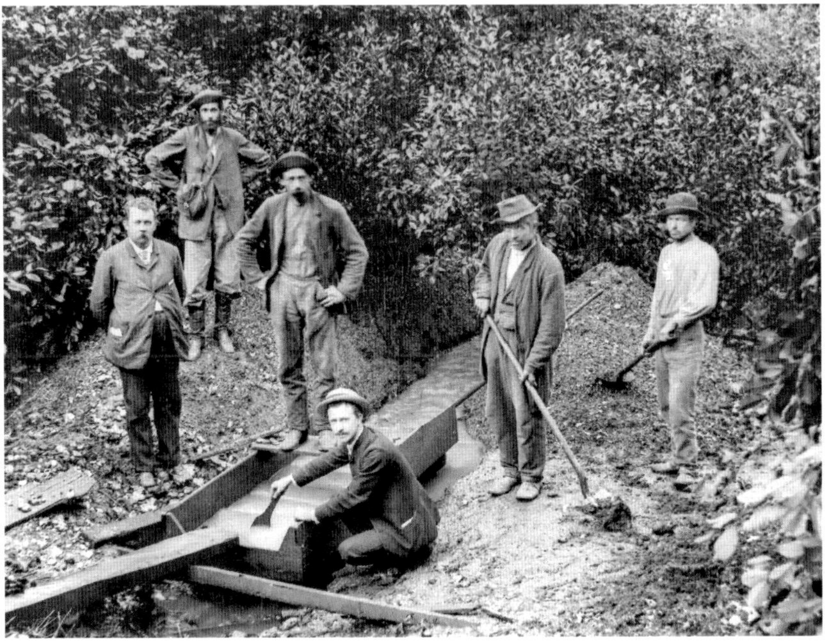

Zircon mining in Green River. *Foreground, squatting*: William Earl Hidden. *Others, from left to right*: Judge H.G. Ewart, Edward H. Freeman, ___ Ward, Levi Jones and Jeff Jones. *Courtesy of Henderson County Genealogical and Historical Society, Inc.*

hit upon auerlite in North Carolina, he named it for the Viennese scientist Carl Auer Freiherr von Welsbach.

Hidden returned to North Carolina from 1902 to 1915, continuing his exploration for commercially sustainable amounts of thorium-rich auerlite. In 1911, at the Freeman mine, he developed an improved hydraulic mining process and constructed a six-thousand-foot ditch lined with boards reaching from Rainbow Falls (aka Silver Falls) to the foot of the "zircon mountain," where previously miners had worked by hand with rocker-type sluice boxes, pans, buckets, shovels, pickaxes and sleds. At its peak, twenty-five workers mined this site. Finding no platinum or sizable deposits of auerlite during his reconnaissance of Appalachia, Hidden abandoned his pursuits by 1915, thus drawing to a close the rage for mining alternative resources in the Green River Valley of Henderson County.

In the company of colleagues Harvey Samuel Firestone Sr. (1868–1938) and Henry Ford (1863–1947), Thomas A. Edison visited Henderson County for two days in the summer of 1906 during a tour of western North Carolina. While in the area, Edison joined Captain M.C. Toms and Charles French Toms (1872–1937), and the three men paid their respects to the Freeman and Jones mines in Green River. The Bell family hosted Edison during his visit.

Octavia Freeman Beddingfield lives in the rock house built by her husband, Maze Cleveland Beddingfield (1913–2001). Maze, a stonemason, harvested yellow and tan rocks from the property and lovingly constructed a home that remains sound and attractive many decades later. Freeman heirs live alongside the access road to this house.

Descended from patriarch Merideth Freeman and Revolutionary War soldiers William Capps (1764–after 1848), William Sentell (1756–1837) and Abraham Kuykendall (circa 1724–1812), Octavia's lineage runs deep in the Green River Valley, where she is a member of Tuxedo First Baptist Church. Her father, Ogilvie, married Alice Capps (1895–1984), worked at the Freeman Grocery Store on Lake Summit and sold fruit trees for Stark Brothers Nursery in Missouri. The couple had four children.

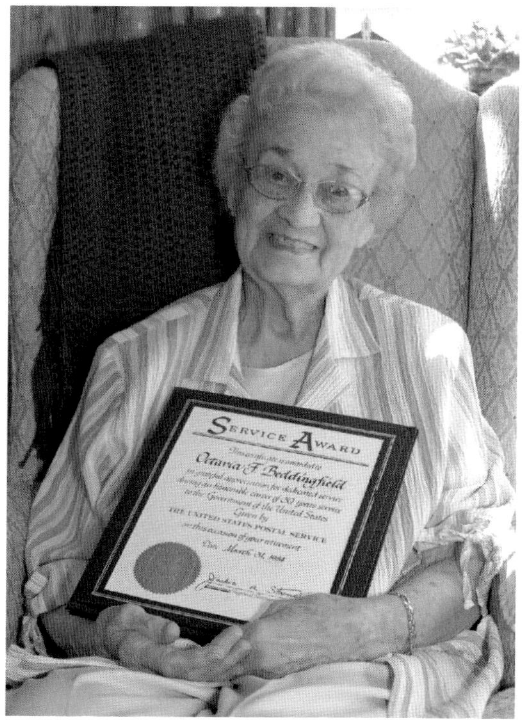

Octavia Freeman Beddingfield with the citation recognizing her many years of service to the Tuxedo Post Office.

As a child, Octavia attended the Tuxedo School and then the Flat Rock High School, "through eleventh grade, because there was no twelfth grade then," she said. For a total of thirty years, she worked at the Tuxedo Post Office, serving as postmaster from 1972 to 1984. The Beddingfields raised two children, Ronald (1947–) and Anita (1949–).

The Beddingfield property includes a stretch of Freeman Creek, as well as Freeman Falls, within a well-kept, park-like setting across the road from the rock house. Skirting a serpentine path, rhododendrons and mountain laurels proffer evergreen foliage and springtime nosegays beneath a canopy of pines, maples and oaks—an idyllic locale graced with the harmony of falling water and rushing stream.

When asked for recollections of the old days, Mrs. Beddingfield said, "It was all delightful to me. No one ever had it better than I did. We were never rich, didn't make a big splash in the world, but we had a wonderful life. We were a close-knit family." She added:

> *On a visit to the little cemetery on the hill as the morning sun shines upon the valley and over the old homeplace, then spreads its rays over the zircon mountain in the distance, it is easy to feel the spirits of these people still lingering along the mountain paths beside the streams they loved and even on the wide porches where they so enjoyed gathering. We see why long ago Anna Sue* dearly loved her old home and named it "Peaceful Valley."*

JOHN BENJAMIN FRANKLIN "FRANK" PACE

Here rests his head upon the lap of Earth
A Youth to Fortune and to Fame unknown.
Fair Science frown'd not on his humble birth,
And Melancholy mark'd him for her own.

Large was his bounty, and his soul sincere,
Heav'n did a recompense as largely send:
He gave to Mis'ry all he had, a tear,
He gain'd from Heav'n ('twas all he wish'd) a friend.

No farther seek his merits to disclose,
Or draw his frailties from their dread abode,
There they alike in trembling hope repose.
The bosom of his Father and his God.
—Thomas Grey (1716–1771)

* Anna Sue Freeman Gordon (1878–1951).

John Benjamin Franklin Pace. *Courtesy of V. Leon Pace.*

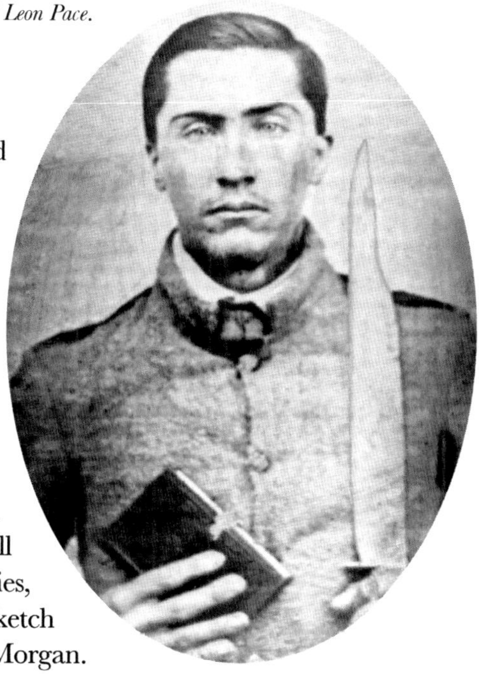

Beyond the verdant pastures and up a rutty roadbed of sallow clay, a field of tributes in marble and granite appears—the Pace Family Cemetery on a knoll alongside the abandoned Green River Full Gospel Holiness Church.

Many of those buried here live on through meticulously kept records, including those archived by V. Leon Pace with his "Pace Family" binder chockfull of documents, photographs, obituaries, correspondence and a biographical sketch written by Pace descendant Robert Morgan. Pace's and Morgan's gleanings concerning their ancestor John Benjamin Franklin "Frank" Pace (1838–1918) portray the early Green River resident as courageous, humble, industrious, kind and generous.

One of eight children of Daniel Pace (1791–1871) and Sarah Revis Pace (1793–1877), Frank came into the world the same year Henderson became a county. In his youth, Frank trapped mink and muskrats, fished the Green River and, with his father and brothers, helped haul the family's farm products to Greenville, South Carolina. He enjoyed reading and learning and amassed an impressive library for the time.

On October 5, 1861, Frank, a Republican, enlisted with the Thirty-fifth North Carolina Infantry Regiment, Company G, Henderson Rifles; was mustered in as a private; and served as a corporal in the Civil War, participating in the Battle of Fredericksburg in December 1862. According to military records, he also served with General James Longstreet (1821–1904) at Chickamauga in September 1863. During the Siege of Petersburg in the summer of 1864, Union soldiers captured Frank Pace on June 17 and transported him with other Confederate prisoners to the prison camp at Point Lookout, Maryland, on June 24; he was later sent to the prison camp at Elmira, New York, on July 27, 1864. Starved and cold, subsisting on a diet of mostly rats, wild birds and soup of potato peelings, Pace contracted diphtheria. Released on June 11, 1865, after taking the Oath of

Allegiance, Pace joined other prisoners on a train to Greenville, South Carolina, from where he walked home to Green River.

Frank married Mary Ann Jones (1838–1880), and the couple had five children: Rosa Elizabeth "Rosie" Pace Staton Queen (1869–1954), Sarah Matilda Pace Morgan (1871–1912), James Lemuel Levi Pace (1872–1940), Joseph Volney Pace (1873–1958) and Robert Franklin Pace (1875–1876). Pace farmed and hunted, set out orchards and employed some of the freedmen of the neighboring Kingdom of Happy Land as hired hands. He owned one of the three Green River Valley zircon mines, which spread between Terry's Creek, Andrews and Green River Roads adjacent to the homesite of Clyde Ray Morgan (1905–1991) and Fannie Geneva Levi Morgan (1912–2010), parents of author and poet laureate Robert Ray Morgan. Serving as an unofficial community doctor, Pace prescribed Native American remedies, including herbal cures. He assumed responsibility for orphaned children and cared for his aged parents.

Invited to speak at the turn of the twentieth century in Washington, D.C., Frank Pace addressed the Bureau of Indian Affairs concerning what he knew about the Hopewell Treaty with the Cherokees and the Siege of the Ninety-Six Line.

Pace, an active member of Green River Baptist Church, transferred title to his land under the church to the congregation. Frank Pace is buried in the Pace Family Cemetery and Mary Ann Pace at Refuge Baptist Church Cemetery.

Provenance of the Surname Pace

A consensus of reports tends to concur that the surname Pace derives from Normandy and England. Possibly the shortened form of the Latin *Paschalis* (*Pax*, *Pacis*, Pascal, Pasquale), this nickname describes a mild-mannered and peaceable person. Several forms of the name spring from medieval English: Pece, Paice, Pacie, Pash, Pacy, Payce and more variations. The surname possibly hails from Cheshire and refers to the French village of Pacy-sur-Eure in Normandy, where inhabitants called Pacy lived prior to the Norman Conquest of England in 1066.

The Paces of Green River Township and other parts of Henderson and Polk Counties trace their lines to the Richard Paces of England and Tidewater, Virginia (near Jamestown), where the family owned a plantation known as Pace's Paines. Descendant John Pace (1732–1780) and his wife, Sarah Pope Burge Pace (1733–1808), removed to Guilford County, North Carolina. Their son Burrell (also Burwell and Burl)

Pope Pace (1758–1816), born in Bertie County, North Carolina, in 1804, removed to Camp Creek in what is now Saluda, Polk County—the sector known then as Pace's Gap. Son of Burrell and Lydia Woodruff Pace (1760–1810), Daniel was the first Pace to settle in Green River.

Levi Jones

Akin to Frank Pace, Levi Jones (1836–1929) also treated ailments with herbal cures and purportedly received medical training during his military service. Jones enlisted on December 1, 1863, and served as a captain in the Second North Carolina Mounted Infantry, Company H. According to a document issued and signed by the Henderson County Tax Collector's Office on June 27, 1908, Jones received a license to prescribe drugs and "to carry on the special trade or business of physician," earning for him the salutation of "Doctor" by many of the early residents of Green River and the neighboring counties of Polk and Transylvania. He paid five dollars for the license.

Also akin to Pace, Captain Levi Jones owned one of the Green River zircon mines. With Captain M.C. Toms, he also leased mineral rights on a section of Reasonover Creek in Transylvania County.

One of ten children born to John Jones (1815–1864) and Elizabeth Hamilton Jones (1814–1894), Levi Jones married Rosannah Jane "Rosa" Pittillo (1837–1926). The couple bore ten children.

Jones acquired more than one thousand acres in Green River between 1869 and 1920, some of which he sold to P.J. Hart, J.O. Bell and several others. Jones purchased one hundred acres of this land from Mordecai Morgan (1812–1881) and his wife, Sarah H. Morgan, in 1869.* (Morgan was married first to Mary Nancy Heatherly, 1811–1852.) Much of Jones's land was later covered by Lake Summit, alongside which he had operated a combination saw- and gristmill. Levi Jones sold about an acre of land for one dollar to the deacons of Crossroads Baptist Church. He and his wife are buried in the cemetery at this church.

* *Henderson County Deed Book* 8: 697, 1869.

TUXEDO AND LAKE SUMMIT

According to the *French Broad Hustler* in May 1908:

> *Through Flat Rock you ride and then you climb, higher and higher, the Blue Ridge standing like a green-covered giant's fortress before you. At last the summit is reached and from there a panorama of scenic beauty unfolds. Then down and down you go, taking advantage, if you please, of the very excellent new roads the chain gang has made, passing the convict camp, where you see B.B. Souther, gun on hip, cigarette in mouth, keeping a vigilant eye on the convicts, whose chains clank-clank seem to but ill accord with the holy Sabbath calm of the beautiful morning. You see Joe Rhodes, now serving a sentence for cutting Joe Bryson on that election day of a year ago. You wonder, mayhap, at the privileges accorded a convict, but just then, coming in sight of the*

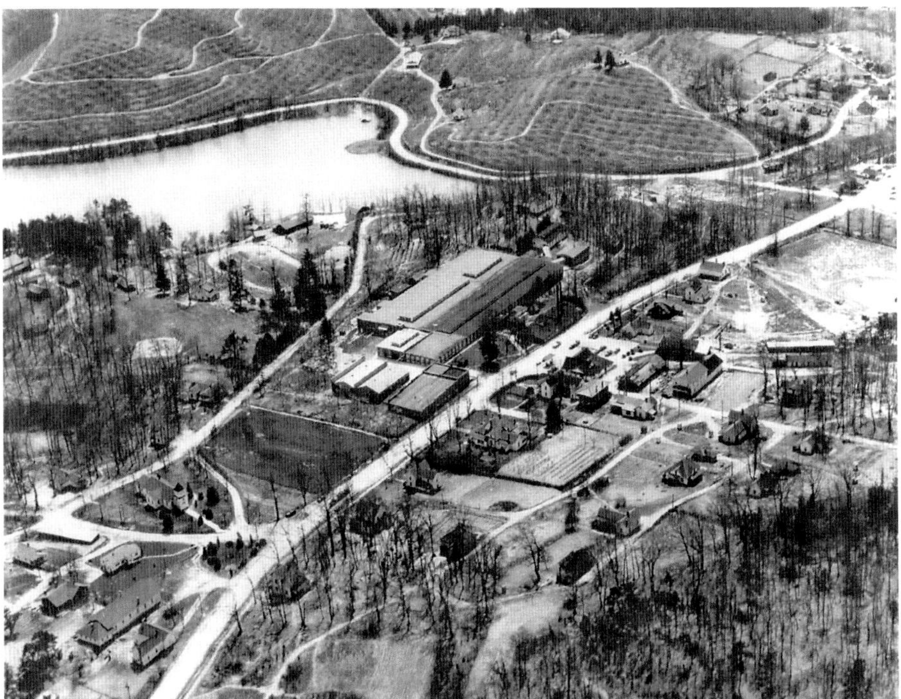

Aerial perspective of Tuxedo with the Green River Manufacturing Company at center, Tuxedo First Baptist Church on the left and Lake Summit in the background. *Courtesy of Henderson County Genealogical and Historical Society, Inc.*

> *new factory of the Green River Manufacturing Co., you forget all about such things in admiration of the men who have caused so great a building to be erected here seemingly so far away from everywhere… You look around and see streets laid out, comfortable cottages, ample grounds. You notice Mr. J.O. Bell's handsome residence and next to it, a big fourteen-room house, just now occupied by only two lone men, Mr. Callahan and Dr. Smart, who complain somewhat of being crowded for room—poor men! You drive on and the road, close overhung with trees and masses of laurel is still beautiful. You see a dead rattler in the road, beautiful and repulsive. You pass a wagon loaded with the everlasting chestnut wood—one cord—four dollars. The oxen have been taken out and yonder in that field of gold, are resting peacefully on this Sabbath. Soon you come to Zirconia Church. Many are already there. Soon more come—in wagons, in buggies, on horseback. The building is full. The sweet sounding organ, the fresh strong voices of the young men and girls seem well fitted to the surroundings. A prayer earnest and simple, then Judge Pace talks and is followed by Col. Pickens. Mr. J.O. Bell occupies a front seat.*

Power companies in the western Carolinas began around the turn of the twentieth century to supply electricity to the region's burgeoning textile mills. Since the end of the Civil War, the South had clamored to develop an industrial economy, resulting in a mania for cotton mills that sprang up between 1880 and 1930. By 1905, the Piedmont Carolinas boasted over 20 percent of the nation's spindles, powered then by steam. By 1913, southern textile mills consumed more cotton than those of New England, and by the 1920s, southern mills achieved national supremacy.*

The potential power of the Green River enticed visionaries at the turn of the last century, and as a consequence, a village grew up in the midst of farmland and unpaved back roads. Soon after, Henderson County would boast its largest industrial enterprise, bringing jobs and also housing, more churches, a school, a library on wheels, a company store and post office, camps and a lake to the hub of Green River. In 1919, J.O. Bell constructed a company pavilion near a waterfall on land his son J.O. Jr. later developed as Camp Arrowhead. The bell that called shifts and served as the village fire alarm now hangs at the adjacent Camp Glen Arden.

---

* Durden, *Electrifying the Piedmont Carolinas*.

In March 1909, the *French Broad Hustler* informed its readers:

> *$250,000 POWER COMPANY NEAR HENDERSONVILLE*
> *Messrs. George E. Ladshaw, Gabriel Cannon and A.L. White, Spartanburg, have incorporated a company, which will build a $250,000 power plant on Green River, at Potts Shoals, seven miles from town. The offices of the company will be in Hendersonville. The incorporation papers were received from the Secretary of State Wednesday and are now in Judge Pace's office. Work on the plant will start immediately. The company will furnish power for any purpose, manufacturing, illuminating and operating. Streetcars!*

In 1907, Joseph Oscar Bell Sr. (1866–1939) bought interest in the Freeze-Bacon Mill at Hendersonville, securing funding with his colleagues J.A. Durham and S.B. Tanner. The three men formed a textile mill, which they named Green River Manufacturing Company, alongside the Green River, with Tanner president, Durham vice-president and Bell secretary, treasurer and resident manager of the fledgling company. Early operations included an on-site brickyard and sawmill for the construction of the plant and its ancillary structures. Dana resident Buford H. Hill (1883–1950) operated the sawmill.

According to an April 1907 *French Broad Hustler*:

> *As a large force of men work on the Green River cotton mill, cottages are being put up, streets laid out and graded, and already a very definite idea of the size of the town may be had from the work done. The brick used in the construction of the buildings is being made on the grounds. The mill will be in operation by December first and will then employ a large force of hands. The company is putting in a sidetrack from Zirconia to the mill, at a cost of $50,000. The railroad company eventually refunds this amount to the mill company, when a certain amount of freight has been shipped. The mill will cost $250,000. The main building will be 1,000 feet long and 100 feet wide, and will be built of brick, two stories high. There is a scarcity of labor, which is delaying the company somewhat. The payroll of the company will be over $1,500 a week, when it starts up, and it is believed will approximate that amount within 30 days.*

Between 1907 and 1910, Bell orchestrated the construction of a sustainable mill village of more than fifty houses and oversaw the erection of a dam above Green River Falls to power the mill with a hydroelectric plant. Before

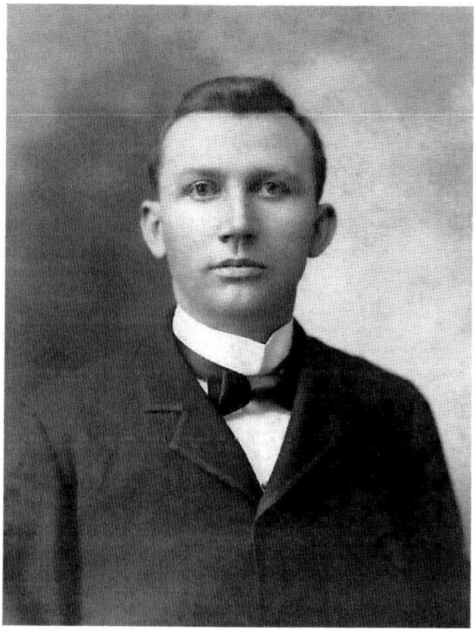

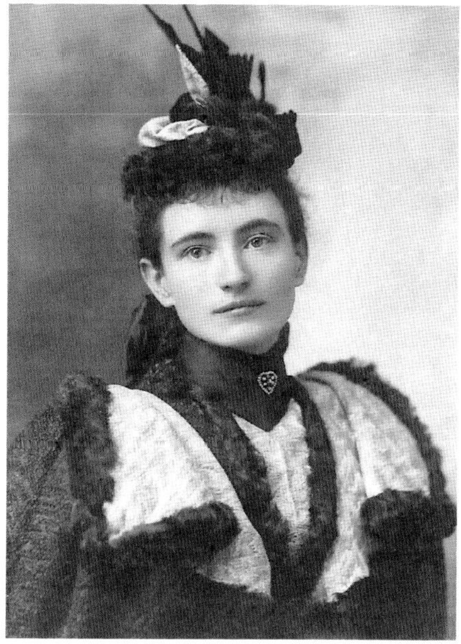

Joseph Oscar Bell and Lillias Durham Bell. *Courtesy of Edwin Bell.*

settling into his own home, Bell and his family lodged with the Freemans. Bell, born in Due West, South Carolina, had come to Green River from Edenton, North Carolina, with his wife, Lillias Durham Bell (1869–1959). Bell named the village Lakewood, changing it to Tuxedo in 1910, the year the Southern Railway opened a depot in the village. Mrs. J.O. Bell, who kept an apartment in the historic village of Tuxedo Park, New York, suggested the name, which she drew from a hat during the informal process to name the Green River Township's mill village.

In February 1910, the *French Broad Hustler* reported:

> *Mr. J.O. Bell, manager of the great mill at Zirconia, or Lakewood, likes to tell the story of a river that ended nowhere. "A man wanted to sell me a certain water power," said Mr. Bell. "I asked him a number of questions concerning it and finally inquired about the fall of the river. He had already given a glowing description of the waterpower but now he became enthusiastic and said, 'Why, that water falls so far it never gets to the bottom. No, sir, it falls so far that it just becomes a fine spray and the sun's rays, of course, naturally draw it back to the river again. And so it never gets anywhere at all. It falls over the ledge and always comes back.'"*

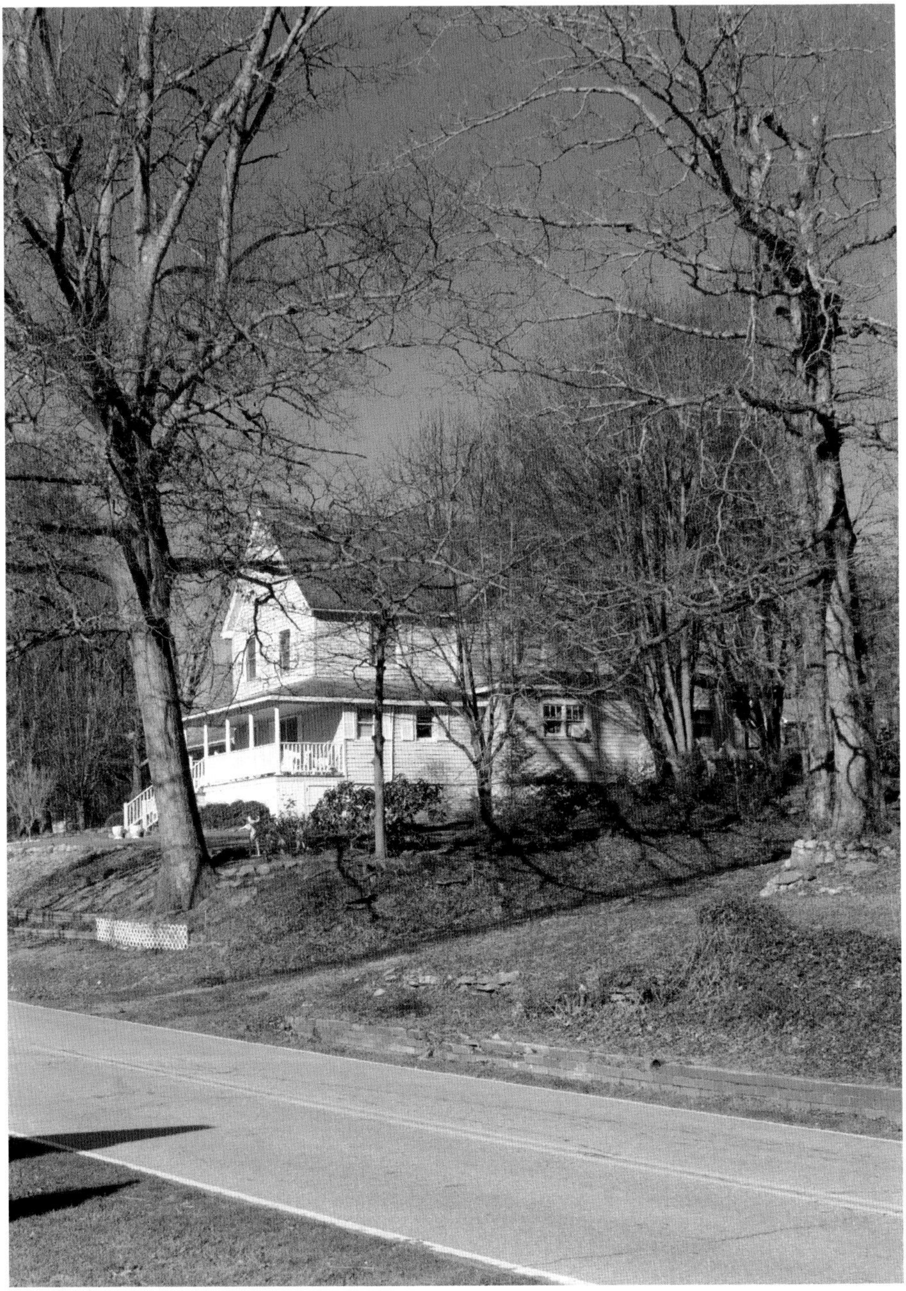

The Jim Andrews home, one of Tuxedo's original mill village houses.

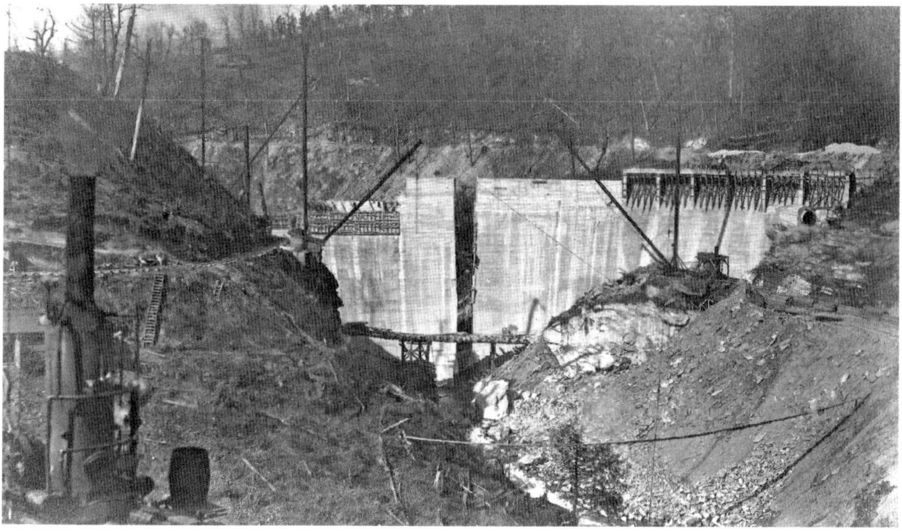

Dam construction at Tuxedo. *Courtesy of Henderson County Genealogical and Historical Society, Inc.*

Prior to all of this, John Adger Law (1869–1950) had dammed the Green River to harness its power to drive mills in Spartanburg County, South Carolina, a major textile center at the turn of the early twentieth century. With other industrialists, Law formed the Manufacturer's Power Company in Spartanburg, which reorganized into the Blue Ridge Power Company, absorbing Hendersonville Power Company. The merger financed two dams, one of twenty feet in Polk County forming Lake Adger and the other a 254-foot single-arch concrete dam in Green River creating Lake Edith, the predecessor of what would be called Lake Summit—the Tuxedo Hydroelectric Plant—placed in operation in 1920.

Bell's company maintained a livery stable for the purpose of transporting cotton to the mill and finished products to markets beyond via mule teams and an ox cart to and from the Southern Railway station. Bell built a village store that stocked everything from general goods, hay and hardware to clothing, shoes and caskets. The village boasted resident physician Frank Cranford (1884–1932), and dentists came from Hendersonville to perform their services at the boardinghouses. Cranford, from Kings Mountain, resided at the boardinghouse of Frances Arminta Taylor (1860–1936), which was later operated by Bertha McPeters Barnett (1898–1976).

The *French Broad Hustler* in May 1909 noted:

> *STRIKE AT THE GREEN RIVER MILL*
>
> *Last Friday sixteen expert workmen employed at the Green River mill struck for higher wages. Mr. J.O. Bell refused the men's demands and they are no longer employees of the Green River Manufacturing Company.*

Before officials filled the lake in 1920, they evacuated the valley of a wee community known as Happy Hollow, the Crossroads Baptist Church and Levi Jones's grist- and sawmills. Work began in 1919 to elevate the railroad tracks eighteen feet for about a one-mile stretch, for had this not transpired, the tracks would have been submerged. Blue Ridge Power Company paid for the concrete trestle.

In April 1915, the following news appeared in the *French Broad Hustler*:

> *FATAL WRECK AT TUXEDO DUE TO BAD TRACK CONDITION*
>
> *Derailment of a Southern Railway train near Tuxedo, N.C., on August 12, 1914, which resulted in the death of the fireman and injuries to nine passengers, was attributed to track conditions, in a report issued today by the interstate commerce commission.*

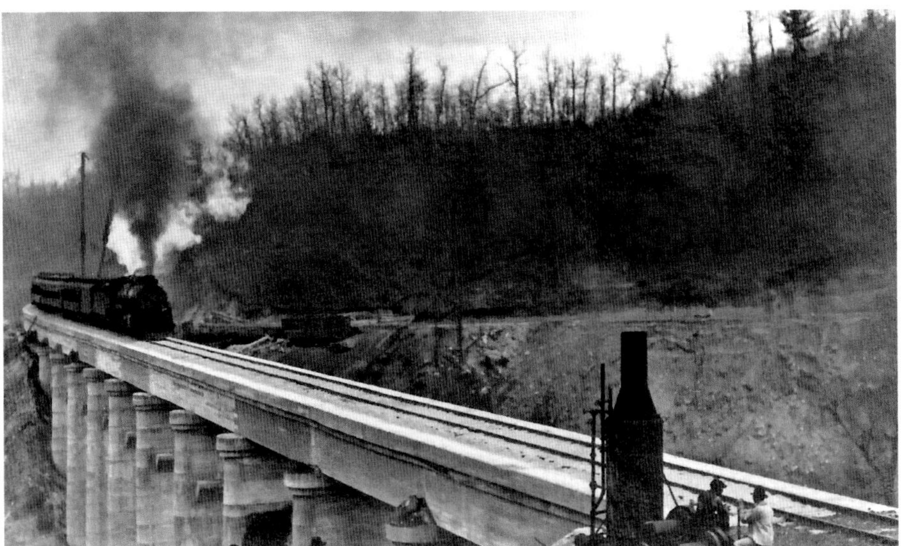

The trestle at Tuxedo. *Courtesy of Henderson County Genealogical and Historical Society, Inc.*

When completed, Lake Summit covered 324 acres, with nearly ten miles of shoreline, the largest lake in Henderson County. Four-hundred-horsepower steam turbines replaced water power, and a Duke Power Company subsidiary purchased the power site in 1929.

Summer dwellings and then year-round homes sprang up around the lake, as did campgrounds. J.O. Bell, considered the founding father of Tuxedo, gave much to the community. More than a magistrate and civic leader, he served as a school committeeman, postmaster, road commissioner, trustee of Fruitland Institute and, later, a North Carolina state senator. Bell, who amassed vast parcels of land in Green River between 1910 and the early 1920s, donated land for and served as the original trustee of Tuxedo First Baptist Church, and he operated the first Tuxedo school, leaving his fingerprint on the town. He built the Classical Revival–style Aloah Hotel, completed in 1919—later expanded and known as the Carson Hotel and Hendersonville Inn and now as Inn on Church—in downtown Hendersonville.

At its peak, the mill employed nearly three hundred people, some of them children. Octavia Freeman Beddingfield's mother worked at the mill at the tender age of fourteen. "There were no labor laws then," she said.

In August 1913, the *French Broad Hustler* printed the following notice:

> *THE PLAN AND PURPOSE OF THE TUXEDO CLUB*
>
> *We propose to convert a magnificent tract of 300 acres of land into one of the most beautiful resorts to be found anywhere. We propose to sell 100 memberships in the Club for $150 each, payable $30 upon signing application for membership and the balance in monthly installments of $10 each. We propose to erect with the money received from the sale of memberships, a modern clubhouse on a suitable location on the club estate where the members and their families will be furnished board at actual cost. We propose for the protection of club members and the protection of the entire community, to adopt strict building regulations covering the cost of buildings erected by members, the sanitary conditions of premises and purposes of buildings so erected. The home of the Tuxedo Club is in the very heart of nature undefiled—a rugged, monstrous mountain as wild, as rugged and as wildly beautiful as the day the Indian hunted the bear, which made its home on its slopes. It is, to repeat, Nature undefiled, Nature in her grandest, most inspiring mood—and it is all very, very beautiful.*
>
> *Officers:*
>
> *D.S. Pace, President, real estate broker*

J. Fuller Lyon, Vice President, Bond Clerk, State Treasury, Columbia, S.C.
R.H. Staton, Attorney, Mayor of Hendersonville, N.C.
Directors:
D.S. Pace, Hendersonville, N.C.
J. Fuller Lyon, Columbia, S.C.
Mrs. J.F. Lyon, Columbia, S.C.
Mrs. L.M. Cullen, Miami, Fla.
R.H. Staton, Hendersonville, N.C.

The proposed resort never came to be, but by virtue of the number of campgrounds in Green River Township, the officers' and directors' descriptions rang true.

GREEN RIVER SUMMER CAMPS

The bucolic Green River Valley with its manmade lake and rushing streams and cascades has hosted a number of campgrounds since the early 1900s, with the Bells of the Tuxedo textile mill spearheading some of the first efforts. Camps in the region include:

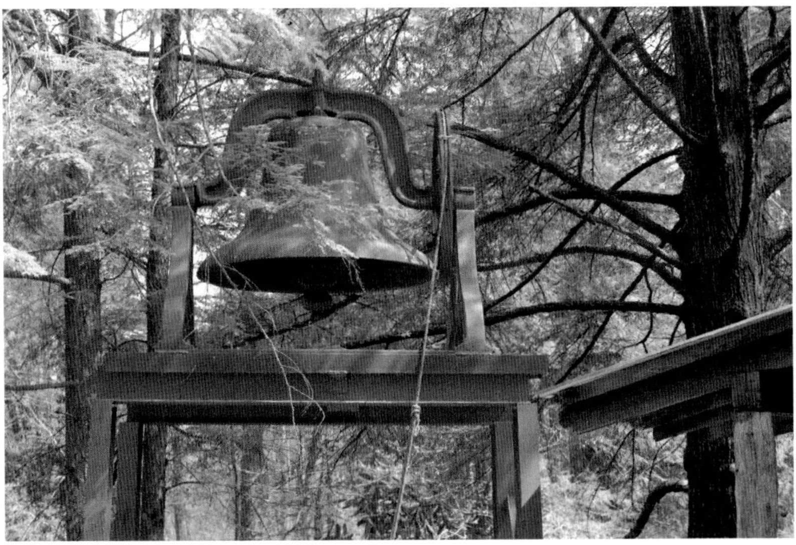

This bell at Camp Glen Arden once called the workers and served also as a fire alarm at J.O. Bell's textile mill. *Photographed with permission.*

- Camp Greystone for Girls (Christian), founded by Dr. Joseph R. Sevier (1920) and operated by his daughter Virginia Sevier Hanna and her husband, Joe Hanna, of Spartanburg, South Carolina (1945). The Hannas' daughter Libby Miller and her husband, Jim Miller, took over in 1968, and their son Jim "Jimboy" Miller Jr. currently operates the camp with his mother.
- Camp Mondamin for Boys, founded and operated by Frank Bell (1922), succeeded by Frank Bell Jr. and currently operated by Andrew Bell.
- Camp Arrowhead for Boys (Christian), operated by J.O. Bell Jr. (1937). Jim Frady currently operates this camp.
- Camp Green Cove for Girls, opened by Frank Bell and operated by Mrs. Frank Bell (1945). Nancy Bell currently directs the camp.
- Windy Wood Camp (1957–86) operated by Joanne Hafner and William Howard "Bill" Waggoner (1957) on the site of the Lake Summit Playhouse.
- Camp Falling Creek for Boys, founded by Jim and Libby Miller and once operated by Chuck McGrady (1969) and currently by Yates Pharr.
- Camp Glen Arden for Girls—listed with the National Register of Historic Places—founded by Mrs. J.O. Bell Jr. (1951–1971) at the Christ School in Arden and moved to a section of the Camp Arrowhead property in 1972. In 1990, Arrowhead moved to a nearby site. It has been operated since 1996 by Glen Arden Associates and directed by Carol "Casey" Thurman and Elizabeth "Liz" McIntosh.
- Green River Preserve, a summer coed camp for gifted students, operated by Sandy and Missy Schenk (1987).
- Noah's Ark, a short-lived, now-defunct camp for boys and girls at the junction of Green River Road and Riverwood Drive, operated by Ellen Woodside Richardson of Jacksonville, Florida (1940s), and currently the site of Summit Landing River Park.
- North Carolina Elks Camp for Boys (1945), which began in 1924 as Camp Bonnie-View for girls, operated by Professor and Mrs. F.E. Elliot of Ohio and currently owned by Boyd "Bub" Hyder and Loren Wells. Now Talisman Camp.
- Mountain Cabin Camp for Girls and Mountain Cabin Camp for Boys, operated by Ellen Woodside Richardson (1927) in Flat Rock and then moved to Lake Summit in 1929. It closed in the mid-1930s.
- Camp Flintlock, Zirconia, a short-lived tent camp (1966–89) owned by William C. Ross of Spartanburg, South Carolina.

According to a June 1911 *French Broad Hustler*:

> *RESULTS SHOWN ON GOOD ROADS*
> *Perhaps one of the best examples of what a road overseer can do in a very short length of time in Henderson County is clearly shown in the magnificent piece of roadwork lately completed between Flat Rock and Green River.*

After World War I, an economic downturn triggered inflated cotton prices, making it difficult for the Green River Manufacturing Company to compete in the market, and the business passed between different managers after the company's bankruptcy in 1927. By the late 1920s, the stretch of highway through Tuxedo sported a paved surface, with four lanes completed by 1979.

In 1933, Robert W. Boys (1870–1949) bought the textile plant and renamed it Green River Mills, Inc., which was continued under that name by Boys's son George Waring Boys (1901–1977) until 1958, when it closed. (A union strike in 1955 had an impact on the business at hand.) For family members of mill employees, the Boys family hosted activities including a summer day camp, Fourth of July celebrations, a baseball team and gift giving at Christmastime for students of the Tuxedo School. In 1959, textile giant John Peters Stevens Jr. (1897–1977) added the enterprise to his J.P. Stevens & Company, Inc. chain of mills, renaming the Green River facility J.P. Stevens Company and utilizing the plant for the manufacture of synthetic yarns. West Point–Pepperell bought the plant in 1988. When operations closed in 1990, 250 people lost their jobs. Thereafter, the site reopened as Farley Textiles, a cloth-recycling plant, and in 2000, Brittain & Sons Recycling took over the building. After just over one hundred years, the great enterprise faded to memories when workmen demolished the condemned structures in 2010—but a village, a lake and world-class campgrounds exist today as corollaries of J.O. Bell's vision. Soon, a community park will occupy the site of the mill.

Norma Rae

The 20th Century Fox movie *Norma Rae* (1979), based on a true-life union-organizing campaign at the J.P. Stevens & Company mill in Roanoke Rapids, North Carolina, drew its inspiration from millworker Crystal Lee Sutton (1940–2009) and union organizer Eli Zivkovich. Sally Fields (1946–) played the lead character, Crystal, and Pat Hingle (1924–2009), one-time resident of Saluda, North Carolina, played the character Vernon.

After operating the Old Mill Playhouse in the Rhett Mill on Highland Lake, Robroy Farquhar (Robert William Smith, 1911–1983) and his Vagabond Players opened the Lake Summit Playhouse in a vacated schoolhouse at Tuxedo in 1948. The production company moved back to Flat Rock in 1952, changing its name to the Vagabond School of Drama, forerunner of the Flat Rock Playhouse and YouTheatre.

Worshipful Places

It took three things to run the Church of God: Grace, grit and greenbacks.
—Reverend John Lynch Brookshire (1851–1926)

Green River hosts a number of churches, each of them Baptist with the exception of one. The first, Green River Baptist Church, begun in 1835, was formally organized in 1837 as an offshoot of Mud Creek Baptist Church for Green River Baptists, with Reverend James W. Blythe (1808–1897) its first pastor. In 1856, members built another log meetinghouse farther down

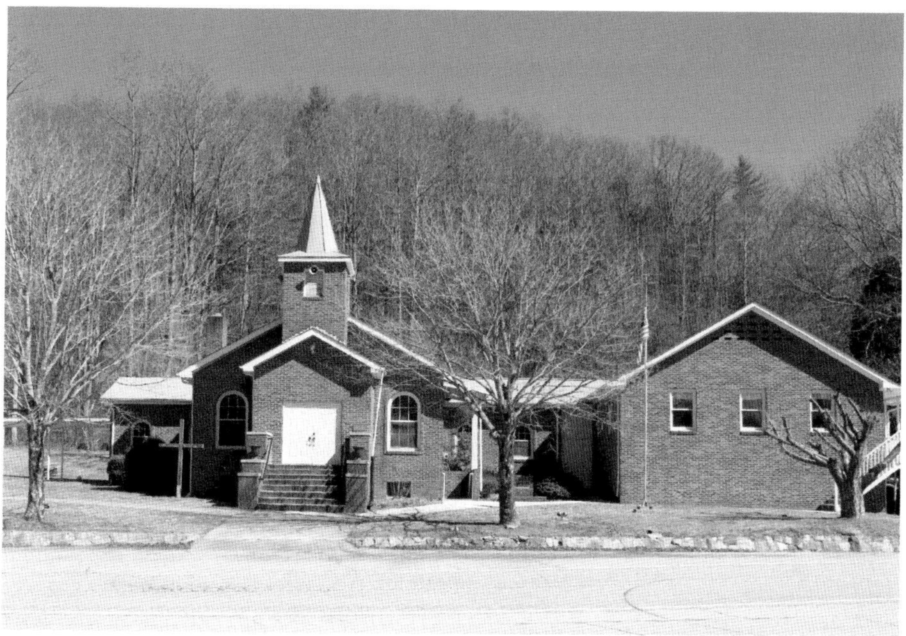

Green River Baptist Church.

the valley—in the vicinity of the current church—where they held services monthly. The congregation joined the Salem Association in 1859, changing to the Transylvania Association in 1867 and joining the Carolina Baptist Association after its founding in 1882. Utilities included a wood stove and coal-burning oil lights, and men frequently carried their guns to services. Early members included the Merideth Freemans, the P.J. Harts, the Daniel Paces, the Nathaniel Beddingfields, the Corns and Nixes, Andrews, Statons, Osteens, Levis and Wards. In 1890, John Benjamin Franklin "Frank" Pace donated an acre of land for a new meetinghouse. A weather-boarded church replaced the smaller building in 1927 under the supervision of Leland T. Pace (1894–1980). Enlargement, wings, a baptistery and a pastorium followed in 1949, 1953 and 1967, and the complex was brick-veneered in 1970. Pastors have included W.B. Johnson, L.W. Berry, James W. Blythe, James McDowell, J.R. Rhodes, J.J. Boone, J. Peyton Corn, Jesse Osteen, Virgil D. Jones, J.L. Mullinax, D. Lewis Staton (great-great-grandson of Frank Pace), Stuart McCall and Robby Henderson. Reverend Seth Nichols currently pastors the church.

CEDAR SPRINGS BAPTIST CHURCH rises from a knoll above one side of Green River Road, and on the other side, its fellowship hall and picnic grounds flank the rolling Green River. Founded in 1853, this church was formally organized in 1847 by a group that broke off from Green River Baptist Church, which granted the request on January 16, 1846, in a document signed by clerk John Davis. Members, who first met in the Rock Creek schoolhouse, built their first church near a spring and a large cedar tree about one and a half miles from the present one. The next structure, built shortly after 1900, stood next to the current one, which members dedicated in 1968, when they razed the old church, making room for a parking lot. Pastors have included William Anderson, John Lynch Brookshire, Robert Hamilton, J.S. Holbert, Jesse Osteen, Marion Clayton Cheatwood (1892–1986), Ed Kuykendall, Henry Mace, Paul Chandler and Bill Tinsley. Reverend Dan Holbert currently pastors the church.

Named for two adjacent springs, DOUBLE SPRINGS BAPTIST CHURCH began as a log meetinghouse in 1871. A new structure was built and dedicated in 1883 on land donated by William C. Ward (1829–1891) and the current one begun—with financial assistance from J.Z. and Agnes Cleveland—in 1924 and completed in 1926 with pillars of native rock. The first church featured two front doors—one for men and the other for women, who sat on opposite sides of the room. Organizers included B.S. Jones, M.E. Smith, E.J. Mullinax, M.M. Duckworth and H.K. Pace, with charter members Bartlett,

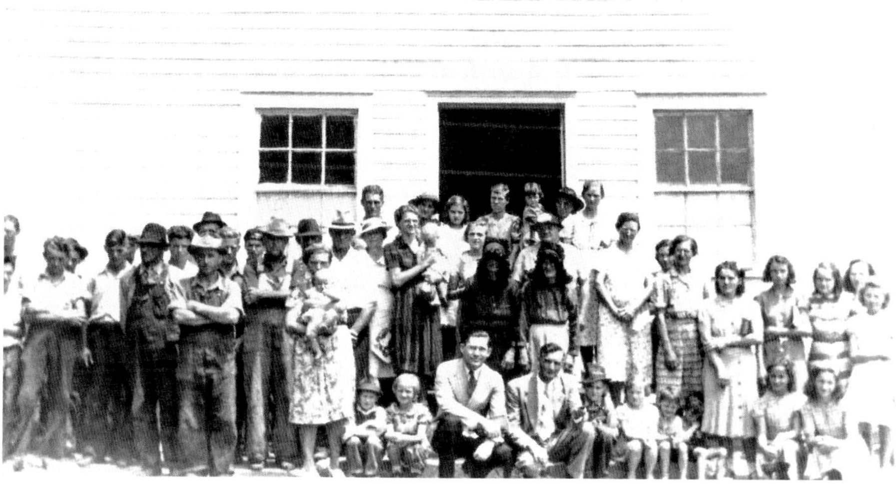

Cedar Springs Baptist Church, with Reverend Marion Cheatwood (squatting, right of center), Reverend Cobb (left of Cheatwood) and members of the Capps, Ward, Morgan, Peace, Allen, Kelly, Bane and Osteen families. *Courtesy of Arnetta Osteen Mullinax.*

William, W.C., Nancy, Jemima, Lucy and Manervia Ward; George B. Hudson; J.H. Morgan; Easter S. Morgan; Nancy Hargrove; and Margaret Shipman. Elder B.S. Jones moderated the first service. Pastors have included M.E. Smith, T.F. Nelson, J.A. Dill, John Lynch Brookshire, E.J. Mullinax, J.S. Holbert, A.B. Jones, J.J. Gentry, George D. Greer, Elmer Adolph Kilstrom, Zeb Brookshire, General Beddingfield and Larry Henderson. The Carolina Baptist Association was formed here on October 19, 1877—a new body with six churches taken from the Transylvania Association and located in the Green River section of Henderson County. Tradition suggests that this came as a result of disagreement among the preachers of the Transylvania Association. Reverend Joe George currently pastors the church. The Bartlett Ward Cemetery lies across the road.

Mount Olivet Baptist Church began—in an open-sided shed on a slope of Mount Olivet in 1870—from Mud Creek Baptist Church under the leadership of Reverend John Wesley Anderson (1845–1899), Noah Webster Corn (1843–1917), Wiley Jones (1843–1916) and others of the Mount Olivet community. The first building, constructed of logs and completed in 1882 on grounds now occupied by the cemetery, burned in 1895 after being struck by lightning. Piety H. Jones (1881–1882), daughter of Wiley Jones (1843–1916) and Martha Jane Neal Jones (1845–1926), was the first to be buried in the cemetery. A framed building replaced the

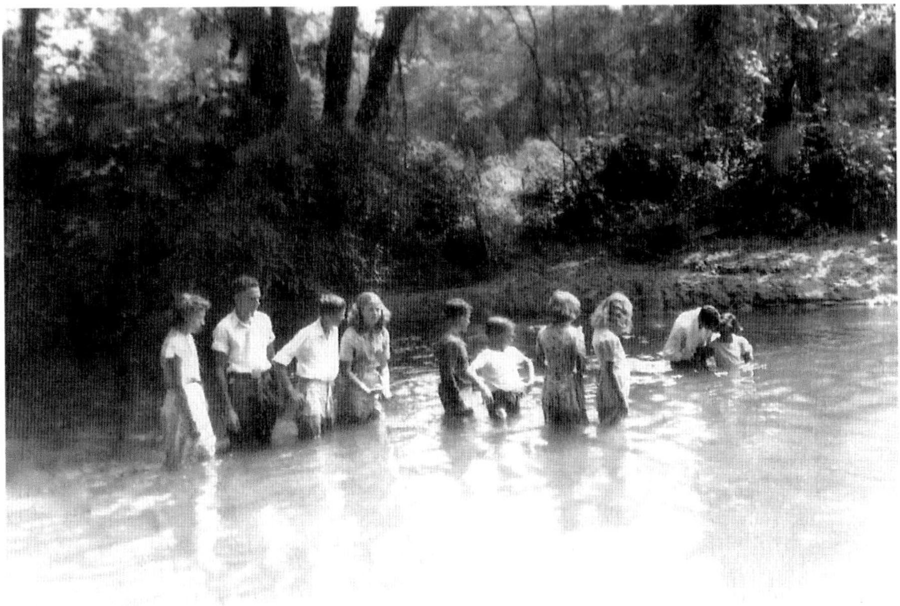

The baptismal pond of Mount Olivet Church. *Courtesy of Octavia Freeman Beddingfield.*

log church, but a fire in 1945 destroyed it as well. Fire claimed the third church also, in 1968.

In January 1914, Reverend John C. Ward wrote in the *French Broad Hustler*:

> *Mr. John L. Orr of Hendersonville visited the church at Mt. Olivet last Sunday and made quite an interesting address, and was greatly enjoyed by the congregation. The organ, which was recently purchased for the church was placed in last Saturday. Next Sunday is our regular monthly meeting and our new pastor will be here on Saturday and Sunday. Reverend Willie Blackwell of Flat Rock was a visitor at Mt. Olivet Sunday and also made a very interesting talk on Sunday school work. Sherman C. Ward will leave Mt. Olivet soon to enter Fruitland Institute for the spring term.*

In the church's early years, John F. Ballard (1853–1930) built a pond on his land with water directed from a stream that ran through the property. This served as the baptismal pond for more than thirty years for the ministers and members of Mount Olivet Baptist Church. Reverend John Sentelle (1859–1935) baptized Duffie R. Corn (1895–1974) in 1909, the first to be christened in Ballard's pond. Ministers of Mount Olivet also performed baptisms at Lake Falls, Camp Ton-A-Wandah and in the Green River until a baptistery was added to the 1960s sanctuary. The contemporary church of brick was completed in 1969 and its steeple added in 2006. Reverend Billy Lewis currently pastors the church.

Established in 1860, the original Crossroads Baptist Church held services in a house that stood on a bank of the Green River—a home that served also as a schoolhouse. Charter members included Phillip Allen Kuykendall (1837–1912) and wife, Rachel Heatherly Kuykendall (1839–1916), and Noah Webster Corn and wife, Sarah Matilda Capps Corn (1843–1916), with Matthew William Corn (1845–1885) as the first pastor. Levi Jones deeded land for Crossroads Baptist Church in 1911. Memory A. Ward (1881–1954), David Levi Beddingfield (1881–1968) and John Cecil Pace (1882–1968) raised a small frame church—described as forty by twenty-four feet with a fourteen-foot ceiling—when the fellowship relocated before 1920 to higher ground above the northern slope of what would become the lake. Ward's general store stood nearby, as did a spur of the train station. Several pre-1920 inscriptions in the Crossroads Cemetery suggest that many graves had been moved to this site before officials began filling Lake Summit. One of those included the grave of Benjamin Franklin Jones (1872–1910), son of Levi and Rosa Jones. Ben purportedly drowned in the Green River while seeking a baptismal spot. Before the current church was built in the early 1960s, the fellowship sat on slatted benches, and at times the clatter of passing trains momentarily interrupted services. Members moved the 1920 structure aside to make room for the new one, rolling the framed building on logs. Although the relocated building stood unlevel against a slope, members nevertheless worshiped there until the completion of their new sanctuary. Early pastors included Robert F. Hamilton, Jesse E. Osteen, J.P. Corn, Albert Rhodes and Tony Youngblood. Eddie Conard Jr. has pastored the church since 2002.

Members called it Poplar Springs Baptist Church when they founded it in 1915, using a small log structure at the Old Pearson-Ward Cemetery (now Mountain Valley Baptist Church Cemetery) until 1919. Members began constructing a larger building in 1917 and occupied it from 1919 until 1932, when they began building a larger church about a half mile distant, just north of the bridge over Bell Creek. Acting as moderator in 1932, Reverend Duffie R. Corn suggested renaming the church Mountain Valley Missionary Baptist, and this name branded the church completed in 1933. Mountain Valley Baptist Church offered foot-washing services twice a year and hosted revival meetings once or twice yearly. Early pastors included J.P. Corn, Pink Corn, J.E. Sentelle, N.W. Corn, Jesse E. Osteen, William Nelson, J.S. Hobert and W.M. Blackwell. The structure of brick was completed in 1972. Reverend Shannon Owen currently pastors the church.

Perched on a lofty bank above the Greenville Highway, Zion Hill Baptist Church began as a union church when it met in a canvas tent in 1914. Members next worshiped in a private home and then in a building that had formerly served as a clubhouse in the Zirconia community, with Doc Kuykendall, Dick Anders and J.C. Pace as organizers and Reverend James Jefferson Gray (1860–1932) as pastor. The group formally organized as a Baptist church in 1916. Building expansion took place in 1940, and successive pastors included Howard Hudson and Luther Capell. Arthur Eugene Taylor (1903–1995) helped build the church. After expansion and brick veneering, the current building was dedicated in 1987. Reverend Blair Stewart currently pastors the church.

In the heart of the village stands Tuxedo First Baptist Church. Early congregants met in one another's homes, reliant at first on pastors from Hendersonville. Early on, Methodist pastors Litaker and Moore served from the Hendersonville pastorate, and Reverend Newell served from Tryon. Other early Methodist pastors included Reverends Coble, Burgess and Shelton. Members withdrew from the Methodist Conference in favor of the Baptist denomination and organized a church in 1910 with twenty-four charter members meeting in various homes until J.O. Bell deeded to the group the present site, giving the use of the textile mill's community house until a sanctuary could be built. Before long, the members erected a small church served by their first Baptist pastor, Reverend Brown, succeeded by Reverend Slattery. Successive pastors included King, Foster, A.B. Jones, M.L. Lewis (first resident pastor), George Greer, Wade W. Worley, E.M. Walker, Wayne Peek, Harold McKinnish, W.M. Belcher, Randall Joines, Grady Hamby, R.A. Pate, Homer Couch and Leo Bell. A new church replaced the old one in the 1960s, with worship services held in the educational building during the interim period. Members dedicated the new building in 1970. Mikell Bennett currently pastors the church.

On land purchased from Joseph O. "Joe" Bell Jr., Mountain View Baptist Church, organized in 1946, stands above Lake Summit. Baxter Heatherly (1888–1978), Hilliard Wilkie Heatherly (1918–2002), Charles Ed Ballew (1920–2003), Reverend Grover Davis (1890–1966), Peter Paul Shipman (1883–1971) and Leroy Levi (1934–) completed construction of the church in 1948. Early pastors included Ansel Merrell, L.V. Allison and Bob Marshall. The current church of brick, completed in 1967, sports a bell from a train. Tuxedo First Baptist Church Cemetery shares the land of Mountain View Baptist Church. A new church replaced the 1948 structure and has been enlarged and updated three times. Until 2000, pastors of Mountain View baptized members in the Green River and, since then, in a portable baptistery on the patio. Reverend Sherrill Moore currently pastors the church.

Bob's Creek Baptist Church, organized in 1948, began as a brush arbor where evangelist William Roy Hester (1916–1987) conducted revival meetings and performed baptisms in nearby Bob's Creek. Eugene Wood counted among the early pastors. Sarah, Addie and Philip Jones donated land for the first church, built in 1949. Before construction of a classroom, teachers led Sunday school classes in the surrounding woods. The church's first funeral service celebrated the life of Addie Jones (1885–1959). In 1989, members purchased land from Cheryl Davis and began construction of a larger sanctuary in 2008, with completion expected in 2014. Reverend A. Dale Holloway currently pastors the church.

Robert Elias Ballard wrote in his book *My Tuxedo No Longer Fits—Memories of a Mill Village Brat*:

> *Most of these churches were begun when travel was limited to horse and wagon…therefore a church would be built where a centralized population existed. Some had their beginnings as a result of a church split, others where an old-fashioned brush arbor had been built. Bob's Creek* [Baptist Church] *had its beginning* [under a brush arbor.]

Members organized Zirconia Missionary Baptist Church in 1953 and built a sanctuary in 1954. George William "Jack" Dryman (1927–1985) and Frank Pitts (1875–1973) helped build this church, first pastored by John Harvey Stanberry (1888–1961). Dennis William "Bill" Brosnan Jr. (1903–1985), general manager of the Southern Railway Company in Washington, D.C., presented members with its bell from a train. Reverend Travis Parker currently pastors the church.

The area's only non-Baptist church, Green River Full Gospel Holiness Church, formed in 1948 following a revival led by Reverend Frank Crawford of Arden, North Carolina. Members cut logs for construction of a church, but the group lost interest until, in 1949, Reverend Joe Southers revived the fervor and led meetings in the home of John Paul Staton. Rosa Pace

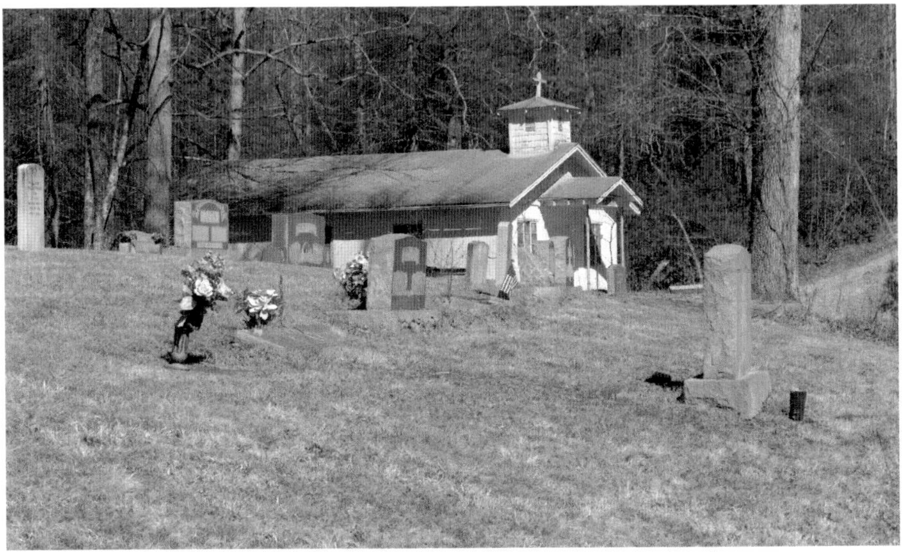

Green River Full Gospel Holiness Church and the Pace Family Cemetery.

Staton Queen* donated one-half acre of land adjoining the Pace Family Cemetery for the purpose of building a church, which, under the name of Green River Full Gospel Holiness, was completed and dedicated in 1951. Reverend Albert Greene pastored the congregation. In 1953, the Southern Railway Company donated a bell. Members changed the name to Green River Holiness Church in 1955. Reverend Ted Huntley succeeded Albert Green as pastor in 1956, followed by Reverend David Lewis Staton. Dan and Betty Smith took charge after Staton's resignation, followed by Reverend Frank Crawford, the founder. Reverend Larry Atkins succeeded Crawford, followed by Bill McDonald, Hubert Hadley and William Bradley. Presently, the church stands abandoned.

According to sketchy accounts, blacks in the area worshiped in a cabin at the Kingdom of Happy Land and, from the time of World War I to the early 1920s, attended religious services and school lessons in a home in a section known as Possum Hollow. There existed also in Green River a chapel by the name of Bane or Bayne. At a bend in the Green River, not far from the homeplace of Clyde and Fannie Morgan, many baptisms have been performed in what locals call the "Lemon Hole."

* Rosa Pace Staton Queen was the daughter of John Benjamin Franklin Pace and Mary Ann Jones Pace.

Green River Schools

Before the days of formal education and consolidation, Green River youngsters attended classes in churches and homes. Early one-room, one-teacher schoolhouses (subscription, old-field schools) included Cedar Springs, Crossroads, Double Springs, Green River and Mount Olivet, the latter the last one-room school for white children in Henderson County. In this era, it was not uncommon for children to walk as many as three miles to school, a time when farm and factory work many times preempted students from attending regularly. Green River old-timers have also mentioned a one-room school in the area called Coon Cove, which operated for only a few years.

Established in the mid-1800s, Double Springs School counted among the earliest learning institutions in Henderson County. Emblematic of its era, this schoolhouse was constructed with logs and rebuilt later as framed buildings, including the last one in 1916. The school boasted one of the county's first libraries. Its teachers included Lawrence Augustus Anderson, Captain James Henry Beddingfield, Margaret Burge, Bessie Fore Capps, Mable Capps, Fred Edney, Walter Justus, Earline Markham, Ludith Ledbetter Osteen, Leonard Revis, Christine "Kitty" Shipman and Leonora Lanning Ward.

Early teachers at Green River School included Miss C. Andrews, Cannon Andrews, Emma Andrews, Mary Brevard, W.T. Clark, Flora Marshall, D.L. Potts, G.F. Powell, Kitty Shipman and Mamie Shipman. Originally located near Green River Baptist Church, the Green River schoolhouse was moved a short distance, enlarged and faced with rock, serving now as a private residence.

The first Tuxedo schoolhouse was built in 1916 on two acres of land sold by the Green River Manufacturing Company to the Henderson Board of Education. Previously, classes had been held in mill buildings. When a larger school was built from 1923 to 1924 on another site, the 1916 three-room school became a residence, later part of the Camp Windy Wood property. The larger school of brick suffered interior fire damage in 1928 but was quickly repaired. The Tuxedo School included grades one through seven, with eighth grade added after World War II with some high school subjects offered. Seventh and eighth graders moved to the junior high school at Flat Rock when consolidated county schools opened in 1960.

The Tuxedo School of brick was completed in 1924, a vision of J.O. Bell Sr. for the purpose of educating the children of his mill village. Bell's wife, Lillias, one of its first teachers, went on to be the school's principal. Estelle Jones Osteen (1908–2005) and Ruth Edna Hill Mullinax (1918–2002) counted among the Tuxedo School's beloved schoolmarms. Other teachers included

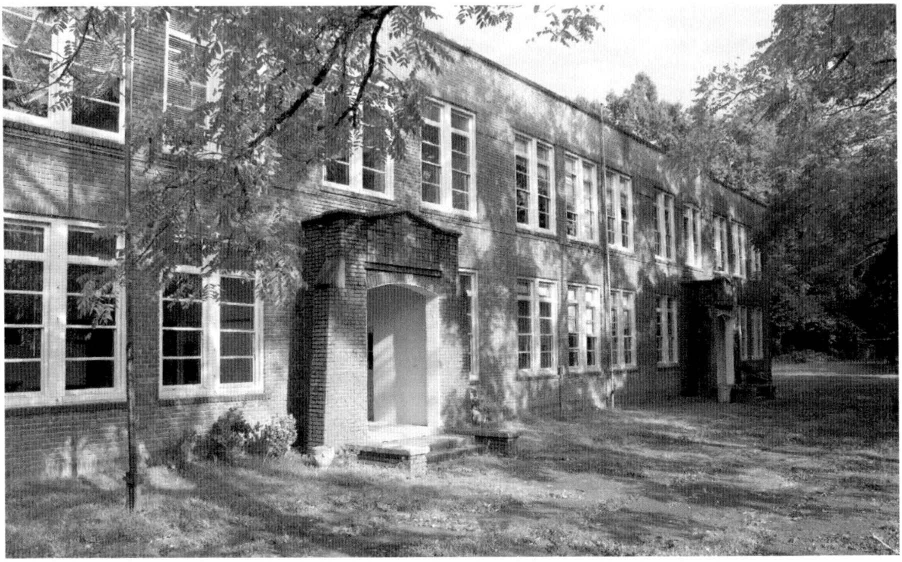

The abandoned Tuxedo School, designed by prominent local architect Erle G. Stillwell.

Bertha Ashworth, Ida Bell, Mary Lowe Bell, Lillis Carwill, Margarette Evans, Jo Hart, E.L. Ponder, Sallie Robinson, Kate Shipman, Mary Theresa Taylor and Dean A. Ward (1904–1991), who also served as one of Tuxedo's principals. The township schools consolidated in 1935. When the Tuxedo School closed in 1993, its pupils transferred to Upward Elementary School, and the old building became an alternative county (extended day) school until 2004, when it closed.

GREEN RIVER POST OFFICES—A CHRONOLOGY

1853: Merideth Freeman, first postmaster at Green River
1866: Green River Post Office closed with Reconstruction
1869: Reopened with Martin Hamilton as postmaster
1871: Closed
1875: Reopened with Philip J. Hart as postmaster
1879: With the coming of the railroad, name changed to Coleman
1882: Name changed back to Green River
1887: Splendor established, with Joseph Warren Ward (1851–1931) as postmaster
1889: Capps Post Office established, with James Clingman Capps (1859–1940) as postmaster

1890: Lead Post Office established, with Berry (Barry) Davis Summey (1865–1939) as postmaster
1895: Capps closed
1890: Green River Post Office changed to Zirconia
1905: Splendor closed
1907: Lead closed
1908: Lakewood Post Office opened with Joseph O. Bell Sr. as postmaster
1910: Lakewood changed to Tuxedo
1984: Zirconia Post Office built by Royce Phelps "Bo" Thomas (1932–1997) at its present location on the Greenville Highway. The structure that housed the previous post office still stands, converted into a private residence. Town folk refer to this area as the top of the "Frog Level."
1991: Tuxedo Post Office moved to Green's Six Oaks Mall as a contract post office
2006: Tuxedo Post Office closed

Additional Green River Township postmasters included Thomas E. Hughston, Ulysses Grant Staton, Andrew J. Newman, Edward A. Edwards, Montraville Lafayette "Mont" Jones, Charles Vernon Waters, Bertha Pace Waters, Joan Gaynelle Isaacs, Pat Lindsey, June Metcalf Orr and Vergie Jane Russell Jones Anders (1920–1988).

Postmasters at Lakewood/Tuxedo included Lillias Durham Bell, Katherine Shipman, Samuel M. King, Sampson W. Bane, James T. Barker Jr., Fred Huggins, Frank D. Bell (son of J.O. and Lillias Bell), Hardee C. Butler and Octavia Freeman Beddingfield.

Country Stores

Since its heyday as a textile mill village, Tuxedo has enjoyed a community store, beginning with a general merchandise emporium established by J.O. Bell Sr. in the core of the mill property. During the Boys' ownership, Donovan Wilkie (1893–1967) managed the store. Known as the "Company Store," this emporium, heated with coal and lighted with kerosene lamps, served many of the community's needs. When the company closed the store, Theron Ernest Mullinax Sr. (1917–2001), who owned the Tuxedo Grocery,

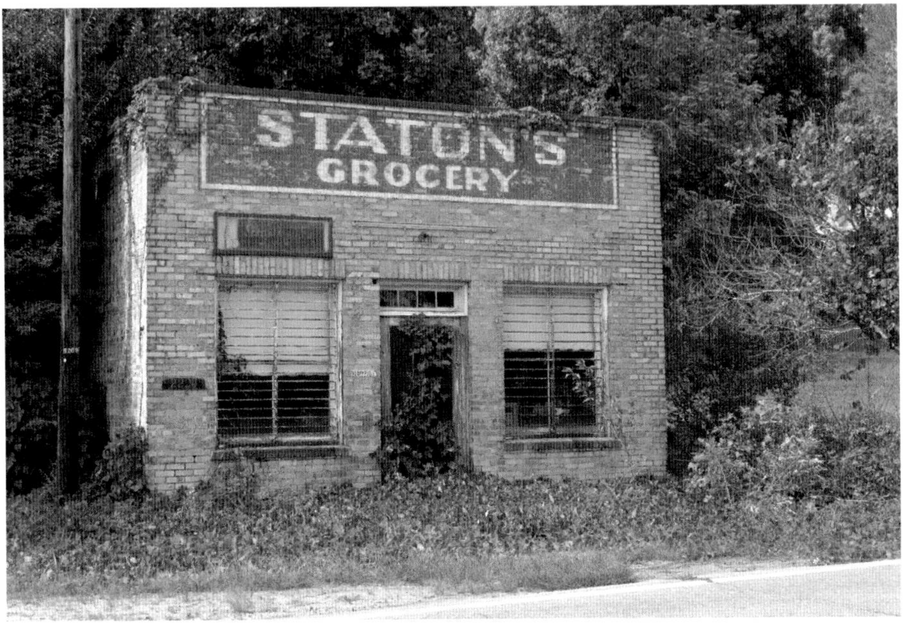

Staton's Grocery.

reopened it. Today, the brick structure houses small businesses, including a beauty parlor and antiques shop.

After 1920, Ulysses Spurgeon Staton (1891–1964) built a general store on the old Greenville Highway, which, before road-widening, he moved a short distance to its current location on Old U.S. Highway 25. Father of noted woodsman, conservationist and trapper John Paul Staton (1917–1992), Ulysses also sprang from a long line of hunters and trappers. In addition to dry goods and candy, Staton sold hides, furs and wild herbs. Staton, also a barber who performed dental procedures, operated the store until his death, succeeded by his wife, Effie Jones Staton (1895–1981), who managed it until her death, after which Steve and Lisa Waggoner sold antiques from the space. Staton's Grocery has been abandoned for several years. The Statons are buried in the Pace Family Cemetery.

The *French Broad Hustler* reported:

> *A BUSINESS DEAL!*
> *I have purchased the store of goods at Zirconia owned by Mr. U.G. Staton. I will continue the business there. I am prepared to offer the highest market prices for chestnut wood, crossties, chickens, eggs, herbs*

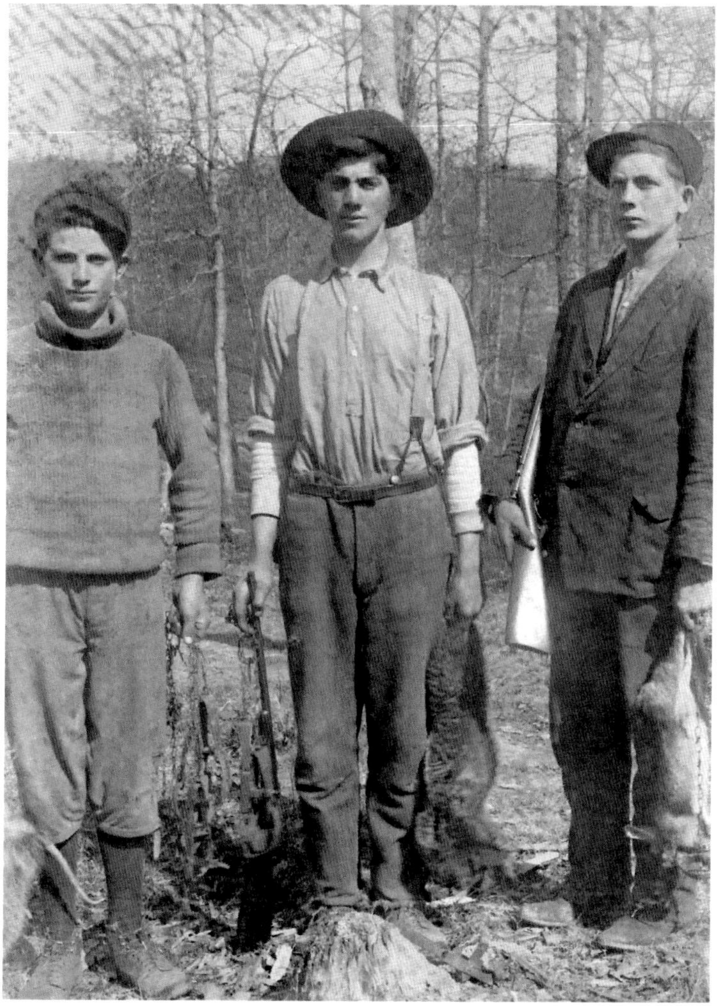

Staton brothers Lewis Avery (1895–1917), Ulysses Spurgeon (1891–1964) and David Edison (1892–1966), sons of Jesse Rhodes Staton (1865–1911) and Rosa Elizabeth Pace Staton (1869–1954). *Courtesy of Gayle Hamilton Stepp.*

and in fact anything you have to sell. I will carry a full and complete line in general merchandise at reasonable prices. I assure the public of courteous treatment and honest values at close prices. All I ask is to give me a trial. Good weights and good measures guaranteed. I promise efficient, prompt, polite and honest service. Yours for fair dealing, C.E. Hypes, Hendersonville, N.C., Dec. 7, 1910.

Other commercial enterprises in and around the village of Tuxedo included the Freeman Grocery on Lake Summit, a barbershop owned by Ernest Craig Lowe (1885–1964), a store operated by Zeb Swann (1911–1974), the Tea Room, Freeman's Lunch (now a barbershop) and Henry's Restaurant. Up in the "Frog Level," between the northwestern shore of Lake Summit and the Zirconia Post Office, additional enterprises once thrived in the days of the depot, including a general store owned by Nathaniel W. Maybin (1913–1983), Rambling Red's Gift Shop owned by musician Ray Flonnoy Boyd (1924–1995) and Rhodes' Antiques & Gifts.

Civic-minded Roscoe Jay Green (1937–1999) of Fruitland volunteered land and materials for the Green River Library. He and his wife, Nancy, opened in 1980 Green's Six Oaks Mall, which continued the tradition of serving the community of Tuxedo and encompassing population centers by supplying everything from general merchandise, seed and feed, gasoline and chuck-wagon grub to postal services, banking for campers and counselors, a community bulletin board and even a sheriff's office and "town hall." Farmers, other residents and summertime campers called Roscoe's the "heart of Tuxedo"—a community hub offering a link to the past and a sense of fellowship for all who enjoyed shopping, dining and gathering there.

An accidental fire destroyed Green's Six Oaks in 2011, but with the help of raised funds, the Green family rebuilt their store fourteen months later and continue to operate the beloved landmark.

With milling but a memory in Green River, the business of agriculture and nurseries perseveres. More than 250 homes and cottages with boathouses trace the shoreline of Lake Summit, where during the season, pontoon cruisers, sail and power boaters, paddlers, skiers and swimmers make the most of the largest lake in the county. Many of the camps endure, and residents of Tuxedo have restored and preserved the old mill village homes in what remains a cordial small town in the midst of pastoral bliss.

Green River Township: proffering glimpses of the past in living color, imparting a manifestation of rural life as it has been lived for decades, where natives seek to hold on to the old ways and values and traditions in the face of recent changes.

II

WHERE APPLE SEEDS AND METHODISM TOOK ROOT IN HENDERSON COUNTY

Edneyville: Latitude 35.394, longitude -82.341, population 2,367, 10.71 square miles, 2,244 feet above sea level.
Fruitland: Latitude 35.396, longitude -82.393, population 2,031, 8.03 square miles, 2,215 feet above sea level.
Clear Creek: Latitude 35.350, longitude -82.441, population 4,616, 16.7 square miles, 2,221 feet above sea level.

In September 1911, the *French Broad Hustler* reported the following:

> *FRUITLAND AND CLEAR CREEK*
> *This is a very busy place these days, with most everyone in their fodder fields. Mr. N.A. Melton preached an excellent sermon at the church Sunday night. Mr. J.N.B. Lanning has been very sick for several days but is slowly improving. A party of young people of this place took a pleasure trip to Chimney Rock Saturday and returned on Sunday. They spent the night at the Red, White and Blue Hotel and all reported a splendid time.*

These lands boast a heritage of some of the earliest settlers in Henderson County. A drive through this fertile vale in springtime proffers vistas of pale-pink petaled orchards, and come late summer through autumn, traffic backs up with carloads of apple gourmands and seekers of cider and other locally grown products.

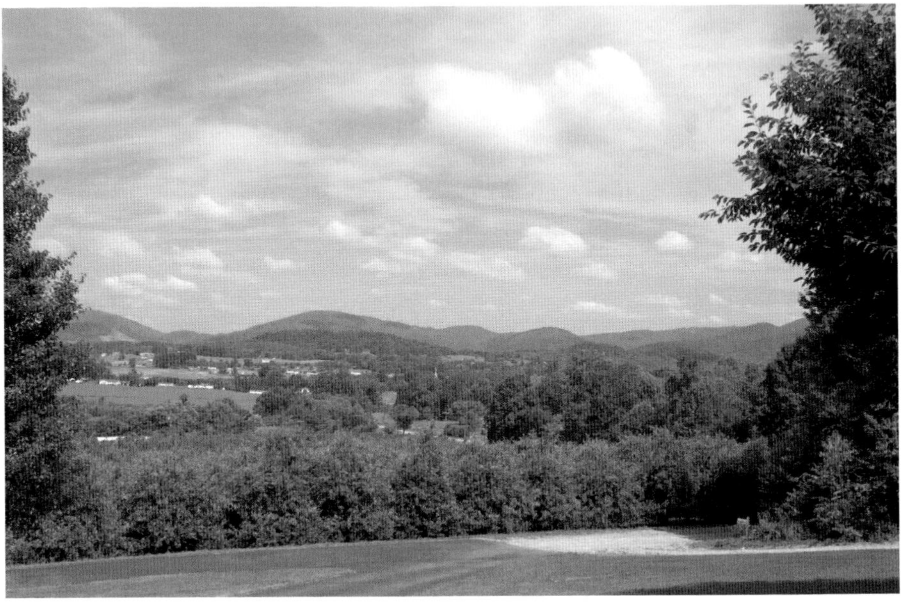

Mountains and orchards appear seamlessly sewn into the scenery of Edneyville. *Photographed with permission of Nancy Dalton Bishop.*

In his 1970 book *Postmarks*, Lenoir Ray stated, "The words 'apple' and 'Edneyville' are almost synonymous." Forty-four years later, the analogy still rings true. Ray referred to pioneer William Mills as "Billy Appleseed," crediting the early settler as the pioneer of apple production in what would become Henderson County. "Mills would become the father of the apple industry in Henderson County," Ray stated. Mills wasn't the only early settler to plant apple trees, and it wasn't until access to and from the mountains via improved roadways, the railroad and modern equipment arrived that the region's apple industry surged, pushing it to become top producer in the state and one of the leading producers in the nation.

In 1883, Wilbur G. Zeigler wrote:

> *The apple finds a congenial home among these southern mountains…Horticulturists are just beginning to appreciate the advantages of the thermal or "no frost" zone…Like conditions of climate exist nowhere on the continent…The climatic conditions with respect to moisture are favorable, and in some respects superior to famous fruit growing districts.*

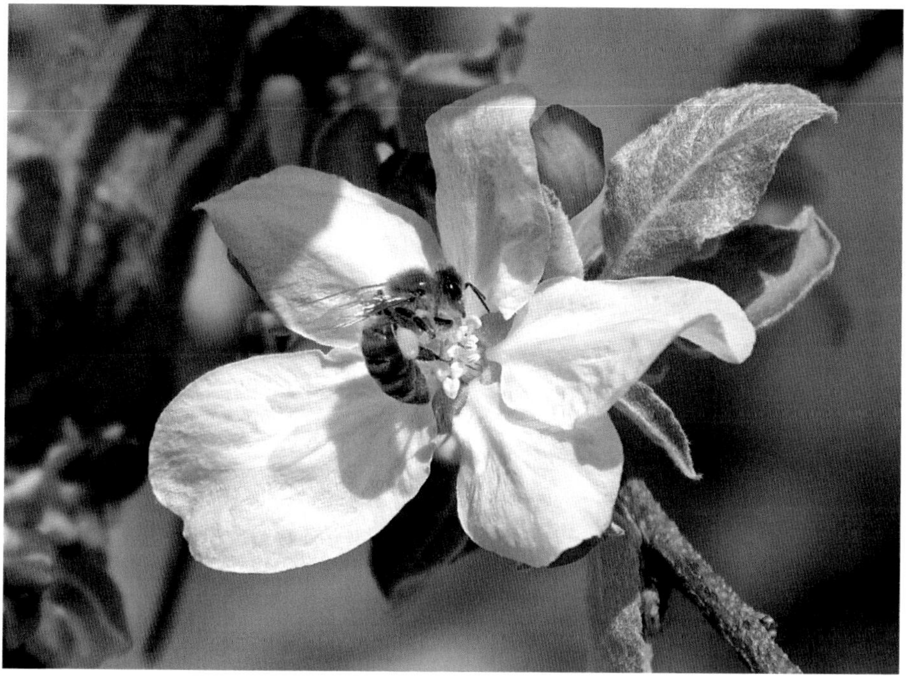

Honeybees prove invaluable to orchardists when by mid-April the county's rural acres burst forth in a flutter of pastel pink and white.

Although early settlers of Henderson County planted apple trees for subsistence and barter, the industry would not gain traction until much later. Apple growers expanded their markets with products surpassing other county crops by the 1950s. Among the first to commercially process apples in Henderson County, orchardist and philanthropist Melvin Lane (1902–1988) organized the Dana Co-op in the 1930s. As a means of apple storage, Lane also built the first refrigeration facility in the county and was one of the first orchardists in the county to subject his crops to government inspection before laws made this a mandatory procedure. In the mid-1940s, part-time residents James Roy Thomas (1897–1961) of J.R. Thomas Produce and H.E. Baxter (1898–1981) were the first in the county to utilize the commercial packinghouse. Orchardists formed the Blue Ridge Apple Growers Association in 1936 and the North Carolina Apple Growers Association in 1954.

Apple growing expanded through the mid-1930s and then slowed down until the 1950s and 1960s, when enhanced techniques and technology

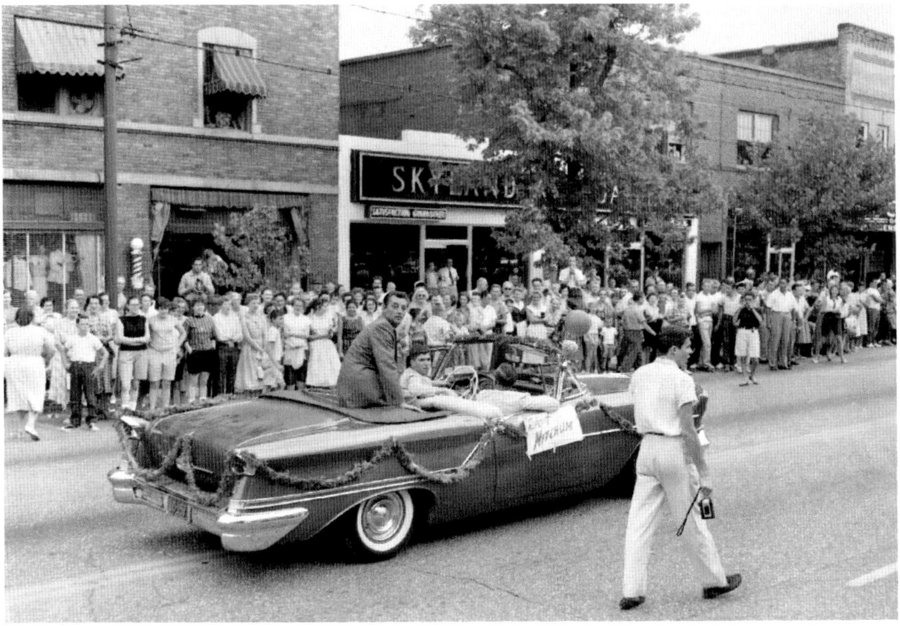

Movie star Robert Mitchum as grand marshal of the 1957 King Apple Parade, Main Street, Hendersonville, North Carolina. *Photo by David Cooley, courtesy of Henderson County Genealogical and Historical Society, Inc.*

such as reduction in tree spacing, speed sprayers, lifts and automatic power pruners accelerated production. Before 1950, orchardists typically spaced their trees thirty to thirty-five feet apart in each row, with rows ranging from thirty to thirty-five feet distant, later spacing them ten to fifteen feet apart with row widths of sixteen to twenty feet. The Hendersonville Chamber of Commerce, together with the Blue Ridge Apple Growers Association and the Henderson County Agricultural Extension Service, organized the Apple Blossom Festival in 1947, held in April, later changing the season to late summer and the name to North Carolina Apple Festival, which climaxes each Labor Day with the King Apple Parade on Hendersonville's Main Street—a boon for local growers and merchants. By 1952, Henderson County had tallied more than 180,000 bearing apple trees, and in 1958, Gerber selected a site in the county for processing local apples and other crops. But how and why did this vast agricultural enterprise take root in Henderson County with Edneyville standing in good stead among the top-ranking apple producers in the Southeast?

"The Mountain Section" in *North Carolina and Its Resources Illustrated* (1896) noted:

> *This is the region of high plateaus and elevated valleys between the Blue Ridge on the east and the Great Smoky range that separates the state* [of North Carolina] *from Tennessee. This region is the home of the apple, and is destined to become the greatest apple-growing region in America when its capabilities in this respect are fully known to fruit growers. Though the apple thrives here under the most negligent treatment and produces unfailing crops, there have been few attempts to grow the fruit in a systematic manner…From the early settlement of the country apples have been grown there from seed, and there is an embarrassment of riches in the shape of varieties that is unknown elsewhere. Many of these native seedling apples are of fine quality, while many are of inferior varieties, there having been a great tendency to grow seedlings of the Limbertwig class, because of their productiveness and keeping qualities, though of a very inferior quality. The Buff, a dry poor apple of the showy Ben Davis style is also largely grown. But that any of the finer apples can be grown there to great perfection is beyond doubt, as has been shown by those who have planted them. Then there are many of the native apples that are of such quality as to deserve propagation and increased cultivation. Here too the Winesap and the York Imperial reach great perfection and here too they should be largely grown. The size to which apples trees attain here is a source of wonder to those who have been accustomed to the trees in the North. In one orchard in Haywood County was measured a tree that had a girth of eleven feet and nine inches, and in the same orchard, which had never been cultivated there were a hundred other trees that were full three feet in diameter of trunk, and all in the most luxuriant health. All that is needed here is a population of fruit growers who understand the culture and handling of winter apples. Apples of the northern varieties grown in Watauga County are hardly recognizable because of their greater size and beauty. With good railroad connections southward (the natural market for the fruit of this section) the growing of apples cannot fail to be profitable. And when is added to this the general fertility of the soil, the pure cold water, fine grasses for dairy purposes, and the superb mountain scenery with the phenomenally light snowfall, we have a region that combines all the advantages of the North in its bracing climate, with the added advantages of a short winter, abounding sunshine and little snow. It is a paradise for the stock raiser, the dairyman and the fruit grower. It must not be assumed that the apple is the only fruit*

> *that will thrive in these valleys and elevated plateaus. In some parts of the mountain region the peach grows to great perfection, while in some parts it is not as successful as farther east. But cherries, plums, quinces and pears are perfectly at home, and the grape reaches a high degree of excellence, and wine of the finest kind is being made. In Buncombe County, Col. Hoyt reports that he is succeeding in growing the Vinifera grapes by grafting them on the native roots, and the wine from his vineyards is gaining an enviable reputation. Small fruits thrive with great perfection, and in the valleys of the northwestern part of this section the cranberry is indigenous.*

More recent statistics—from the 2010 Dana Community Plan Advisory Committee of Henderson County—list 87,936 acres of the county in agricultural land and 11,056 acres of planning area in countywide agricultural lands. According to the committee's reports, county apple production ranked first in North Carolina annually, producing 80 percent of the state's apples, rated as a leading producer of apples in the Southeast. Of Henderson's many packinghouses, only one continues to flourish: Apple Wedge Packing & Shipper, the largest in North Carolina, owned by Greg Nix. Moreover, Henderson County boasts the first and only organically certified apple orchard in the Southeast: Windy Ridge, managed by Anthony Owens.

Besides apple production, Henderson County ranks high in its nursery, greenhouse and floriculture revenues and also in vegetable production, silage corn and cattle. Recent agricultural endeavors also include wineries and breweries. Trends illustrate declining agricultural lands in the county due to parcelization, a scattered real estate development pattern, farmers' inability to compete successfully for land because of increased value, the economic hardships on farming and the loss of farmers due to age and lack of heirs interested in continuing family enterprises.

Nevertheless, a mild spring and record rainfall in 2013 led to a bumper crop of apples with such surplus that rotting fruit swathed the ground under the trees occupying the abundant orchards in Edneyville, Fruitland and Dana, much of it laid to waste. Present-day apple growers include old family names: Barnwell, Coston, Dalton, Edney, Enloe, Freeman, Gilbert, Henderson, Hill, Jackson, Justice, Justus, Lamb, Lancaster, Laughter, Llese, Lyda, McConnell, Merrill, Moore, Moss, Nix, Staton, Stepp and Waters.

But Edneyville's heritage includes so much more than apples. As Bob Rhodes (1939–) said, "Living in Edneyville is a religion in itself."

Provenance of the Surname Edney

Opinions shared through genealogical sources differ on the origin of the name Edney, some of them citing Old Norse, English or Scottish as possible springboards. Adney and Edney count among English surnames found in sixteenth-century church records, originating from the West Midlands hamlet of Adney—the name meaning "Edmund's Island"—near the market town of Newport in the county of Shropshire near Wales. (Church records were not established in Shropshire before 1570.) Welsh genealogy relates the surname Edneyfed in the line of King George II. Certain researchers claim that the names Adney and Edney date from as early as the sixth century, others suggesting the name hails from the English village of Gedney (*Cyddan-ea*, meaning Gydda's Island) in the county of Lincolnshire, well before the Norman Conquest at Hastings in 1066.

Surnames became necessary when governments introduced personal taxation, in England known as the poll tax. Over the centuries, surnames evolved into scores of variants, with versions of Edney including Adeney, Adney, Adneyr, Edeney, Edny, Edonea, Edony, Ideny, Idone, Idonia, Idony, Ydany, Ydeneye, Ydenia, Ydon and Ydonea.

Sources citing Old Norse as an origin suggest the name *Idhuna* (*idh* for "work" or "labor") from the Latin *Idoneus*—moniker of the goddess of springtime and also meaning apt, capable, substantial and sufficient. Other sources offer "Ednie" from "Son of Idonia." (Idonia was a popular girl's name in the fourteenth and fifteenth centuries.)

The 2013 Hendersonville telephone directory included 23 entries under the name Edney, and the 1995 *Henderson County, North Carolina Cemeteries* book lists 149 Edneys and 1 Edny.

Edneys have played a major role in the development of Henderson County before and since its development, beginning with the locally and regionally acclaimed brothers Samuel and Asa, sons of Samuel Wrensher (alternatively spelled Rensher) Edney Sr. (circa 1725–before 1790) and Mary Ellen Kelly Edney (circa 1737–1800). Samuel Edney Sr. was a son of Robert Edney (circa 1700–before 1758), a planter, and Anna A. Wrensher (1700–1762) of Virginia. Robert and Anna located to North Carolina, settling in 1724 on 200 acres in South Mills, Pasquotank County, on a plantation known as Wolf Creek Necke, which Edney later expanded until his holdings exceeded 1,600 acres.

The Brothers Edney

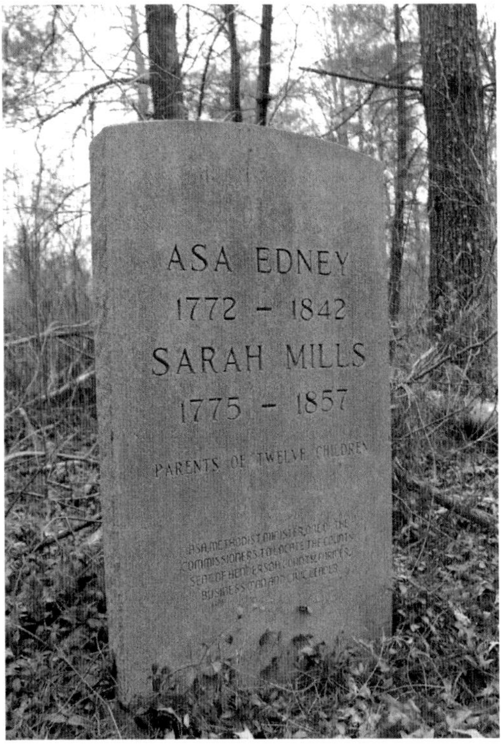

The graves of Asa and Sarah Edney, Asa Edney Family Cemetery. (Sarah's dates are questionable.) *Photographed with permission.*

Edneyville was named for Reverend Samuel Edney (1765–1844)* and Reverend Asa Edney (1772–1842). The brothers, born in Pasquotank County, North Carolina, became Methodist ministers who had a significant impact on what would become Henderson County. Samuel was admitted to the Holston Conference in 1791, assigned to the Bladen Circuit and stationed at New Hope (extending from Long Bay, South Carolina, to Cape Fear, North Carolina, including New Hope, Bladen and Yadkin) in 1792. A year later, when the Lincoln Circuit divided into the Union and Swannanoa, Edney earned the status of minister in charge of the newly created Swannanoa Circuit—including western North Carolina and Tennessee—known later as the Black Mountain Circuit. Edney also preached and taught at the Newton Academy in Asheville, North Carolina.

As he traced his route, Reverend Samuel Edney had occasion to lodge with hospitable settlers, including William Mills. Edney, as well as Bishop Francis Asbury, preached at meetings held on Mills's property, where Edney met and fell in love with one of William Mills's daughters, Eleanor "Nellie" Mills (1776–1842). The couple married in 1793. Mills gave them land on the east side of his holdings, where by 1794 Samuel had built his family home in what would become known as Edneyville, considered by many to be the

* Certain genealogical sources give 1765 as the birth year of Reverend Samuel Edney, and others state 1768. The date of 1765, quoted above, complies with the obituary penned by Reverend Samuel Edney's son James Madison Edney.

Newton Academy

Before 1793, Robert Henry (1767–1863) organized a school in Morristown ("Moriston" on old maps; today's Asheville), the progenitor of Newton Academy, known first as Union Hill School and then Union Hill Academy, which followed a classical curriculum and enjoyed popularity throughout the South. William Forster Jr. (1748–1830) allowed Henry to build a school and a church on his land. When Henry, the first instructor, resigned, Reverend George Newton (1765–1841), the first Presbyterian preacher in Buncombe County, operated the institution from 1797 to 1814. In his expeditions through the area, the Methodist bishop Francis Asbury (1745–1816) spent nights in the Newton home. In 1814, Reverend Newton removed to Bedford County, Tennessee, where he served as pastor of the Shelbyville Presbyterian Church and principal of Dickinson Academy. Buncombe County's Union Hill School occupied a log structure, replaced by a more substantial building of brick and renamed—by an act of legislature—Newton Academy about 1805 and enlarged about 1857. Reverend Francis Hamilton Porter (1786–1845) succeeded Reverend Newton. The academy discontinued classes around the turn of the twentieth century, and after 1921, the City of Asheville built a public school on the site. Razed in the late twentieth century, the campus passed into the hands of Mission Memorial Hospital.

The Newton Academy graveyard has been preserved, maintained by an endowment trust of the Community Foundation of Western North Carolina. This hallowed ground, established about 1818 at the corner of present-day Biltmore Avenue and Unadilla Avenue, contains at least 295 (205 marked and 90 unmarked) grave sites, some of them with the remains of early settlers in the area, including James McConnell Smith (1787–1856), reportedly the first white child born in the region. George Charles Swain (1763–1829), father of North Carolina governor David Lowry Swain (1801–1868), counts among others buried there, as do Colonel John Patton (1765–1831) and the familiar Asheville families Alexander and Stevens. The younger Swain attended the Newton Academy and was also president of the University of North Carolina at Chapel Hill.

"Cradle of Methodism in Henderson County." Edney gave up circuit riding before 1796 to settle permanently with his wife. He owned seven slaves, served as road overseer for his community and conducted a school in his home, the first in Edneyville (circa 1802) and one of the first in what would become Henderson County. He later built a one-room schoolhouse.

In 1804, Edney became justice of the peace of Buncombe County. He hosted Blue Ridge camp meetings on his property, preaching up to the time of his death. The Edneyville United Methodist Church credits its genesis to services held on the Edney property. Bishop Asbury, who preached in Edney's home in 1806 and 1812, ordained Edney as an elder in 1813—this being after Edney had dismissed his slaves. The first church of logs stood about a mile from Edney's home. The present church was built after 1880 and remodeled in the 1940s.

As stated in the *Minutes of Some Conversations Between the Preachers in Connexion* [*sic*] *with the Rev. Mr. John Wesley*, Baltimore, April 24, 1780, "All preachers should promise to set slaves free...All preachers should rise at four or at least at five and disown practices of distilling." In the same year, Wesley passed a resolution against slavery. Minutes taken at annual conferences of the Methodist Episcopal Church for 1785 resolved to "hold slavery in abhorrence."

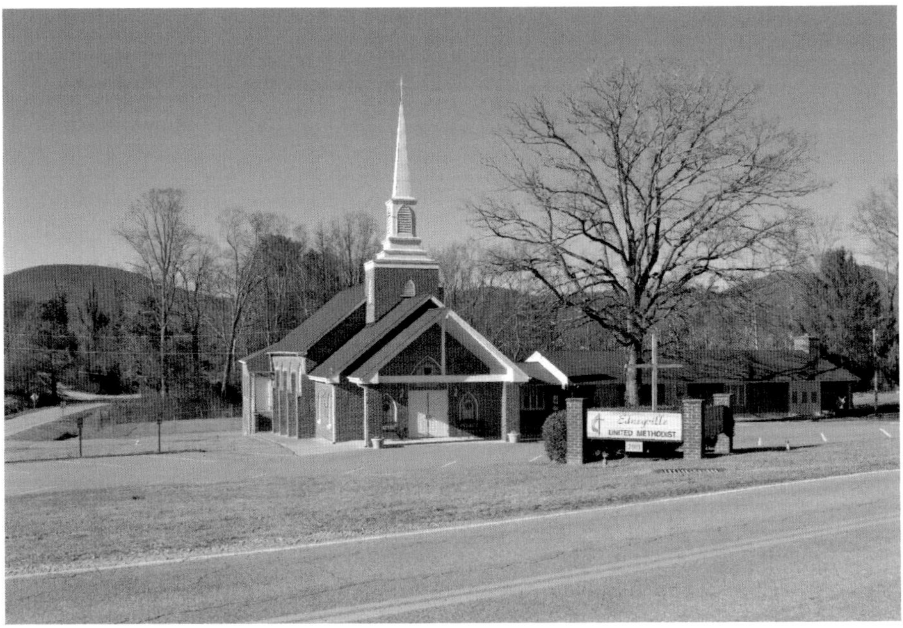

Edneyville United Methodist Church.

Post Offices

Edneyville: 1828 (private post office), Samuel Edney, first postmaster; 1842, U.S. Post Office, James Madison Edney, first postmaster
Liberty: 1883/Maxwell: 1883–1905, Cary Maxwell, the only postmaster
Fruitland: 1883–1906, David J. Merrell, first postmaster
Love: 1883–84, George W. Love, the only postmaster
Lyda: 1886–88, John Stepp Lyda, the only postmaster
DeWitt: 1889–1906, Nancy Juno King Edney, the only postmaster
Uno: 1899–1905, Hattie K. Drake, first postmaster
Roosevelt: 1900–07, Thomas Andrew Washington Lyda, the only postmaster
Horace: 1901–13, James M. Jackson, the only postmaster
Ottanola: 1902–24, William F. Merrell, first postmaster
Fairbanks: 1904–07, Columbus Monroe "Lum" Dalton, the only postmaster

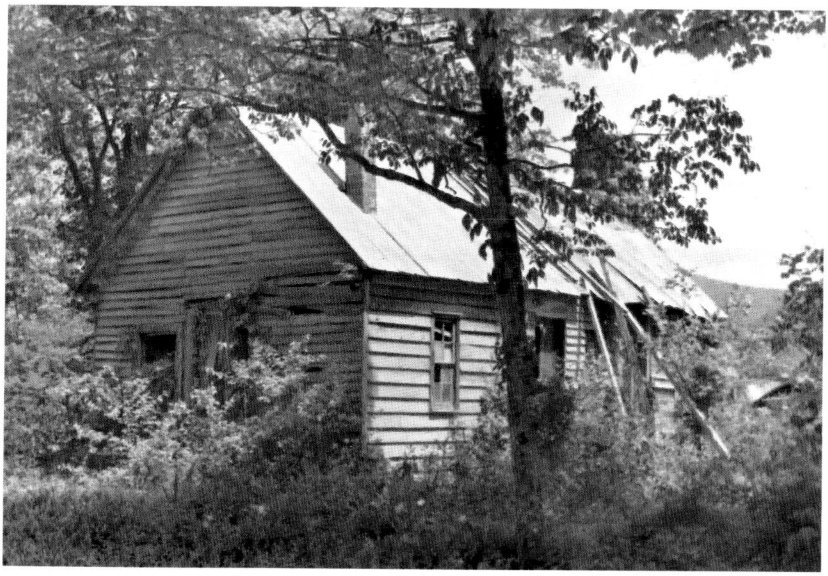

Fruitland Post Office. *Courtesy of Henderson County Genealogical and Historical Society, Inc.*

Because the government did not approve Samuel Edney's appeal for a post office in his community, he opened a private one on April 15, 1828—antedating the formation of Henderson County by a decade—and served as its first postmaster, operating it at his own expense for fourteen of its sixteen-year tenure during his lifetime. (The last two years—and from that point on—it operated as a U.S. Post Office.) James Madison Edney (1814–1866), a son of Samuel, was appointed postmaster at Edneyville, from 1842 to 1846, and later relocated to Asheville, where he published the *Highland Messenger*, the city's first newspaper (subsequently renamed the *Spectator*). The younger Edney's assorted trades in Asheville included singing master, auctioneer, house painter, merchant and broker. He then relocated to New York, where he worked as a publisher and newspaper editor and was said to have practiced medicine. Samuel Rufus Edney (1816–1897), another of Samuel's sons, opened a store in Edneyville and succeeded his brother as postmaster in 1846. Successive postmasters included Winston McKinley Edney (1852–1926), a son of Samuel Rufus Edney, appointed in 1872.

Daniel K. Bennett, in *Chronology of North Carolina* (1858), wrote:

> *He* [Samuel Edney] *unintentionally gave great offense while preaching the funeral sermon of one of a numerous family by the name of Stepp, during which, while in the height of his sermon, with great emphasis, he exclaimed, "Yes, and after all these warnings from God, you will go on, step by step, 'til you all go down to hell!" An explanation afterwards was necessary to redeem them from so terrible an end. He maintained his Christian walk for fifty-six years and his ministerial for fifty-four. It was his custom to supply some appointment on Sabbath all through life. He preached monthly for a number of years at the Newton Academy near Asheville, a distance of twenty miles from his residence; was a regular attendant of camp meetings; the first one ever held in the county was upon his possessions, and his house was always the preacher's home…He was an acting magistrate for forty years, and perhaps tried and disposed of more cases than any other man in his county or state. He was the first, and continued postmaster at Edneyville for twelve years. He inherited and raised a number of slaves, but not being able to govern them without chastisement, he parted with them, and shared the common toils of his neighbors in the support of a large family, whom he loved and cherished until death. He fought a good fight…often exclaiming with a holy triumph in his old age, "I have served God over fifty years, and have never seen the moment that I regretted it, or was willing to look or turn back to the beggarly elements of the world."*

According to certain writers, Reverend Samuel Edney sold his slaves, who had been given to him by his father-in-law; other writers claim that he freed them at the urging of his friend Bishop Asbury.

Interestingly, David K. Bennett wrote in his *Chronology of North Carolina* that William Mills's wife, Eleanor Morris Mills, had practiced Methodism for over fifty years and therefore might have been the first Methodist in Edneyville.

The lengthy obituary of Reverend Samuel Edney, written by his son James Madison Edney, read in part:

> *He was neither blessed nor cursed with a classical education, but his mind was naturally good, and by close application, much prayer, and extensive reading, he was at all times enabled to bring forth things new and old out of the words of eternal truth. To what extent his humble labors reached in the conversion of souls the Judge of quick and dead only knoweth, but many now living can testify of his instrumentality in their salvation…in the last sermon he ever preached, which was from these words, "But sanctify the Lord God in your hearts; and be ready always to give an answer to every man that asketh you a reason of the hope that is in you with meekness and fear."…The Law of kindness, forgiveness, peace, humility, and love was engraven in every ligament of his nature…Samuel Edney lived and died a plain, whole-souled, cross-bearing Methodist, but he extended the right hand of fellowship to all evangelical denominations, and often officiated in their altars and invited them to his…Signed, J.M.E., September 4, 1844.*

The obituary appeared in the Asheville newspaper the *Highland Messenger* and in the *Jonesborough Whig*, *Rutherford Republican*, *Raleigh Register* and *Hamburg Journal* in 1844.

Samuel and Eleanor Edney had twelve children; one of them, Balis (also spelled Bailus, Baylis, Balous, Baylus, Baylous or Baylus) McKendrick Edney (1811–1865), was an attorney and North Carolina senator known as the "great persuader." In 1850, President Zachary Taylor appointed Edney as U.S. counsel to the port of Palermo, Sicily, where he served for one year. In 1852, President Millard Fillmore appointed Edney to be chargé d'affaires of the United States to the Republic of Guatemala. According to an 1860 census report, Edney owned four slaves. With news of the portent of the U.S. Civil War, Edney—a secessionist—resigned from his diplomatic duties and returned to Edneyville, where he organized a cadre known as Edney's Greys, which became part of Company A of the Twenty-fifth North Carolina

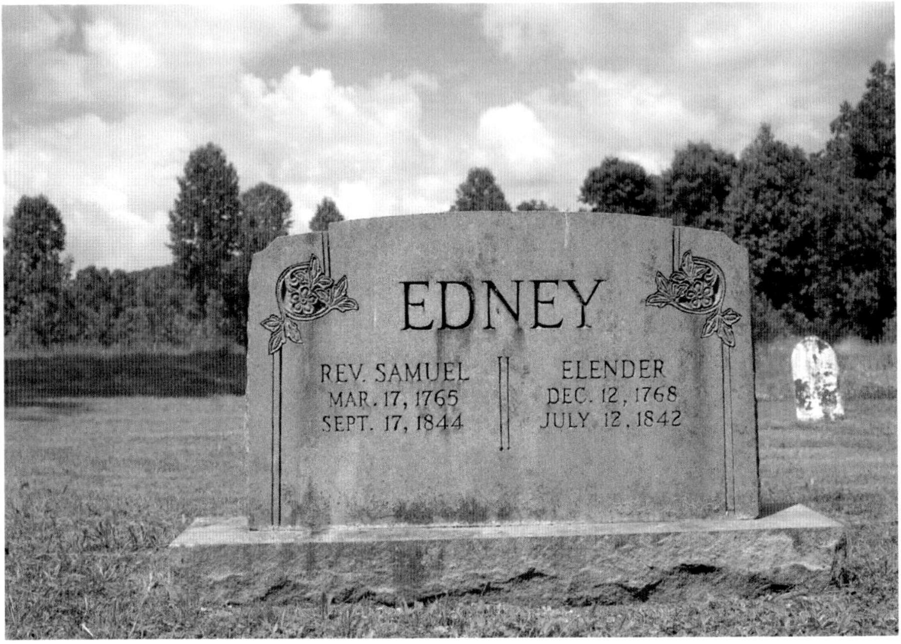

The graves of Samuel and Eleanor "Nellie" Edney, Edney-Coston Cemetery. (Eleanor's dates are questionable.)

Infantry Regiment, with Edney serving as its captain and commander during the Civil War. Captain Balis M. Edney was assassinated by Union troops near his home during the last week of the war.*

Samuel, Eleanor and Balis Edney are buried at the Edney-Coston Cemetery near their homesite. A North Carolina historical marker previously stood at the site of their home near the cemetery.

In his article "Roaming the Mountains" for the *Asheville Citizen-Times*, John Parris wrote:

> *He* [Balis Edney] *lived in an era before statesmen deteriorated into politicians...Edney was a man of fine appearance, his features dominated by the prominence of his jaw and chin. And he cut quite a figure in his swallowtail coat, doeskin pants, silk vest, soft calfskin boots and tall silk hat.*

---

* Some have written that bandits assassinated Balis M. Edney. Others have written that he resigned his post at Palermo to return to North Carolina to participate in the Civil War. According to congressional records (mostly spelling his name "Balis" and sometimes "Bailey"), he served in Guatemala after resigning from his post at Palermo in 1851—a decade before the onset of the Civil War.

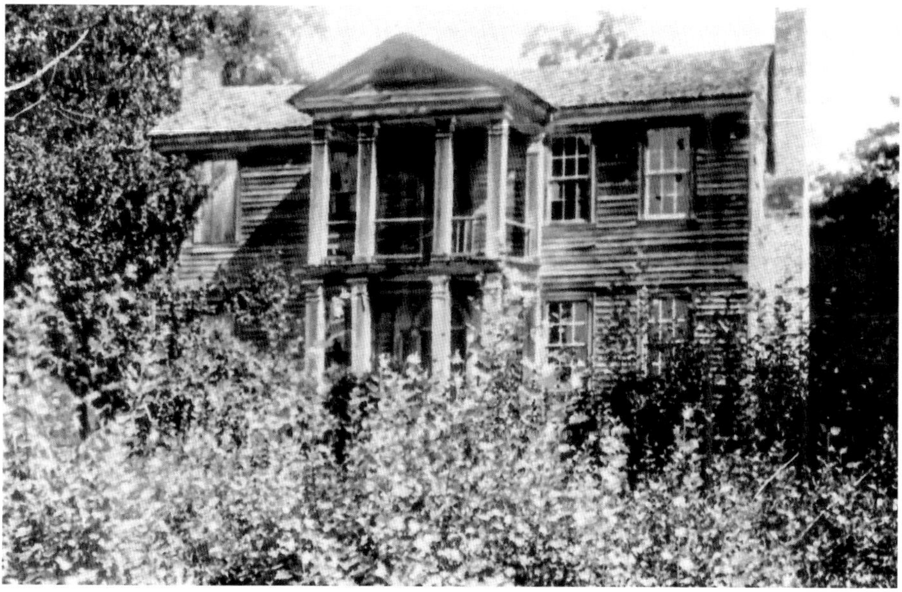

The William Coston house—no longer extant—occupied the property of James M. Edney's homeplace. This was "the largest and most imposing of the early houses in the Edneyville section," as written in a report in the Elvert M. Davis Collection, Arts Division, Library of Congress. The home sported an imposing façade with its portico and second-story pediment supported by squared Doric-style pillars. *Courtesy of Robert and Doris Marlowe.*

For the sum of $2,000, William Baxter Coston (1839–1910) bought 625 acres of the Edney property "with the exception of the mills…opposite Rufus Edney's and ¼ including graveyard above the house…and all the woods, ways and watercourses…between James M. Edney of Buncombe County and William Coston of Henderson County."* The wording suggests that the Coston house was once the home of one of Samuel Edney's sons, most likely James. This was "the largest and most imposing of the early houses in the Edneyville section," as written in a report in the Elvert M. Davis Collection, Arts Division, Library of Congress. The home sported an imposing façade with its portico and second-story pediment supported by squared Doric-style pillars.

William Coston, an early Edneyville schoolmaster, served as postmaster at Edneyville from 1851 to 1856. A Confederate veteran (Twenty-fifth North Carolina Infantry Regiment, Company A, Edney's Greys), Coston was wounded at the Battle of King's Schoolhouse at Oak Grove, French's Field, during the Seven Days' Battle in Virginia and discharged in 1863. He reenlisted

* *Henderson County Deed Book* 5:188, January 20, 1853; registered May 16, 1853.

in 1864 and was captured at the Battle of Five Forks during the Appomattox Campaign; imprisoned at Point Lookout, Maryland; and released in 1865.

Samuel Edney's brother Asa, who arrived in Edneyville shortly after Samuel's coming, married Sarah Mills (1775–circa 1848), another daughter of William Mills, and owned land on both sides of Clear Creek, where the couple kept their homeplace on the first wagon road through the area, the "Edneyville Highway"—known today as South Mills Gap Road—and their home supplied a drovers' stop along this ancient stage way that opened a route from Rutherford County through Edneyville and up to Hoopers Creek and Asheville. Sarah inherited slaves from her father.

Asa, a Methodist minister, farmer, politician and civic leader, was appointed as one of the site commissioners for the county seat of Henderson. Two parties existed for the purpose of choosing a location, with one (the Road Party) favoring its present position and the other (the River Party) favoring a site in present-day Horse Shoe. Leader of the Road Party and a friend of Judge Mitchell King (1783–1862), Asa Edney proved influential in convincing King to donate fifty acres, the larger of the parcels of land gifted for the purpose of founding Hendersonville.

Some accounts state that Asa and Sarah had "eight or more children." In the Henderson County Original Estates documents in the North Carolina State Archives at Raleigh, a lengthy probate case concerning Asa Edney's last will and testament states "twelve children," the same number as his brother Samuel.

Methodism in Western North Carolina

Writers and lecturers on western North Carolina history have sketchily tossed around the name "Bishop Asbury" and the phrases "Holston Conference," "Swannanoa Circuit" and "Newton Academy," mostly without further definition or explanation. So who was Asbury and what did he and others have to do with the conference and circuit?

The Holston Conference

Methodism took root in England at Oxford University in 1729. Forty-four years later, the sect had reached the "Holston Country," the rugged American frontier region where Indians posed resistance. One of the principal rivers in southwestern Virginia and eastern Tennessee includes one named for Revolutionary War captain Stephen Holston (1729–1814), son of Scandinavian immigrants to Virginia.

In an era when Methodists were many times despised and persecuted, Methodist circuit riders came to the wilderness to preach among the sparsely settled region—the advance guard of civilization and morality, at times described as the most self-sacrificing breed of men known to American history. More than preaching, circuit-riding ministers also presided over funerals, ministered to the sick and performed wedding ceremonies. Besides his Bible and possibly Isaac Watts's hymnal, the circuit rider might tote with him a book on herbal cures, a volume such as John Wesley's 1747 *Primitive Physik* and a gun.

Dr. Thomas Coke (1747–1814) came to America under the auspices of—secretly having been ordained as a bishop by—John Wesley (1703–1791), the "father of Methodism." Thomas Ware (1758–1842) was the first circuit rider to come to the Lower Holston; Elizabeth Russell (1749–1825), sister of American Revolution Patriot Patrick Henry, earned the title of "first lady of Methodism" on the Holston; and William McKendree (1757–1835) was the first American-born bishop of the Methodist Episcopal Church.

Bishop Francis Asbury (1745–1816) of the Parish of Handsworth, near Birmingham in Staffordshire, England, took up Methodism at the age of thirteen and at eighteen became a preacher. Three years later, John Wesley received him into the itinerant Methodist ministry. The British Conference admitted Asbury in 1768, and he sailed to America, landing in Philadelphia as a missionary in 1771. In 1775, Reverend Asbury assumed the title of bishop and became the first circuit rider in America, taking Methodism to the colonies and the frontier. John Wesley gave Asbury authority to conduct church affairs in America as he saw suitable, and under Asbury's sway, Methodism expanded.

Asbury had reached North Carolina by 1788 and helped organize the Holston Circuit. During his journey, he wrote, "Steep as a rooftop...we walked, crawled and prayed." Considered the founding bishop of American Methodism, Asbury established the precedent for circuit riding. With his coach driver and partner, "Black Harry" Hosier (circa 1750–1806), a freed slave, Asbury covered 270,000 miles and preached sixteen thousand sermons during his ministry. Circuit riding ended sometime before the Civil War when Methodist Episcopal congregations had become well established.

Samuel Edney, who had been licensed to exhort and preach in the Methodist faith by 1790, was assigned circuits in eastern North Carolina. Appointed minister in charge of the newly formed Swannanoa Circuit in 1793, his assignment included all of western North Carolina and parts of eastern Tennessee—a territory counting approximately seventy Methodist families. During his visits in the area of what is now Henderson County, Edney would lodge with William Mills, as did Bishop Asbury.

Bishop Asbury crossed the Allegheny Mountains sixty times, ordaining over four thousand ministers and presiding at 224 conferences. After Asbury's death, William McKendree became senior bishop. Asbury was buried at Mount Olivet Cemetery in Baltimore, Maryland.

In 1824, provisions for the Holston Conference included parts of Tennessee lying east of the Cumberland Mountains, parts of Virginia and North Carolina embraced in the Holston District and also the Black Mountain and French Broad Circuits formerly belonging to the South Carolina Conference. At the time, the organization boasted 42 ministers and approximately 14,934 members.

Preachers on Horseback

Braving the elements through all manner of weather, the primordial ministers of Methodism endured treacherous trails and the menace of attacks by bear, wildcats, venomous snakes and disease-carrying insects. Traveling great distances on horseback between their flocks, these brave and zealous men rested and took sustenance where they could. In their journals, some of the circuit-riding preachers mentioned incidents of fleas, lice and bedbugs. A circuit preacher's salary averaged about sixty-four dollars per year.

The assigned "circuits" they journeyed—referred to as "charges" today—included miles of sparsely populated wilderness between the two or more local meetinghouses or churches in the circuit. The ministers met annually at conferences where, in most years, their bishops would appoint them to new circuits.

"Circuit riders" they were called by some and "saddlebag preachers" by others, although officially they were traveling clergy. Preaching venues included private homes–usually cabins–and meetinghouses (predecessors of churches), meadows and fields, barns and courthouses. In some cases, it took a preacher several weeks to cover his assigned circuit. Nevertheless, this arduous work ultimately boosted Methodism to the status of largest Protestant denomination in America at the time.

William Mills

Major William Mills (1746–1833), a Tory, was born to Colonel Ambrose Mills (circa 1722–1780) and Mourning Stone Mills (1725–1761) of James River, Albemarle County, Virginia. The Millses immigrated to Maryland from England in the 1720s, then to Virginia and finally to Wateree, South Carolina, in the 1740s, when William was a child. William survived an attack when Indians slaughtered his mother and siblings at Pine Tree Hill, Camden County, South Carolina, during the Indian War of 1751–61. Ambrose later married Anna Brown (circa 1748–1805) and had six more children.

William Mills fought with his father in the King's Army during the American Revolution at the Battle of Kings Mountain, sustained wounds and was left for dead. Ambrose, a Loyalist originally of Derbyshire, England—captured and hanged in battle—gave his life in defense of his motherland. Local historians have written that William Mills hid in a cave near World's Edge on Sugarloaf Mountain until his wounds healed, after which he fought against the Patriots in the Battle of Cowpens on January 17, 1781. After the Revolutionary War, Mills took the oath of allegiance to the new nation after renouncing his treasonous activities. By 1787, he had arrived in Buncombe County—in what is today the township of Fruitland within the intermountain plateau of Henderson County—where he amassed considerable land through grants for his service during the war and later acquired thousands of acres through dealings as a land speculator. He married Eleanor Morris (circa 1739–1843) and had eight children. In his *Chronology of North Carolina*, Daniel K. Bennett described William Mills as "small in stature but compact, sinewy and hardy."

Contradicting Sadie Smathers Patton and other earlier writers, contemporary historians agree that William Mills was *not* the first settler

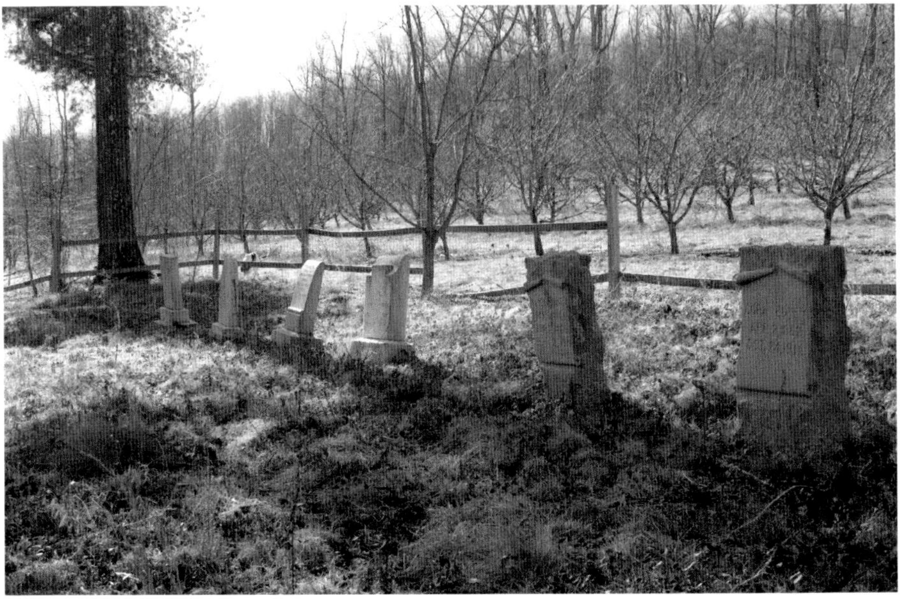

Mills Family Cemetery. *Photographed with permission.*

in what would become Henderson County. Other pioneers included James Andrew Miller (1750–1808), Matthew Maybin, Joseph Henry (1763–1840), John Peter Corn (circa 1751–1843), James Johnson (1771–1852), Abraham Kuykendall (circa 1724–1812), Baptist preacher Reverend Joel Blackwell (1755–1839), Jacob Shipman (1746–1794), William Capps, Jesse Rickman (1770–1860), Elijah Williamson (1755–1837), Samuel King (1746–1828), William Sentell (1756–1837), James Brittain (1769–1841), Merrimon Featherstone (circa 1760–1844), James E. Stepp (1744–1821) and Jacob Lyda (1778–1860). Mills is credited for having named many of the natural features of what would become Henderson County, including Mills Gap Road, Bald Top, Bearwallow and Sugarloaf Mountains.

On a placid knoll in the midst of apple orchards on private property, a crude sign of wood reads: "Mills Cemetery Est. 1800–1902 William Mills Rests Here." Fieldstones and timeworn tombstones mark many of the graves, including those of slaves.

Fruitland Institute

Martha F. Sullinger, teacher and "lady principal" at Fruitland Institute for thirty-five years, stated:

> *Spirituality was the aim and thoroughness the watchword.* [Fruitland Institute] *believed that development of Christian character was the chief function of education. The Bible said, "By ye fruits ye shall know them." That was Fruitland's goal.*

According to an early twentieth-century Fruitland Institute catalogue, it all began about seven miles from Hendersonville in the Clear Creek Valley on an acre of land donated by Nathan Drake (1798–1876) and his wife, Emily B. Davies Foulds Drake (1821–1880). In a log schoolhouse on the site built by Absalom Garren (1798–circa 1879), William Gunaway Brownlow "WGB" Morris (1840–1891) taught the first session in 1870. Morris worked to secure a Peabody grant to finance the nonsectarian community school named Green Mountain Academy. In 1885, Reverend Amos Isaac Justice (1851–1945) dedicated and became the pastor of Green Mountain Baptist Church. Justice, an alumnus of Hendersonville's Judson College, appealed to the Carolina Baptist Association in 1899 to promote and finance the school, renaming it at that time Fruitland Institute. Justice served as the first principal, with his daughter Grace May Justice Grisett (1877–1950) and Professor Frederick Brown as teachers. Professor Delos Wenford Sorrell (1882–1961), William Seymour Shytle (1869–1925) and Martha F. Sullinger (1861–1939) served as early educators at Fruitland as well. Samuel P. Pittillo (1832–1917) deeded to the school ten acres in 1900 and an additional acre in 1904.

William Frances Powell (1877–1959) came at the recommendation of Wake Forest College to serve next as principal. Powell and Justice worked diligently to promote and secure funding to grow the institution as a Baptist associational high school, effecting a generous donation from Samuel Jerome Benjamin Franklin "Rome" Freeman, who had recently sold his Chimney Rock property to Dr. Morse. Freeman gave $2,000 of the $5,000 he received from the sale of his property, enabling Justice to erect an administration building, which he named Freeman Hall in honor of its benefactor. Freeman later served as one of the institute's trustees.

The Carolina Baptist Association incorporated the Fruitland Institute, two years after its founding date, into a system of mountain schools under the Home Mission Board, enabling the school to procure financial

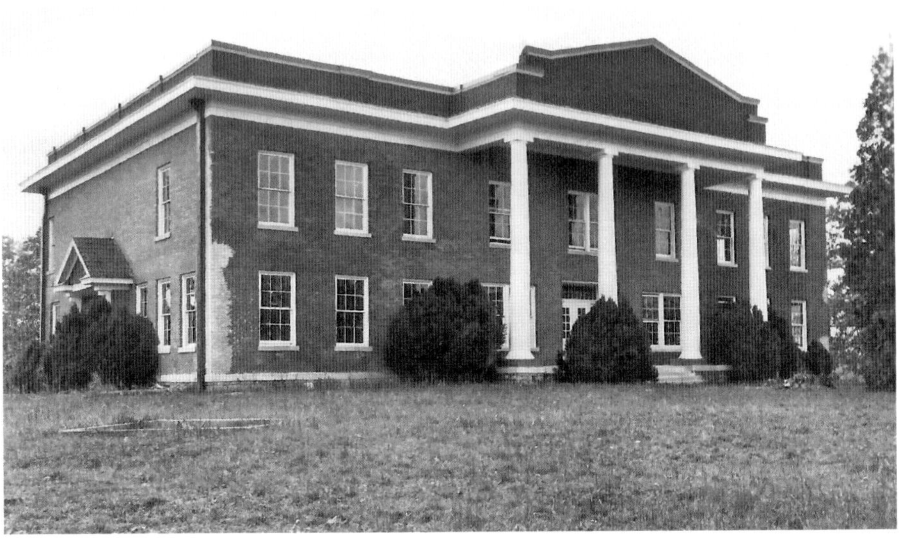

Fruitland Institute's administration building, early 1900s. *Courtesy of Henderson County Genealogical and Historical Society, Inc.*

assistance. Prior to this funding, the school operated from the old one-room subscription schoolhouse and another small building with a partition between its classrooms. Soon, an administration building, a dormitory for girls and a two-story educational building counted among the growing campus's facilities. A boys' dormitory was also added, and after a 1923 fire destroyed the administration building, which had been converted into an annex to the girls' dormitory, a new building replaced it.

According to an early 1900s Fruitland Institute catalogue:

> *The school exists for the training of Christian leaders, for giving the best literary culture under Christian influence through the high school period and meeting college entrance requirements. Fruitland Institute stands for a well-rounded Christian character. Only those who have a real purpose in life may hope to be satisfied and happy here.*

Besides the fundamentals, the school's curriculum included Bible studies, Latin, music, drama, art and athletics and boasted its own baseball and basketball teams—and literary societies, Phi and Chi for the young men and Theta and Sigma for the young ladies. The institution served grades eight through eleven with auxiliary college preparatory courses, adding later a junior college. In its early days, Fruitland Institute charged tuition of two dollars per month for the first year, two dollars and twenty-five cents per month for the second year, two dollars and fifty cents enrollment fee and a dormitory fee averaging eleven dollars and twenty-five cents per month. Fruitland offered free tuition to young men who had been licensed to preach and half tuition to sons and daughters of ministers. An early catalogue described the campus as isolated in the countryside, distanced from "the moral dangers of town life…free from evil influences as any in the country."

The six-building campus drew students from all over the United States and even from abroad. Noted graduates from Henderson County included attorney and Fruitland Institute trustee James Foy Justice (1886–1944); attorney Arthur John Louis Redden Sr. (1907–1982); attorney and U.S. congressman Monroe Minor Redden (1901–1987); Henderson County longtime teacher Irene Mitchell (1904–1994); beloved principal Clara Mae Capps Babb (1906–1999); Yvonne Mann (1919–2008), future spouse of Dana entrepreneur Joseph Hamilton Stepp Jr. (1920–2011); and South Carolina governor and U.S. senator Olin DeWitt Johnston (1896–1965).

Later principals included Reverend Henry Hudson McMillan (1886–1959), Reverend Noah Abraham Melton (1881–1959), Reverend Adolphus Bennett Miller (1877–1931) and Spencer Bidwell King (1880–1954). Alumnus Robert Gibson "R.G." Anders (1882–1968), Henderson County

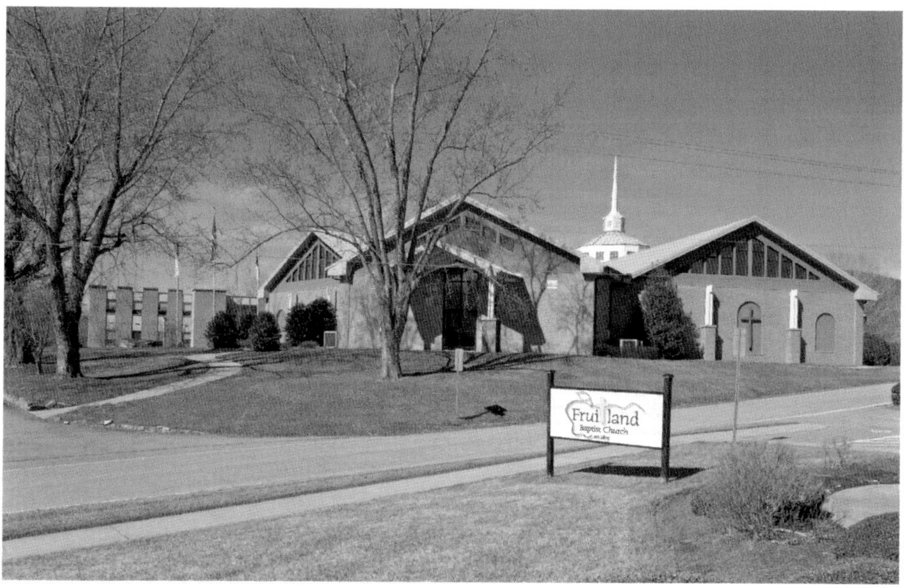

Fruitland Baptist Bible College, 2014.

School Board member and superintendant, served as first president of the institute's junior college.

A piece in a 1936 issue of the *Asheville Citizen* listed the impressive turnout of professionals from the Fruitland Institute, including five hundred who became teachers, seventy-five ministers, one hundred trained nurses, twenty-five missionaries, thirty lawyers and twenty-five doctors.

After its 1936 session, this pioneer in educational development of western North Carolina closed its doors due to insufficient funds. The North Carolina Baptist State Convention purchased the property in 1937, operating there a conference center until 1946, when the facility opened as the Fruitland Baptist Bible College, with John Clifton Canipe Jr. (1922–1975) as its first president. During the 1971 rampage of arsonist James Robert Arrowood (1946–1981), the Justice Building—named for founder A.I. Justice—burned to the ground.

Today, the college counts among the membership of the International Association of Baptist Colleges and Universities. Approximately 25 percent of Baptist pastors in North Carolina have graduated from Fruitland Baptist Bible College.

La Capilla de Santa María

Characteristic of English Norman ecclesial architecture and appearing a great deal older than its years, a most attractive minster in native gray granite stands quite hidden from Chimney Rock Road, northeast of Moore's Grove United Methodist Church and Ebenezer Baptist Church, just beyond the Hendersonville City limits. Tucked away as it is up a gravel road behind a wooded buffer, a sign alongside the highway identifies the site as "La Capilla de Santa María," or St. Mary's Chapel, a Hispanic Episcopal church pastored by Austin K. Rios, rector.

On land originally owned by his Drake grandfather, the Reverend John Creighton Seagle (1871–1947) of Rutherford County began constructing the handsome edifice before 1940, but progress halted during the World War II years. John's brother, the Reverend Nathan Adolphus Seagle (1868–1957) resumed construction, finishing the chapel in 1955. St. Mary's came under the jurisdiction of St. James Episcopal Church and was leased to Mount Pisgah Lutheran Church members, who worshiped there until the late 1980s, when St. Mary's reverted back to St. James and the Seagle family.

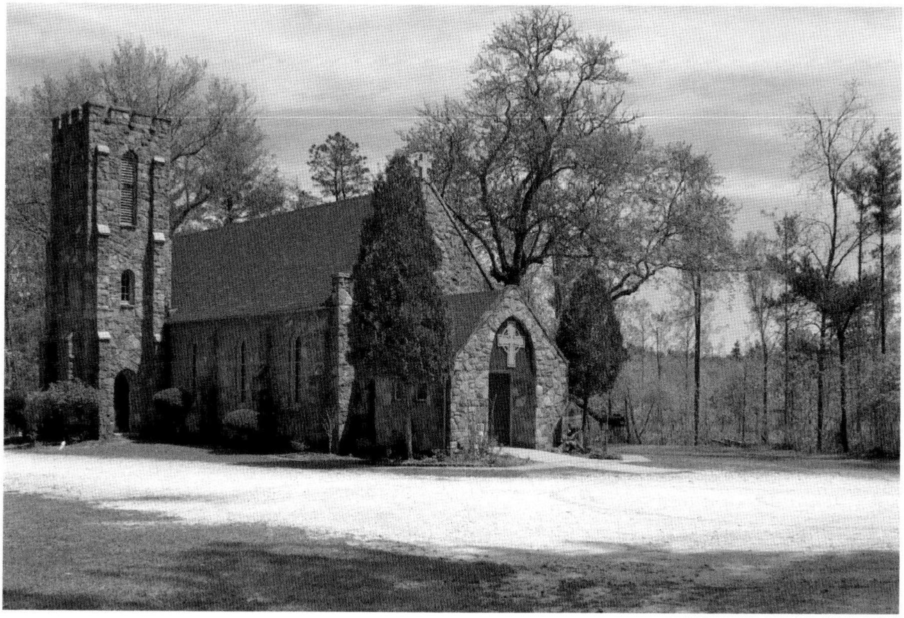

La Capilla de Santa Maria Iglesia Episcopal.

John and Nathan's father, Philip Coon Seagle (1833–1902), a one-time Lutheran, became an Episcopalian later in life. Philip was married to Mary Serepta Drake (1837–1914), John to Ellen Denny Tongue (1871–1928) and Nathan to Marie L. Peckham (1889–1969), his third wife.

The rock house on the property, built by John Seagle, serves as a church study and office. Enclosed by a low wall of granite, the adjacent Seagle-Drake Cemetery frames the graves of Seagles, Drakes, Codys, Harpers, Joneses, Knights, Smiths and Wileys.

Prestwood

A homestead in Clear Creek proffers a snapshot of early Henderson County farmsteads, this one originally owned by Samuel Jerome Benjamin Franklin "Rome" Freeman (1849–1919) and Elizabeth Ashworth "Lizzie" Freeman (1851–1935). "Rome" of Bear Wallow (now Gerton) and Elizabeth of Fairview started a family in Fairview, where, when Reverend Robert Patterson (1809–1876), a minister of Flat Creek Baptist Church, visited the

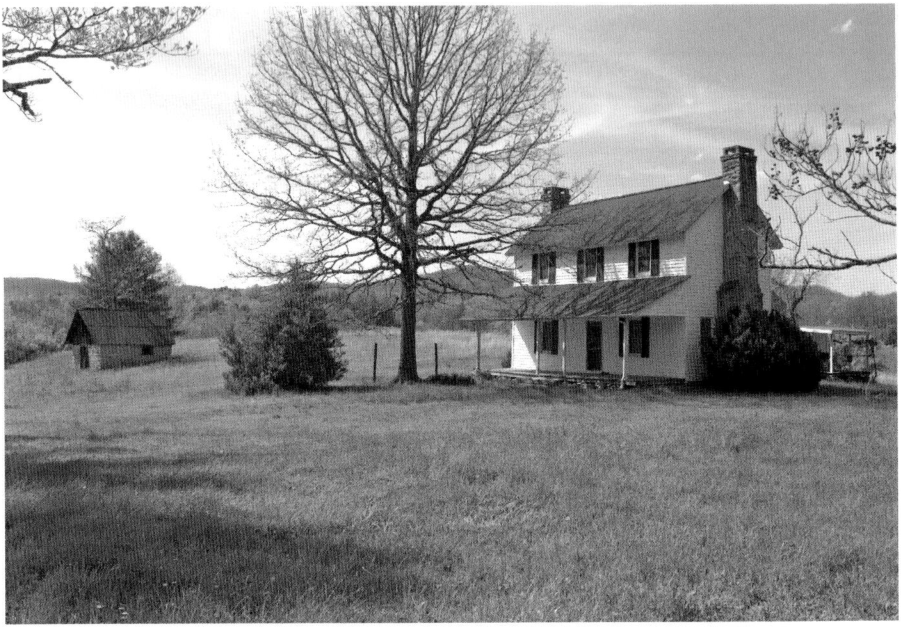

The nicely preserved home and stone outbuilding at Prestwood. *Photographed with permission.*

Freeman home after their son Robert (1875–1974) was born, he said, "His name shall be called Robert Patterson Freeman."

Before the days when Dr. Lucius Boardman Morse (1871–1946) and his brothers Asahel Underwood Morse (1864–1939) and Hiram Boardman Morse (1865–1952) bought the Chimney Rock real estate from Rome Freeman in 1902, Freeman had blazed a three-mile foot trail to the granite "chimney" oddity in Rutherford County and guided groups to the top. From this four hundred acres of land he owned above the Rocky Broad River, Freeman also harvested and sold walnut trees for the manufacture of railroad ties.

The Freemans' home in Clear Creek, known as Prestwood since 1906, stands handsomely preserved today. Asbury B. Prestwood (1857–1928) purchased the classic I-house and its associated ninety-nine acres from Rome Freeman in 1906 for the price of $4,320.* Prestwood also bought additional land in Clear Creek from A.D. Nix, F.A. Thompson, G.L. Norman, James Russell Townsend, William A. Whitesides and Nannie Freeman. Asbury and his wife, Cynthia Clementine Smith Prestwood (1863–1944), moved from

* *Henderson County Deed Book* 53:434.

Lenoir to Henderson County in 1906 to enroll their children at Fruitland Institute. Disappointed that Fruitland had no Methodist church, Asbury worked to raise money for Fruitland Methodist Church and served as one of the trustees of the church, completed in 1910.

Asbury's eldest son, James Guthrie Prestwood (1884–1961), and his wife, Eulalie Stevens Prestwood (1898–1991), next occupied the home. James's brother Albert Asbury Alexander Prestwood (1897–1977) married Nora Azalee Whitaker (1902–1989) and built a home near the family farmstead in Clear Creek. Albert farmed and worked at the Hendersonville Post Office and also as a substitute rural mail carrier. Prestwood descendants still own the home and its remaining acreage and use it for special occasions and as a summer retreat.

TOWNSEND HOME, PITTILLO CIDER HOUSE AND LOVE FAMILY HOME

Alongside the clay track known as Townsend Road off Chimney Rock Road stands a splendid ruin: a circa 1900 two-story pebbledash-stucco home and, adjacent to it, a barn of silvery gray. This was the homeplace of James Russell Townsend (1876–1939) and Mollie Belle Rhodes Townsend (1878–1971), parents of three children: Ollie, Lottie and Ruth. A prominent farmer and orchardist, Townsend grew apples that fetched numerous state fair prizes. Active also in church and civic affairs, James Townsend served on the board of trustees of Fruitland Institute and as superintendant of the institute's Sunday school. He was a magistrate, Clear Creek township constable and a skilled blacksmith. Described as a jack-of-all-trades by his descendants, he was also, perhaps, one of area's earliest conservationists.

The Townsends' blacksmith shop and springhouse stood across the road from their pebbledash house adjacent to a pond used by Fruitland Baptist Church for baptisms. Apple orchards spanned the acreage between the home and Chimney Rock Road. Today, one lone apple tree grows from that forsaken orchard: an unkempt, gnarly reminder of olden times. Between the house and the barn, a nicely preserved apple house of board and batten rests on a granite cellar. Townsend lined its interior with humidity-resistant cork and creosote as a means of preserving his stored apples. Sweeping expanses of pastureland occupied the acreage west of the apple house and the barn. Townsend built all of the structures, including two log cabins, one in a

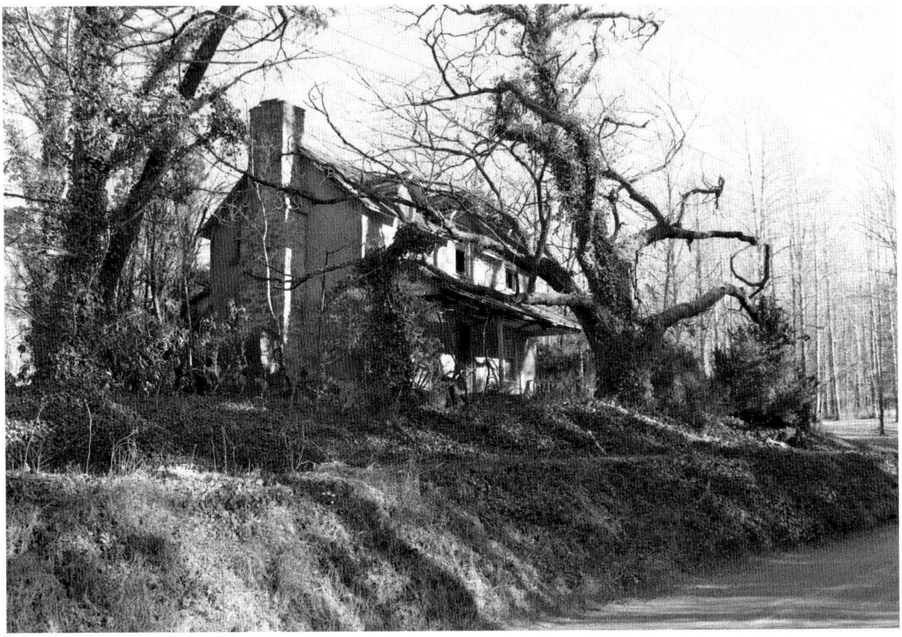

Townsend home. *Photographed with permission.*

ruinous state and the other having burned to the ground. On his anvil, he fashioned hinges and fasteners and also crafted much of his home's furniture and all of its cabinetry.

James's widow, Mollie, abandoned the home five years before her demise, and the ghostly buildings have stood vacant ever since. Stanley Stepp (1959–) and his wife, Jane Lancaster Stepp (1960–), who built their home across the road on part of the old Townsend acreage, own the ancestral property.

Across the way, at the edge of Chimney Rock Road, stone foundations mark the site of the former Cider House, a country store on the homestead of Samuel Joseph "Sam" Pittillo (1874–1946) and Mattie Rodgers Pittillo (1875–1960). The Pittillos, who lived on a slope above the road and store, pressed cider from apples they grew in the back of the property. Their grandson Fred Pittillo (1941–) remembers the cider being so cold it would give him "brain freeze." Sam, one of the original incorporators and vendors of the Henderson County Curb Market, served as first secretary of the market's board of directors.

Provenance of the Surname Pittillo

The surname Pitillo/Pittillo derives from Pitlochry in Highland Perthshire alongside the River Tummel, north of Edinburgh, Scotland. Found first in Fife, the Gaelic name *Pit Cloich Aire* means "place of the sentinel stone," having to do with a Pictish settlement rich in standing monoliths and ancient stone circles. (The Pictish were late Iron Age and early medieval Celtic tribes living in eastern and northern Scotland.)

Variations on the surname include Patilloch, Patillock, Pattillo, Pattullo, Petilla, Pettilla, Petullow, Pitiloch and more. Henderson County's Fred Pittillo traced his ancestry to southeast Scotland. "My ancestors grew potatoes," he said.

A house of wormy chestnut and tulip tree logs, a red barn, a shed and a white foursquare home occupy the property just north of the Pittillo homeplace. Marcia Amschler Kruse and her husband, Darrell, inherited the property from Marica's mother, Gladys Amschler, of Dade County, Florida, and Gaston County, North Carolina—widow of R. Lee Amschler (also spelled "Absher" in some of the deed records)—who owned it since 1967, having purchased the property from heirs of the Loves. A multiplicity of deed records having to do with this property described it in its earlier years as "bordered by the Edneyville-Hendersonville Road" and the "Drake division," "James Townsend," "G.O. Love" and "M.Y. Pittillo" corners.*

Adjacent to the white home and red barn, the circa 1860 log cabin was home to Robert Columbus Love (1843–1884), descended from Robert Love II (1731–1796) of Ireland and immigrant to Charleston, South Carolina. Robert, a private in the Civil War and married to Mary Rebecca Drake (1855–1934), moved from Clear Creek to Farmersville, Texas. He was a son of Robert Love (1803–1878) and Eliza Ewing Love

* Between the tenure of Loves and Kruses, the property and its adjoining acreage passed between a spectrum of owners or part-owners including Nathan A. Drake, S.J. Pittillo, Lula Maxwell, Emma Merrell, William A. Solomon, E.R. Craig, Frank L. Whisnant, James D. Marshall, R.H. Rector, B.F. Nesbitt, Mary Rhodes Jackson and Jerry K. Dotson, the latter grantee having named the subdivision Greenwood Acres. *Henderson County Deed Books* 35, 36, 87, 95, 367, 390, 395, 413, 433, 447, 467, 477, 621, 669, 675, 686 and 703.

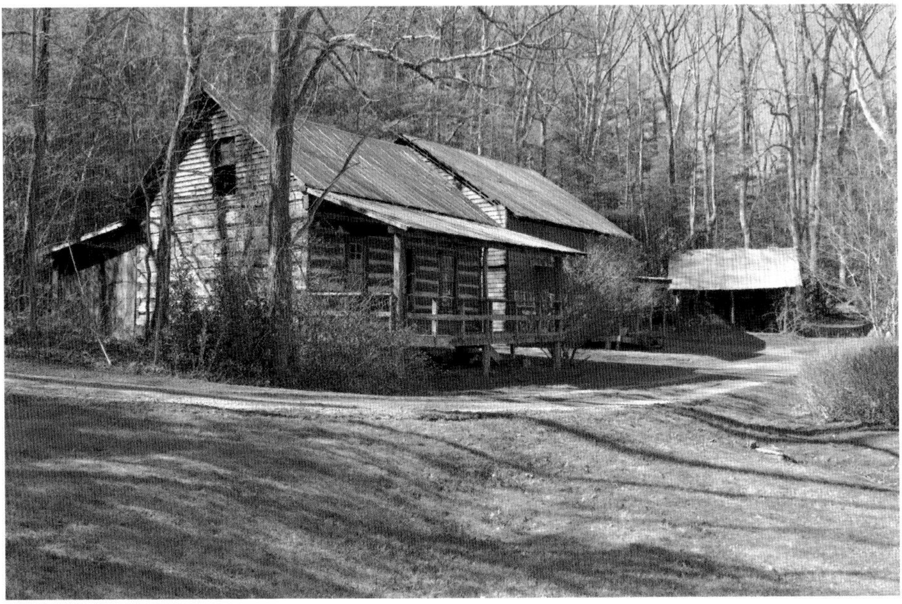

Love cabin. *Photographed with permission.*

(1807–1884). After Robert died, Mary returned to Henderson County with her children William Ernest, George Oscar, Margaret Eliza, Ellen Lavada, Mary Jane and Nancy Juno. Robert and Mary's bachelor son George Oscar Love (1875–1952) and spinster daughters Ellen Lavada Love (1878–1965) and Mary Jane Love (1880–1956) lived in the late-1880s white foursquare farmhouse when a separate structure housed the kitchen and an outhouse served as a restroom. The Kruses, present owners of the property since 1987, added a bathroom and full kitchen, a wing and other modern touches but left original hardware, heart-pine flooring, moldings, root cellar and many such historic features intact.

LET THERE BE PEACE IN THE VALLEY

Beyond fruited slopes and ranchland, a ghost town unexpectedly appears in a nook of the Clear Creek Valley. Longhorn cattle graze the emerald expanse amid Old Clear Creek Road and this village back-dropped by Bald Top Mountain and forested hillocks. A creek named Puncheon Camp cuts a glistening gash through the turf, and a dainty chapel of white nestles into a

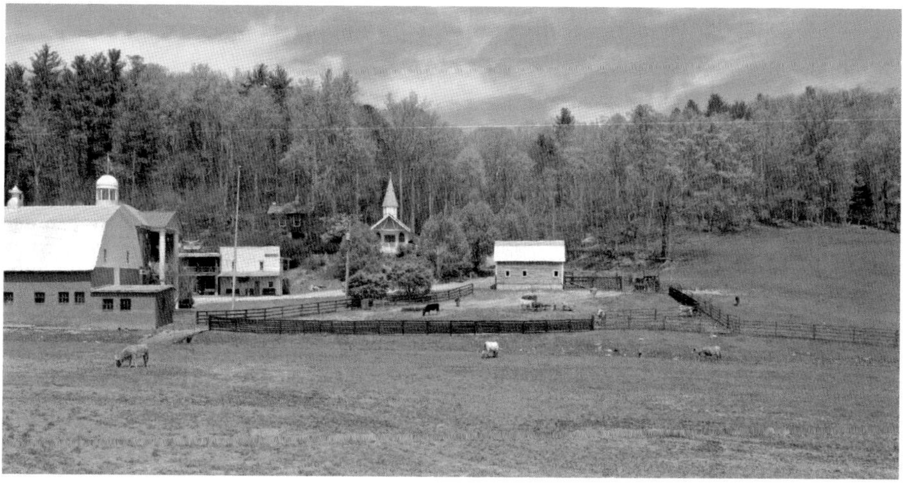

Bub Hyder's Puncheon Camp Creek Land & Cattle Company. *Photographed with permission.*

slope above the town, a five-point star adorning its steeple. Closer inspection discloses a spectrum of picture-perfect barns, sheds and silos; a livery stable; the Longhorn Hotel and saloon; a post office; a general store sporting vintage Pure gasoline pumps; a red schoolhouse; a jailhouse; and a courthouse of brick, the latter incorporating a city hall and fire department. With its stately dome and pilasters, the courthouse possibly drew its inspiration from one of the civil buildings designed by the English architect Richard Sharp Smith (1852–1924). Vintage advertising signs, the towering "Indian Muffler Man," fiberglass steers and an array of antiquities accouter this property.

Boyd "Bub" Hyder (1942–) enjoys building things, so he built a village on land his forebears—Maxwells, Rhodeses and Hyders—farmed in bygone times. Hyder's parents were Leon Doc Hyder (1916–1967) and Carrie Marie Rhodes Hyder (1920–1994). Hyder holds monthly services at the wee church named Marie's Chapel in homage to his mother, a daughter of Harley Bryon Rhodes (1897–1968) and Lexine Merrell Rhodes (1897–1960), who settled on 750 acres at the foot of Bald Top Mountain—land owned by Harley's parents, Thomas Clingman Rhodes (1869–1945) and Elizabeth Maxwell Rhodes (1871–1951). Harley worked a stint at the Beaumont estate in Flat Rock, farmed in Clear Creek, did carpentry, drove a school bus and served on the Edneyville School Board. Edneyville's first scoutmaster, first fire warden and first to operate the fire tower on Bearwallow Mountain, Harley served also as a motorcycle policeman for his uncle Sheriff James Hamilton "Ham" Ballenger (1874–

1940) and as steward of Edneyville United Methodist Church, where his wife, Lexine, taught Sunday school classes.

Bub Hyder, like his maternal grandfather, is a mover and a shaker. In the trucking business since the age of fourteen, he has amassed vast landholdings in Henderson County. Bub purchased a portion of the Puncheon Camp Creek farm in a 1988 bankruptcy sale and has added to it over the years, amassing nearly six hundred acres of that property, where he operates his Puncheon Camp Creek Land & Cattle Company. After restoring the agrarian buildings, he proceeded to build his village.

Alexander Lafayette Maxwell (1847–1926) owned the section of property purchased later by Harley Rhodes and then, in 1947, by Malcolm Donald McNaughton (1889–1949) and Margaret Comstock Cole McNaughton (1891–1963) of Illinois and Florida. Margaret was a daughter of Ernest Chapin Cole (1858–1943), an inventor who held patents on an airtight cooking stove and a damper system. Erle G. Stillwell (1885–1978) designed the McNaughtons' rock-and-sided cottage (1924) across the road from Bub's village. The McNaughtons' son Malcolm D. McNaughton Jr. (1918–1975) next owned the farm, where he raised prizewinning cattle and sold Golden Guernsey milk. William Dalton next owned the property and sold it to Robert and Rosemary Miller, after which Bub Hyder acquired it.

Adjacent to the Hyder holdings—on land owned by Bub's uncle Marvin Rhodes—a structure with a water wheel replicates a gristmill once operated by the Maxwells, predating Harley Rhodes's tenure on the property. Back in the day, Harley turned his Boy Scout troop loose to explore this area graced by a waterfall, today a photogenic setting for wedding receptions and family reunions. Bub Hyder continues the family tradition of scouting by hosting fundraisers for Boy Scouts on the property.

St. Paul's Episcopal Church

The first Episcopal services in the Edneyville area, according to diocesan records, were held at the home of Aaron W. Whiteside (1838–1914) and his wife, Elmira Whiteside (1842–1913), shortly after 1876 with Episcopal missionary and vocational deacon Milnor Jones (1848–1916) presiding. In 1885, Whiteside deeded two acres to the Episcopal Diocese of North Carolina, and a small congregation of Methodist-Episcopalians organized and built a church, naming it St. Paul's, a structure described by one of

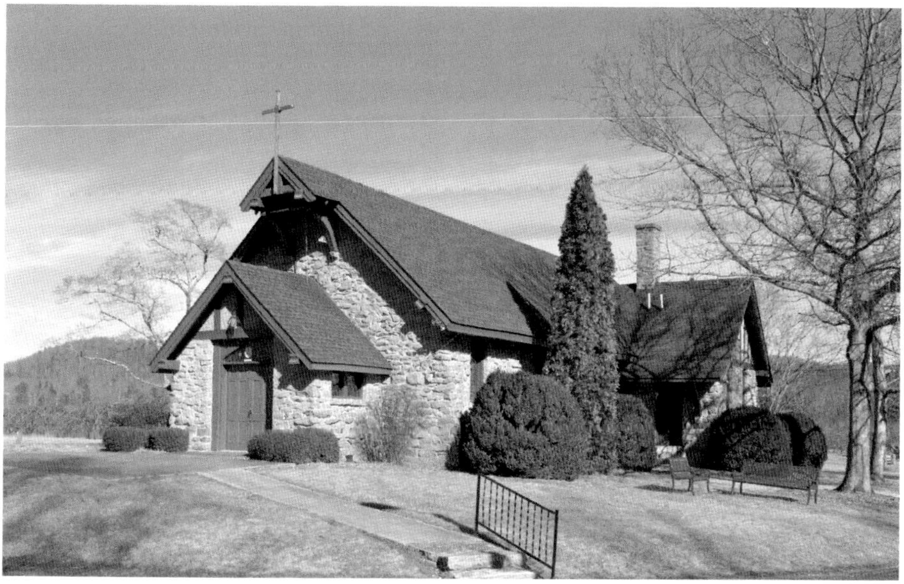

St. Paul's Episcopal Church, consecrated in 1910.

the church's missionary teachers as "a rough shed beyond hope." Jones continued to pay regular visits to the church until 1894, when asked by Bishop Joseph Blount Cheshire (1850–1932) to revive the Episcopal mission at Valle Crucis. The Reverend Dr. Thomas Cogdell Wetmore (1869–1906) next served St. Paul's. After Wetmore's departure in 1900, few services were held.

England-born Reverend Reginald Norton Willcox (1873–1929) came to Henderson County in 1902 to serve St. James Episcopal Church in Hendersonville and the county's Episcopal missions. From 1902, Willcox began performing services every other Sunday on a regular basis at St. Paul's and, in 1903, on alternate Sundays at St. John the Baptist of Upward. At the time, two preaching stations existed—at Adam's Run and East Flat Rock. Willcox also raised money to improve the mission schools.

After violent winds warped the roof and shifted the wood-frame sanctuary from its stacked stone foundations, rendering it unsafe, a fine building of granite replaced it in 1910. Descendants of Reverend Willcox remember that the eldest son of Martin C. Freeman (1870–1960) and Ellen Sarah Owens Freeman (1870–1957) secreted his moonshine under the older church until Ellen caught the young fellow in the act and reported and reprimanded him.

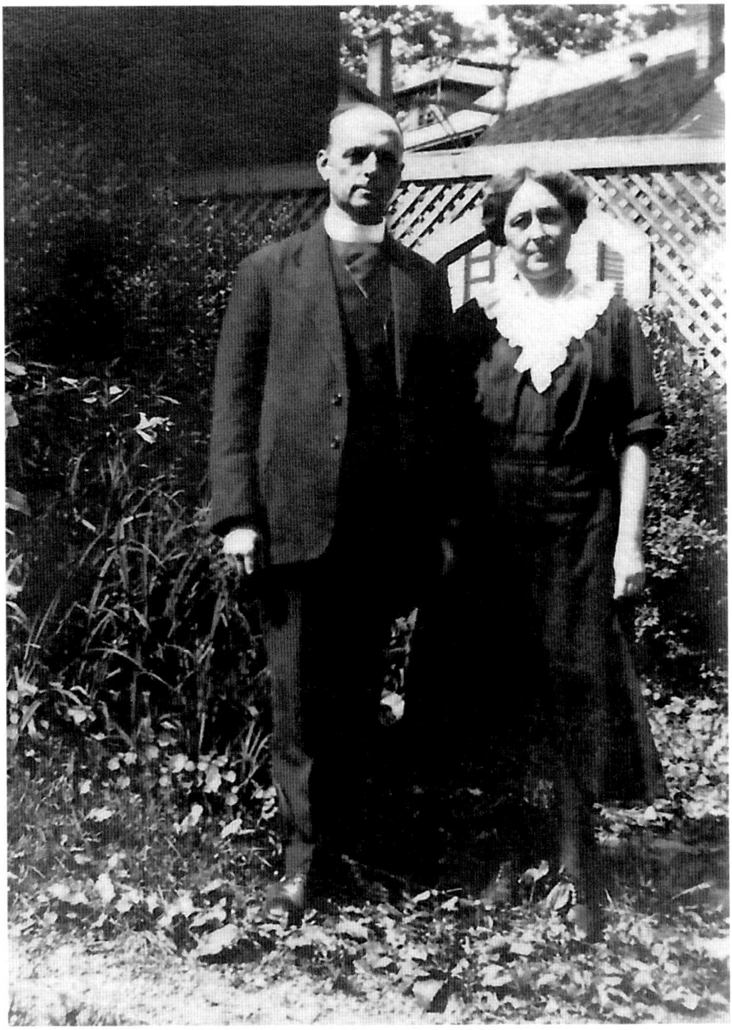

Reverend R.N. Willcox and his wife, Nell. *Courtesy of Henderson County Genealogical and Historical Society, Inc.*

Reverend R.N. Willcox's *The Appalachian Appeal* pamphlet noted:

> *St. Paul's is on the backbone of the Blue Ridge. More than 400 people live within sound of its old locomotive bell. (We need a new bell.) The influence of St. Paul's cannot be estimated. The year's work of Church and School costs about seven hundred dollars, of which the people can raise about three hundred. We therefore need four hundred dollars for this year.*

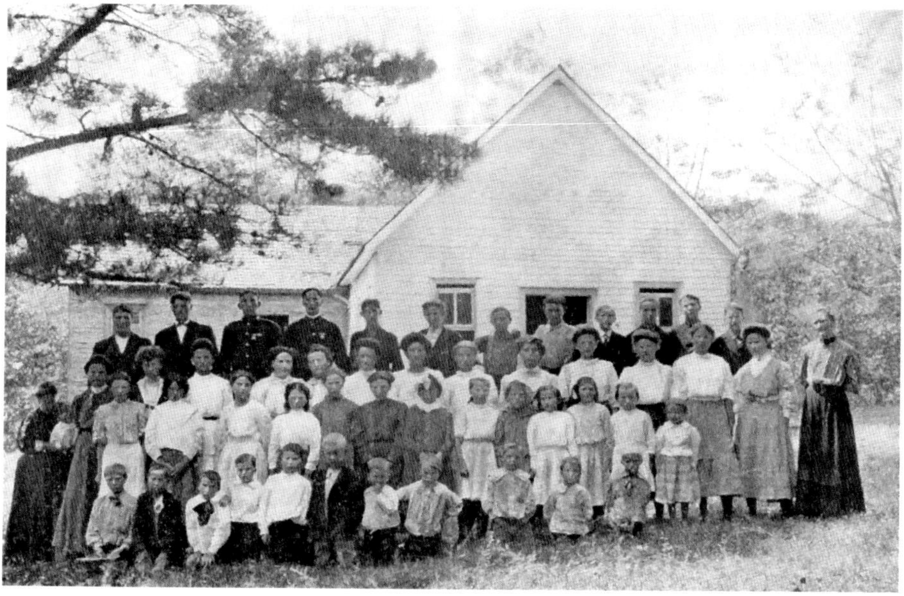

St. Paul's School. *Courtesy of Henderson County Genealogical and Historical Society, Inc.*

> *We also have two mission stations, Adam's Run and East Flat Rock, without property or buildings and no regular service at present. We expect to have regular lay service at these places beginning this autumn.*

With no free rural schools available, Willcox recognized a need for education in the area and dispatched his "Appalachian Appeal for Missions"—a petition to reopen schools in Edneyville—to his colleague Frank J. Frith (1877–1962) of Germantown, Pennsylvania. With the stipulation that such schools be nonsectarian, Frith convinced Bishop Junius Moore Horner (1859–1933) to authorize Father Willcox's request. Frith conveyed $300 to Willcox for the construction and maintenance of St. Paul's Missionary School, which opened in 1905 with Mary "Minnie" McIntosh (1883–1961) as teacher. Until a mission house could be built, the early teachers of St. Paul's lodged with neighbors Andy and Sylvania Lyda. Successive teachers in the two-room schoolhouse included Mollie Arizona Haydock (1886–1963), Louise A. "Ma" Springer (1852–1915) and Sisters of the Transfiguration Margaret and Mary. Assistant teachers included Sallie A. Flack, Cortez Cody, Gracie Whitaker, Estelle Wheelock and a "Miss Madison." St. Paul's Missionary School provided education for grades one through eight with some high school–level courses offered and was open seven to nine months per year in line with available funding. Aline Cronshey

(1901–1982), a nurse from Morris Plains, New Jersey, served as one of St. Paul's missionaries. Miss Cronshey later moved on to South Dakota.

According to Louise A. Springer:

> *On the average there are within a radius of three miles of each of the mission schools about 150 children of school age. The public or county schools are open only about four months during the year and less than half of the children attend. One would think in a state the size of North Carolina that the public schools would be more plentiful and better attended, but the taxable values of the state show that the people have not yet recovered from the stupendous destruction of the Civil War.*

Springer, the first woman to make an address before the Convocation of the Missionary District of Asheville, spoke at the Thirteenth Annual Convention in Lenoir, 1907. "I have been engaged in church work and have dealt with all sorts of girls and boys for the past twelve years," she said, "but I have never been so deeply interested, heart and soul, and felt that my work was so worthwhile, as I do now." She also stated, "When I first began teaching in Edneyville last year I was not quite in sympathy with the idea of giving secular education so prominent a place in the spiritual development of the people, but I have grown to see the wisdom of the plan."

Father Willcox appealed for funds to build a new church of granite from a nearby quarry. Richard Sharp Smith of Smith & Carrier in Asheville drew up the plans, charged a nominal twenty-five-dollar fee for his work and credited Willcox for its design. Willcox oversaw construction performed pro bono or at reduced costs by Hugh Haydock, Virgil Ledbetter, Quincy Nix, Lewis Waters, Mark and Bob Freeman and several Lydas: Andy, John, Grover, Zachary, Mark, Gay, Millard, Austin, Seaborn and Singleton. For a reasonable fee, Frank Brown (1882–1965) raised the stonework, and a retired train bell was installed upon completion and consecration of the church in 1910. During construction, Happy Sylvania Lyda cooked for the crew. The 160-seat sanctuary cost approximately $3,000 to build, not including its furnishings. Laws Stained Glass Studios, Inc., of Statesville, North Carolina, crafted, over the years, the church's resplendent windows, the first ones in 1910 followed by the first picture window in 1951 and then fifteen more between 1972 and 2004.

Elizabeth Willcox Thomson (1915–1990) remembered:

> *On a ridge of the Eastern Continental Divide, with a full view of Bearwallow Mountain, Little Pisgah and the two Chickasaw Knobs is*

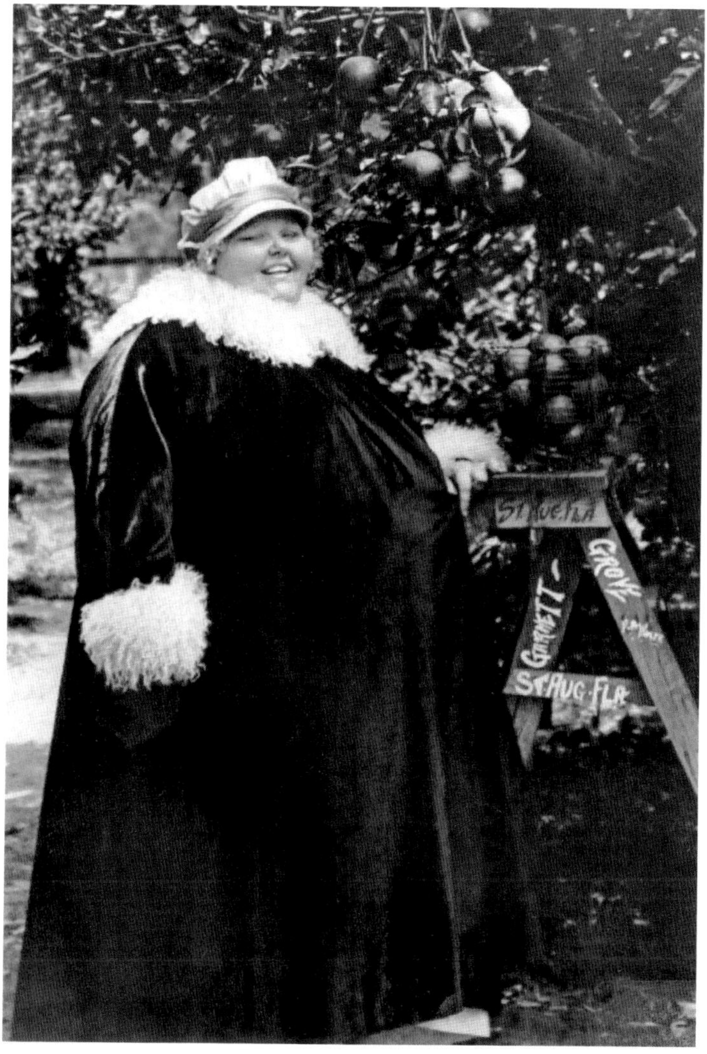

Louise A. "Ma" Springer, teacher at St. Paul's School, 1906–12.
Courtesy of St. Paul's Episcopal Church.

> *situated St. Paul's Episcopal Church, Edneyville. It is a beautiful location and the little stone church gives a feeling of belonging.*

Willcox designed an altar, which he commissioned Frank Wesley Wells Geddes (1888–1951) of Dorchester, Massachusetts, to build and then ship by train to Hendersonville, and after spending a few days in a shop window on

Main Street, the fine piece of furniture made its way from Hendersonville to Edneyville by oxcart. (U.S. Highway 64 remained unpaved until 1924.)

Father Willcox married Nell Thomas Gray (1878–1982) of Shelbyville, Kentucky. The couple had eight children, all of them born in Henderson County and two of them dying in infancy. Father Willcox spent a great deal of time away from his family, ministering to his missions, visiting and treating the infirm and traveling frequently to the Northeast to preach missions and solicit funding. Locally, he trekked by foot and then on the back of Bess, his trusty mare, through all manner of weather, picking his way along unpaved byways and through wooded slopes between the hollers of rural Henderson County. He later bought a motorcycle, and in 1914, he purchased a Hupmobile, one of the first cars owned in Henderson County. Willcox suffered from migraine headaches and was prone to sore throats, and his many letters to his wife revealed his homesickness.

The *French Broad Hustler* of August 1907 reported:

> *Cyril, the infant son of Rev. and Mrs. R.N. Willcox, was found dead in bed, last Saturday afternoon. Dr. J.L. Egerton is unable to state definitely the cause of death, but it is supposed to have been heart trouble. Bishop Horner conducted the funeral services at St. James Episcopal Church on Sunday and interment was in St. John in the Wilderness Cemetery at Flat Rock. This is the second child Mr. and Mrs. Willcox have lost within the past two months, and the sincere and heartfelt sympathy of the entire community is extended to them in their great bereavement.*

Reverend Willcox served as president of the Greater Hendersonville Club. In January 1912, he spoke on behalf of the Patton Memorial Hospital Association, a group formed to generate interest in and funding for the city's first hospital. The *French Broad Hustler* reported that Willcox's persuasive appeal to a packed hall at the courthouse raised $3,500, a substantial sum for the times.

The Willcoxes relocated to New York in 1917. Nell moved back to Henderson County at the age of 102. She died two years later, and her ashes were interred at the Memorial Garden of St. James Episcopal Church of Hendersonville. Her daughter Elizabeth Willcox Thomson's ashes were interred at the Memorial Garden of St. Paul's Episcopal Church. Reverend Willcox is buried under the present church of St. James in Hendersonville.

St. Paul's School continued until after World War I, when pupils transferred to public schools. Mollie Haydock McLaughlin and her husband had reopened the facility and made repairs but stayed for only one year, after which Mary Gorham and Linda Lusby ran the school until 1917, the same year Father Willcox left Hendersonville, having accepted a call to Jamestown, New York. Father Herbert Ross Cary-Elwys (1914–1966) succeeded Willcox. Other pastors included lay minister Floyd William Finch Sr. (1906–1996); Reverend Mark Jenkins (1907–1979) of Calvary Church, Fletcher; Reverend Edgar Ralph Neff (1896–1951); and interim pastors Ladd Fields and Ron Greiser. Reverend Harriet G. Shands currently pastors the church.

St. Paul's Cemetery includes graves of Ballards, Freemans, Logans, Lydas, Sumners, Whitesides and the black families of Freemans, Laus, Littlejohns, Montgomerys, Owens and Waters. Conway McAdams (1900–2002), a farmer, kept a vineyard near St. Paul's Cemetery, where he and his wife were buried in the midst of apple orchards and exquisite mountain views.

The Lyda Family

I don't need to look for the Garden of Eden anywhere else in the world as I have it right here.
—Mitchell Hampton "Mitch" Lyda (1910–1991)

The Lydas, one of the early families to settle in Henderson, augmented the county's apple industry and continue to do so. The family name has become synonymous with apples, and the "Lyda apple" became known as the "Chickasaw apple."

Some local Lydas accept that their ancestry stems from the German provincial counsel Johann Andreas Leidig (circa 1715–1759) and his wife, Elisabetha Haessler Leidig (circa 1718–1759), who immigrated to Pennsylvania from Württemberg in the Palatinate region of Prussia (part of today's Germany). One of the Leidigs' sons, Andrew Jacob Lydick or Lyda (circa 1739–1816), first married Mary Davis (1750–1785) and, second, Sarah Elizabeth Mackey (circa 1754–1807). Andrew's son Jacob "the Pioneer" Lyda (circa 1778–1860)* married Sarah Ann "Annie" Wilkerson (1782–1862). Jacob and Sarah's son Isaac Monroe Lyda (1817–1880), a blacksmith, married Mary Jane Almyra Stepp (1818–1901), and their son

* An 1850 census listed Jacob Lyda at sixty-nine years of age.

James Wilkerson Lyda (1843–1903), a Confederate soldier, married Sarah Anne Lyda (1855–1907). James and Sarah were parents of Andrew Monroe Lyda (1873–1958).

Jacob Lyda owned large tracts of land, including the prominences known as the Chickasaw Knobs. He amassed nearly one thousand acres in the Edneyville area between 1802 and 1835.* Lyda and many of his descendants are buried at St. Paul Cemetery in the midst of neatly pruned orchards.

BEE HIVE INN

St. Paul's Road veers sharply from Chimney Rock Road and then snakes a twisty course between its namesake St. Paul's Episcopal Church and St. Paul's Cemetery to the former sites of grand country inns. This is apple country, and two of the local inns belonged to Lydas. The legacy of Andy and Sylvania Lyda lives on through the abundance of this region's apple crops and through their descendants, who continue to work the orchards and operate guest accommodations on the ancestral land.

Andrew Monroe "Andy" Lyda (1873–1958) surely had an impact on Henderson County's apple industry, more so than "Willy Appleseed," and Lyda left a legacy, as well, in the county's hospitality heritage. Andy and his wife, Happy Sylvania Hill Lyda (1881–1970)—daughter of Hampton Green Hill (1835–1917) and Emily Pike Hill (1852–1918) of Reedy Patch—settled on sixteen acres of woodlands and built there a four-room farmhouse in 1900. They cleared the land with the help of their horse named Charlie and a cow called Mott. After boarding a missionary from neighboring St. Paul's Episcopal Church, the couple resolved to expand their home as a guesthouse in order to accept more boarders—a ten-room, two-story framed structure Andy built around 1907, named by the Lydas the Bee Palace Inn, in keeping with dozens of hives that lined the front porch. Lyda later moved the hives to the back of the property, rocking chairs to the front porch and two-person swings to the surrounding lawns. When Andy—after whom the "Andy June" apple was named—wasn't providing hack service for his guests to and from the Hendersonville train station, he tended the orchards and transported his apples to downtown Hendersonville to sell to business mogul Flave G. Hart (1853–1940) at Hart's jockey lot.

---

* Buncombe County deeds.

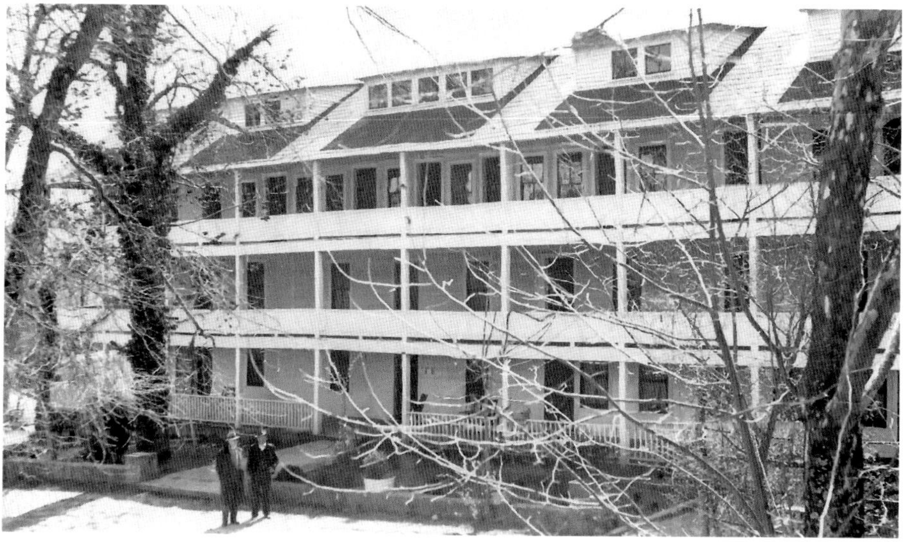

Andy and Sylvania Lydas' Bee Hive Inn. *Courtesy of Barbara Lyda Lackey.*

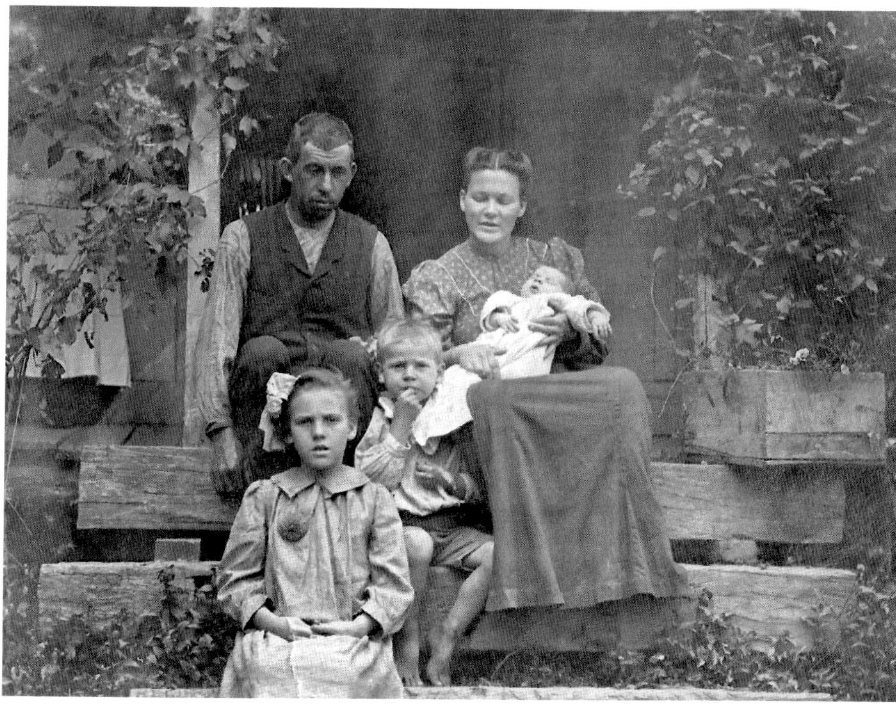

Andy and Sylvania Lyda with their first three children: Cynthia, James and Mary. *Courtesy of Barbara Lyda Lackey.*

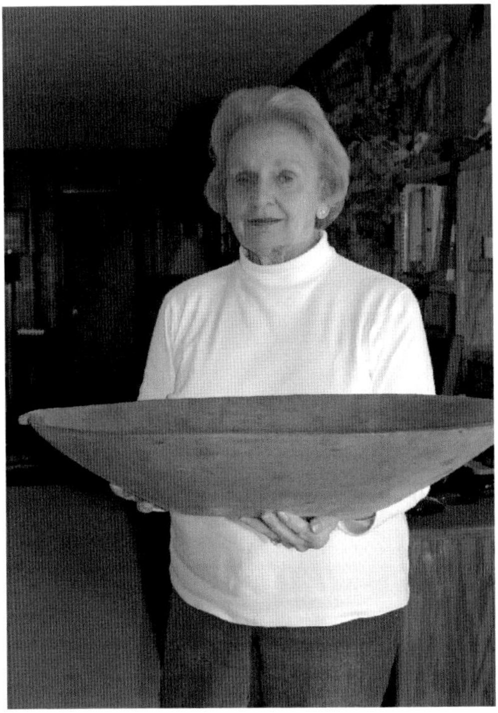

Barbara Lyda Lackey with a wooden bowl her grandmother Happy Sylvania Hill Lyda used for bread making.

Barbara Lyda Lackey (1938–) reminisced, "I remember Grandpa robbing those hives and then bringing the honey inside for his guests. The food tasted so good: country hams with red-eyed gravy, chicken and dumplings, grandpa's fresh honey on grandma's hot biscuits and pancakes and waffles. Most people don't cook that way anymore."

Boarders enjoyed the Lydas' warm hospitality and Sylvania's lovingly prepared meals. Word spread, and soon the ten-room structure expanded into a rambling manse of three stories with thirty-five rooms, which the Lydas renamed the Bee Hive Inn. In the 1940s, log cottages sprang up around the property. Flatlanders affectionately called their hosts "Uncle Andy" and "Aunt Vanie," and guests continued to flock to the hospitable compound, where the Lydas hosted square dances. Andy earned a reputation as an entertaining debater and an optimist and Vanie the status for running a tight ship. Descendants remember Vanie, armed with a rolling pin or skillet, shooing Andy from her kitchen after he would attempt to pilfer goodies prepared for guests.

Mrs. Lackey recalled stories of summer guests traveling with heirloom silver and other valuables. "In chests or trunks," she said. "They worried about leaving their valuables behind so they would bring them up for the summer. Grandpa built a hoist and winch on the roof as a means of conveying heavy trunks to the upper floors." She also recalled the inn's Delco battery system and iceboxes before Duke brought power to the area.

The following advertisement appeared in the 1940s:

> *THE BEE HIVE INN*
> *Furnished Cottages*
> *Fresh Fruits and Vegetables*
> *Top of Blue Ridge Mountains—Altitude 2,500 Feet*
> *Nine Miles East of Hendersonville on U.S. Highway 64*
> *R.F.D. 2*
> *Hendersonville, North Carolina*
>
> *We have a delightful boarding house located nine miles east of Hendersonville, just off U.S. Highway 64, in the Edneyville section of the famous "Land of the Sky." Upon reaching Edneyville, just follow our signs to the inn. We are located just far enough off the highway to enjoy a cool, quiet atmosphere. Our beautiful apple orchard surrounds the inn and there are many interesting mountain trails for walks. Various recreations and points of interest may be reached within a 30-minute drive of the Bee Hive Inn. Each summer we employ an excellent cook who prepares three delicious meals daily. Since our resort is located on our farm, we serve our own fresh fruits and vegetables and our own country cured hams. Our rooms are clean and comfortable and we have good mattresses. There are two bathrooms and a shower per floor and they are kept clean and sanitary.*
>
> *May we have the pleasure of having you as our guest? We will do all possible to make your vacation here a pleasant and healthful one.*

When local farmers finished their work in the fields and orchards, they relaxed at the Bee Hive's annex, playing their instruments—"fiddle, harmonica, bass guitar, mandolin, banjo, whatever they could play," said the Lydas' granddaughter Barbara Lyda Lackey. "And they'd make the grand promenade from the dance floor, down the steps and into the parking lot and then back into the ballroom."

Andy Lyda, the first in the area to spray his orchards, maintained a penchant for growing apple trees, which encircled the Bee Hive Inn. He and his son Mitchell Hampton Lyda (1910–1991) built the region's first spraying apparatus, and Andy convinced neighbors to set in apples and to spray and fertilize them. "He had a vision about the way things should go," Mrs. Lackey added. "He enjoyed teaching young farmers. He taught my father, Mitchell Hampton Lyda. Daddy did the apple orchards and later ran the inn." Mitchell's wife, Ethel Annie Laura Davis Lyda (1919–2012), continued

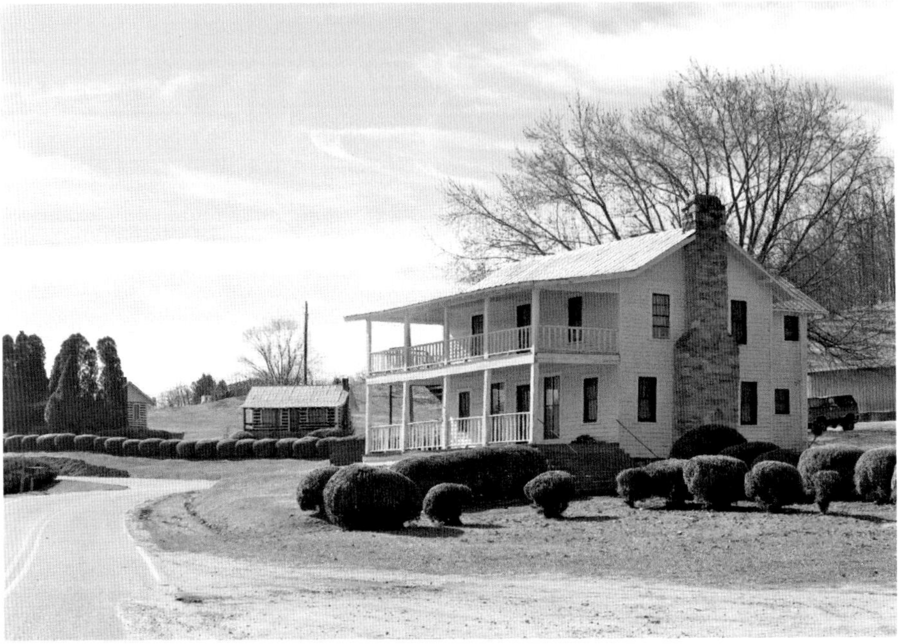

The "annex"—the Bee Hive's dance hall. *Photographed with permission.*

Sylvania's tradition of hospitality. Guests included James G. Martin (1935–), a future North Carolina governor.

Mitchell's sister Louise Lyda (1908–1980) married James Cyfax "Fax" Jones (1897–1977). The Joneses worked as independent farmers and orchardists.

Lyda descendants razed the Bee Hive Inn in 2000, but the dance hall and cottages stand today as the Lydas keep alive the tradition of their ancestors' enthusiasm for hospitality and cultivating apples. The ancestral land passed down to five Lyda grandchildren: Shirley, Barbara, Ray, Mike and Janell, with all but Shirley and Mike (now deceased) living on the property. Today, Mitchell Ray Lyda (1943–) tends the property's beehives and sells honey, and Jeffrey David Lyda and Donovan Barclay Jenks tend the orchards.

Mission Schools

At the turn of the last century, one-, two- and three-room schoolhouses dotted the coves and slopes of Henderson, with possibly more of these

More Lydas of Note

Andrew Washington Lyda (1823–1864) married Nancy Catherine Justice (1825–1904) and served as a private in Company B, Fifteenth Regiment, North Carolina Cavalry. A son of Jacob Lyda, Andrew died of pneumonia in a Union prison during the Civil War.

Thomas Andrew Washington Lyda (1857–1926), son of Andrew Washington Lyda, married Amanda Tow (1862–1930) and served as the only postmaster at Roosevelt when it opened in 1900 and closed in 1907. Thomas helped build the road from Edneyville to Bat Cave in 1913.

Jacob Merrimon "Preacher Jake" Lyda (1842–1922), son of Henry Carpenter Lyda (1811–1849) and Matilda Ballew Lyda (1811–1862) and grandson of Jacob Lyda, was first a Methodist preacher, then a Baptist preacher and finally a Seventh-day Adventist minister. He married Rhoda E. Mackey (1841–1922).

John Stepp Lyda (1861–1915) served as postmaster at the Lyda Post Office from 1886 to 1888. John married Mary Jane Whiteside (1862–1942) and lived in the St. Paul section of Edneyville. John, a rock mason, taught his craft to his sons John Thurmond Lyda (1889–1971) and Millard Lyda (1884–1959). John T. Lyda married Pearl Jane

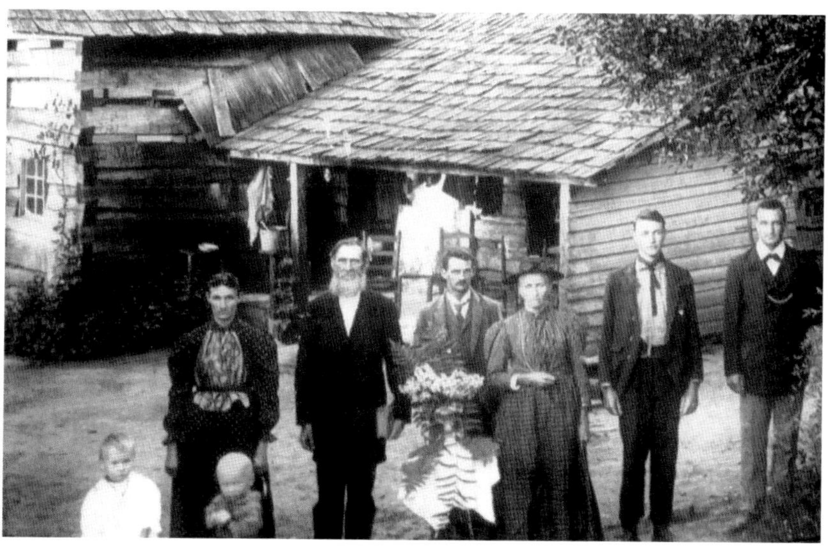

Preacher Jake Lyda and his family at their home. *Courtesy of Norman C. Lyda.*

Brown (1900–1989). Millard and his wife, Nancy Jane Owenby Lyda (1885–1964), worked as apple farmers.

William C. Lyda (1853–1930), married to Mary Jane Gilreath Lyda (1857–1934), and their son James Cebron Lyda (1884–1950) and his wife, Hester F. Byers Lyda (1883–1964), farmed in Henderson County. Cebron and Hester's son Rome Atlas Lyda (1919–2008) and his wife, Mildred "Millie" Lyda (1928–), founded Lyda Farms in 1948. Rome served on the board of directors for the Western North Carolina Apple Growers Cooperative and the Blue Ridge Apple Growers Association and remained active in the Edneyville Grange #1051 for more than fifty years.

feeder schools in Edneyville than in any other part of the county. Before consolidation, a handful of the county's small learning institutions included mission schools.

In 1903, Dorothy Nickells "Dolly" Sharpe (1873–1933)—referred to by local writers simply as "Mrs. Sharp [*sic*]" or "Dorothy Ann [*sic*] Sharpe"—appealed to Reverend Willcox of St. Paul's Church to establish a missionary chapel and school at Reedy Patch/Slick Rock to serve the local mountain people. With the pastor's approval and espousal, this small institution fulfilled Sharpe's dream and became known as the school and chapel of the Good Shepherd.

The few words about Sharpe in older written histories of Henderson County briefly describe her as a druggist dressed in men's clothing and smoking cigars and a pipe. She traveled by foot and on horseback or on a mule to administer to the sick and frail. Further digging—including correspondence between Mrs. Sharpe and Reverend Reginald Norton Willcox collected by Elizabeth Willcox Thomson, daughter of Reverend Willcox—revealed the following: Dorothy N. Sharpe, a graduate, licensed pharmacist from Portsmouth, Ohio, who dealt also in real estate, met Elizabeth L. Baldwin (1864–1921) of Columbia, South Carolina, in New Orleans during Mardi Gras. When Sharpe, mourning the loss of her husband, Amasa J. Sharpe (1865–1902), endeavored to jump from a hotel window, Baldwin and hotel staff managed to halt the suicide attempt. According to Dorothy's account, Amasa had been stabbed to death in a drunken brawl, leaving her a penniless widow. Sharpe and

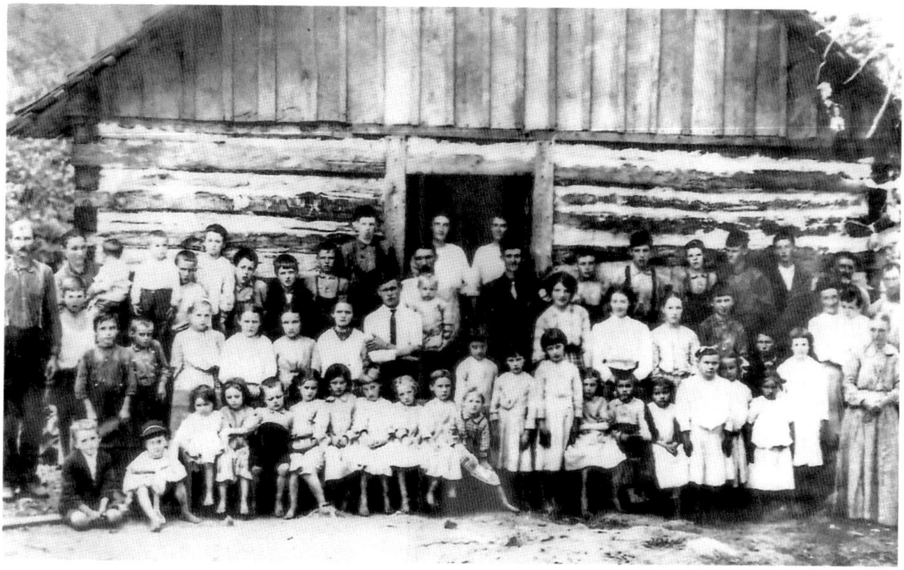

The Good Shepherd School with the Justice triplets seated front and center. *Courtesy of Henderson County Genealogical and Historical Society, Inc.*

Baldwin struck up a close friendship and moved to the Slick Rock area, where they bought, in 1906, a log home on twenty-three acres from John C. Dalton (1868–1937), which they renovated, enlarged and named Inglenook.* They furnished this home with ancestral pieces from Baldwin's family estate in Columbia. Baldwin had grown familiar with the Edneyville/Bat Cave area, having previously lodged at the Edney Inn. She believed a change of scenery would help Sharpe overcome her grief and addictions.

Just below Inglenook, Sharpe and Baldwin constructed a log structure that "Dr. Sharpe"—as some locals called her—used as a dispensary. The couple also orchestrated the building of the tiny Good Shepherd School and chapel at Point Lookout, about three miles from Inglenook. After receiving approval and seed money from Reverend Willcox, Sharpe, noted as a devout Episcopalian, campaigned for additional funding and donations of clothes and toys for needy children, accepting pledges from as far away as New York and New Orleans. This mission building of notched logs, located near Salola Creek on Slick Rock, off what is now Edney Inn Road in Reedy Patch (replaced later with a larger log structure), schooled the locally renowned

* *Henderson County Deed Book* 54: 310.

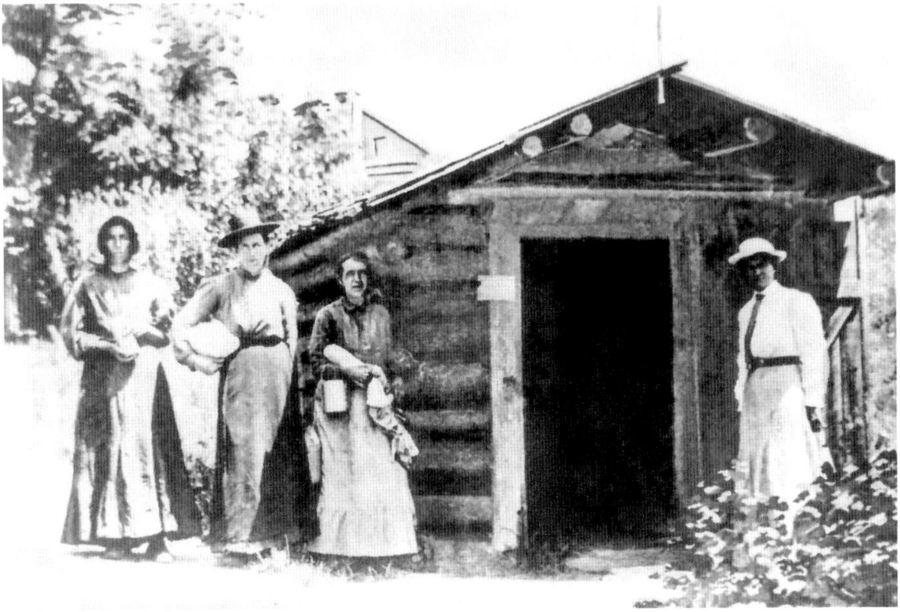

Dorothy N. Sharpe's log drugstore. *From left to right*: Sarah Freeman Barnwell, Ellen Hill Morrison, Myra Nix Edney and Dorothy N. Sharpe. *Vintage postcard courtesy of Richard Barnwell.*

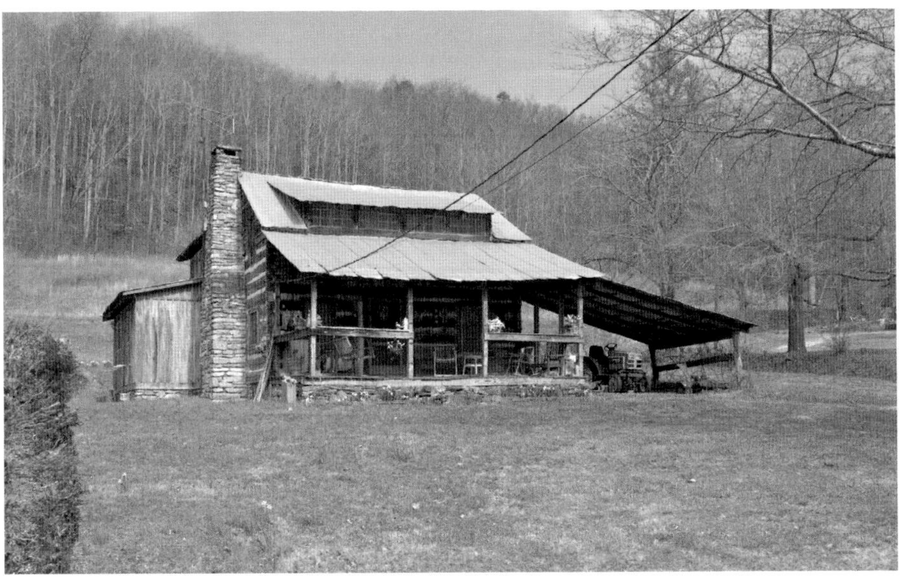

Inglenook, the home of Dorothy Sharpe and Elizabeth Baldwin, retains its isolated setting with unobstructed mountain views. *Photographed with permission.*

Justice triplets Bessie, Dessie and Essie, whose schoolmates nicknamed them "Shoes," "Boots" and "Leggings."*

Moreover, Sharpe and Baldwin established the Mountain Industrial Exchange, a marketplace where locals could sell and barter handicrafts for staples. Baldwin also taught at the Good Shepherd School, as did another of Sharpe's companions, Miss Florence Belva Corey (1883–1970). Sharpe and Corey later ran a small store where they sold school supplies.

Born to Cyrus Hull Baldwin (1822–1906), a prosperous merchant and customs collector, and Lydia Eunice Ford Baldwin (1829–1895) of Columbia, South Carolina, Elizabeth Baldwin held fast to her cultured upbringing. A well-read world traveler, she enjoyed poetry, theater and playing the classics on her mahogany grand piano, which she had shipped by rail from Columbia to Hendersonville and then transported by oxen to Edneyville. Fine antebellum furnishings accoutered the rustic log home known as Inglenook. In her travels, Baldwin at times worked as a translator of German.

Sharpe, a known user of opiates (specifically laudanum), dispensed medical drugs at cost or for no charge to those who needed them. Friends and associates, including Reverend Willcox's wife, Nell, attempted intervention, yet any fervent attempts failed when Sharpe weaned herself off opiates only to take up heavy drinking. Nevertheless, the zealous Sharpe persisted in appealing for donations for the mission she had established and continued visiting the sick, administering pharmaceuticals and medical treatments to the extent of her expertise. Elizabeth Baldwin and Dorothy Sharpe parted ways when Baldwin could no longer tolerate Sharpe's self-medicated fog. Baldwin bought out Sharpe's interest in Inglenook in 1916,† and Sharpe spent the rest of her short life renting in various parts of north Henderson County. Elizabeth Baldwin continued her travels with her adopted daughter, Ellen, in tow.

Another of Sharpe's companions, Ruth Anna Gottlieb (1866–circa 1940), helped administer medical services to local people. Census records list Gottlieb's occupation as "medical student" in Cincinnati, Ohio; "physician" in Covington, Kentucky; "reporter, *Kentucky Post*" in Covington; and

* Bessie M. Justice Jackson Nix (1904–1988), Dessie M. Justice Nix (1904–1986) and Essie Justice Williams (1904–1998), triplet daughters of Thomas Edward "Tommy" Justice (1873–1943) and Laura Effie Searcy Justice (1883–1943), lived as children with their parents and other siblings in a log home tucked into a cove below Mountain Home Baptist Church at the foot of Sugarloaf Mountain.

† *Henderson County Deed Book* 73: 157.

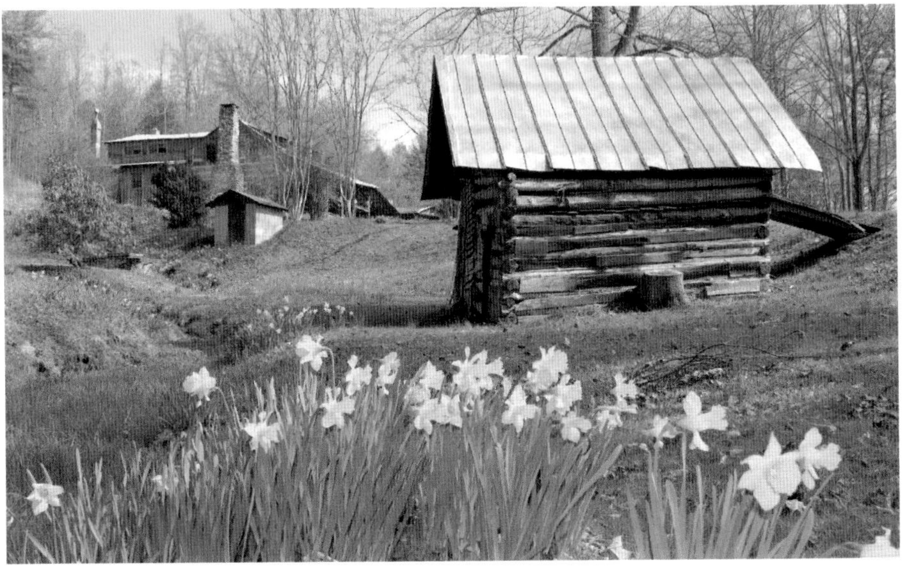

A converted structure on the Inglenook property, possibly the former Sharpe drugstore. *Photographed with permission.*

"teacher" in Cincinnati high schools. The last record to be found for her, in 1940 in Columbus, Ohio, lists Isabel Thompson as Gottlieb's companion.

According to *The Ministries of a Neighbor* (1911), a pamphlet by Clara Louise Webster:

> *Up among the mountains of North Carolina stands a log house not much more pretentious than its fellows. It is the home of a noble Christian woman who, in widowed sorrow, sought health among these mountains. She had a small cabin built near her home, into which she put a stock of drugs. From miles around people come over the mountains to get the medicine, which she sells at cost to those who can pay and gives away to those who cannot.*

Baldwin adopted Ellen Williams (1904–1990), one of five orphaned children of Andy Williams (1864–1905) and Nancy "Nan" Williams (1868–1906), and Dorothy Sharpe adopted Drusilla (1904–1935), nicknamed Cobby, daughter of Florina "Flora" Hill Gilliam Laughter (1879–1906) and Jacob Monroe Laughter (1876–1913). When Sharpe and Baldwin parted ways, they sent Cobby to Glendale, Ohio, to an Episcopal boarding school operated by the Sisters of the Transfiguration. In 1926, Drusilla married Wiley R. Roth (1901–1976), an Ohio farmer, and worked as a nurse. According to her death certificate, Drusilla died of Malta fever and pneumonia. Ellen married Walter Linwood Taylor (1905–1969) of Nash County and had a child named Bertha. She divorced Taylor and married Clyde M. Haydock (1903–1976) of Edneyville, then taught at Stanhope School in Nash County and in Rutherford County for thirty years before retiring to her childhood home, Inglenook. Ellen's daughter Bertha Whitt (1930–) and her family currently use the cabin as a summer getaway.

In April 1914, the *French Broad Hustler* reported:

> *POINT LOOKOUT VIEWS*
> *The old-time singing at Good Shepherd's schoolhouse Sunday was enjoyed by a large congregation. Everybody was invited to meet there again for another old-time singing the third Sunday in May. But don't forget to bring a basket of dinner.*

Good Shepherd School closed in 1914. Dorothy Sharpe later developed severe stomach ulcers and passed away at Mountain Sanitarium, her obituary stating that she died from an attack of acute indigestion. According to her death certificate, the coroner attributed the cause to "acute anemia contributed by twenty years of chronic alcoholism." The certificate listed the informant as Miss Florence B. Corey. Sharpe was buried at St. Paul's Cemetery in Edneyville.

The Missionary District in Henderson County also included—in the area served by the Roosevelt Post Office (1900–1907)—a church named St. Peter's, established in 1911, and a school named Laus, established for black children on land deeded* by F.M. Laus (Frances M. Owens Laus, 1872–1943) and Martin C. Freeman (1868–1960), with Reverend Ira Charles Swanman (1889–1955) in charge (closed in 1946, students transferred to the East Flat Rock school for black children); St. Matthew's of Hillgirt, also established

* The deed concerning land for the Laus School, filed on August 10, 1893, reads: "Between children and widow of George Owens, Mary A. Owens, Lou Howell and husband George Howell, Richard Owens and wife Frances Owens, Ellen Freeman and husband Mart [*sic*] Freeman, Frances Laws [*sic*] and husband William Laws [*sic*], Nancy Littlejohn and husband Pink Littlejohn, Mandy Owens, Emma Owens and Lila Owens desiring to make said deed [to School Committee of the Colored District #1] for a school house site...the sum of five dollars...Reedy Patch creek...southwest from the present school house...including the old school house." F.M. Laus sold one-half acre, and Martin C. Freeman sold one-quarter acre. *Henderson County Deed Book* 30: 364.

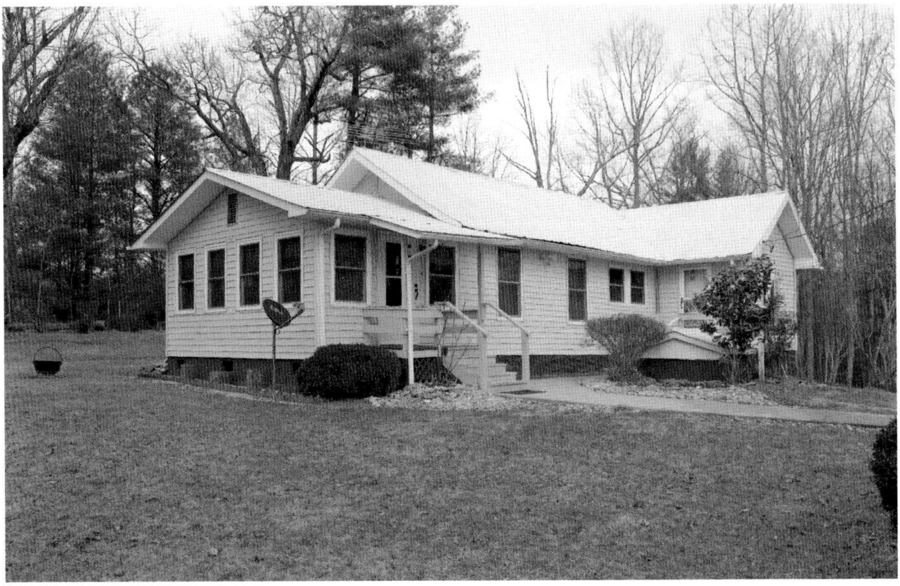

The former Laus schoolhouse. *Photographed with permission.*

1912 (burned in the 1950s); a school at Bat Cave (circa 1906–circa 1915); and an unorganized mission at Etowah. A cemetery was established at St. Matthew's (today, St. Elizabeth Methodist Episcopal Church Cemetery). Martin and Ellen Freeman appealed to Reverend Willcox to start St. Peter's, which, at the peak of its school enrollment, included thirty-seven black students. The diocese assigned Reverend James Burges Sill (1871–1958) of Shelby to St. Peter's, and one of the early teachers was Odie Mills Littlejohn (1891–1968), mother of Ruth Montgomery (1925–), whose husband, John Lee Montgomery (1921–2008), added an enclosed porch, converting the old schoolhouse she attended into their home.

Reverend Reginald Norton Willcox recalled:

> *Besides St. James, St. Paul's and St. John the Baptist the Hendersonville Associate Missions takes charge of St. Peter's, Roosevelt, a community of colored people. These colored people of St. Peter's make very earnest and devout Church people. They have built a handsome frame church. I believe the colored problem in the South would be solved, or at least much simplified if the Church only had the power to reach the people.*

SECULAR SCHOOLS

Edneyville had several feeder schools in addition to St. Paul's, St. Peter's and the Good Shepherd mission schools. The following counted among the roster:

- Barnwell (previously Clear Creek)
- Bat Cave
- Bearwallow
- Chestnut Grove
- DeWitt
- Ebenezer
- Edneyville
- Fruitland
- Hickory (Gerton)
- Lake Lure
- Liberty
- "Little Red Schoolhouse," Bat Cave
- Locust Grove (Hogney)
- Middle Fork
- Point Lookout

The *French Broad Hustler*, in April 1914, informed its readers:

> *It is proposed to consolidate Upper Reedy Patch and DeWitt districts and to form another by the consolidation of Liberty and Barnwell. It would become necessary to build two new schoolhouses and thereby provide for two teachers and greater school efficiency.*

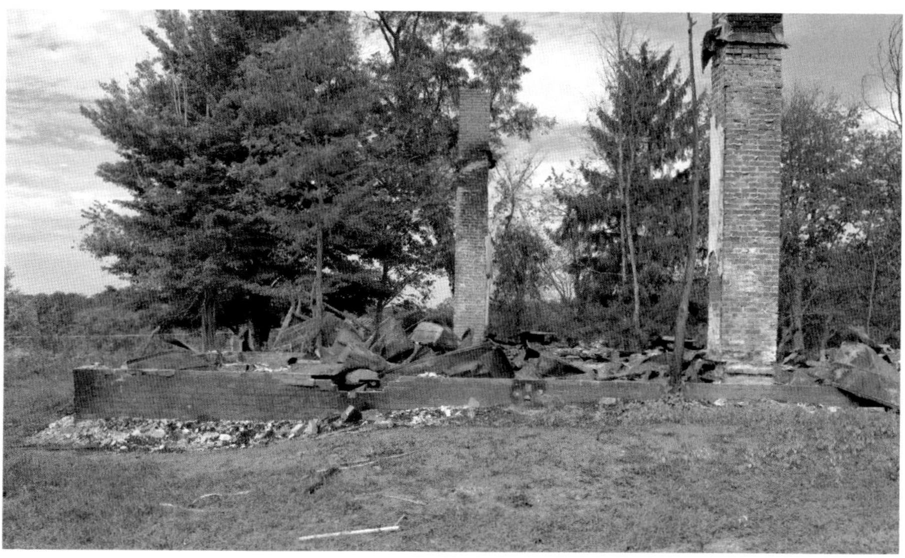

Point Lookout School ruins.

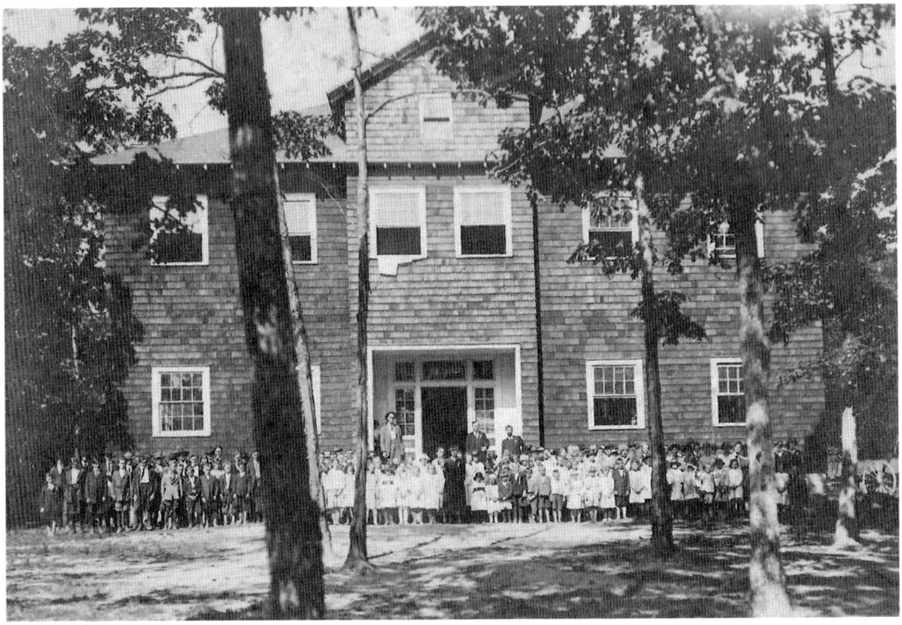

The "Old Brown Building," Edneyville School. *Courtesy of Henderson County Genealogical and Historical Society, Inc.*

In 1921, fifty-one white and eleven black schools represented fifty-three school districts in Henderson County. The feeder schools of Edneyville consolidated with Edneyville School, where until 1927, grade school and high school students shared the same edifice known as the "old brown building." Countywide schools had consolidated to ten institutions by 1930, to six by 1934 and, in 1960, to three: East Henderson High, West Henderson High and Edneyville High.

In *Paradox of Southern Progressivism: 1880–1930*, William A. Link wrote:

> *An important factor behind the opposition to school consolidation was parental fear about their children walking to distant schools. From Henderson County, a North Carolina parent described the treacherous roads of that mountainous region. The present route, he argued, was "very dangerous" and "unsafe for a grown person to walk." He had had "some narrow escapes." Appeals to the county school board had been futile, he maintained, because the chairman had "no relatives on this road" and therefore had little concern for "the life of our little ones."*

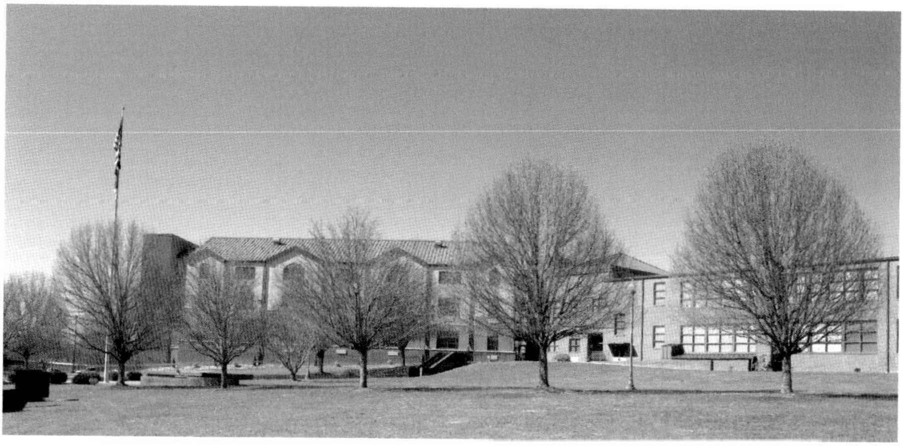

Justice Academy.

> *Frustrated by this unresponsiveness, he took his case to the governor as "a Democrat and a man that voted for you…to see that we get this bus for the protection of our little ones."*

The county school system added grade twelve to the curriculum in 1946 and built a separate high school for Edneyville students in 1951 at the corner of U.S. Highway 64 East and St. Paul's Road. Black students integrated into the system in the early 1960s. In 1970, a new brick building at Edneyville housed elementary students, grades four to six moved from Edneyville Union School to Edneyville Elementary on Pace Road in 1982 and a separate building for junior and high school students was completed in 1984 at the U.S. Highway 64 East/St. Paul's Road campus. Edneyville High School consolidated into North Henderson High School on Fruitland Road, completed in 1993, and Edneyville middle school students began attending Apple Valley Middle School. The old campus was repurposed as the Justice Academy in 1998 and named in 2004 Larry T. Justus Western Justice Academy, in honor of North Carolina representative Larry Thomas Justus (1932–2002). The Justice Academy facilities, with an eastern campus at Salemburg, provide training programs for criminal justice personnel and afford technical assistance to criminal justice agencies.

WHAT'S IN STORE?

In August 1911, G.W. Lyda, road supervisor, reported to the *French Broad Hustler*:

> *Good roads at small expense will have to be brought about in this way. The supervisor at Edneyville has been spending about $10 every two years to keep up the bridge at J.J. Freeman's. Under the advice of T.C. Rhodes overseer, they hit upon the idea of employing Mr. Henry Rogers to build a culvert over said stream at the small expenditure of $16. It is done for life. Come on brother supervisor of other townships and see what can be done in the way of curtailing taxes.*

Country stores mushroomed alongside the "good roads" through Edneyville—hubs of activity in days of old. Such a store was tucked among Hunsinger's Cottages at the corner of Chimney Rock and Pace Roads. The Boy Scout Hall housed Nesbitt's Grocery and, later, Bill Wilson's Grocery, as well as the post office run by Foy Carl Hill (1917–1990) and his wife, Roscoe Sarah Frances Townsend Hill (1916–2007). Other stores included Uno Grocery, Kerr's Grocery and Edneyville General, as well as Ted's High Value, 64 Bait 'n' Tackle, Mr. T's, Griffin's, Nix's, Turner's and Hoots Grocery & Garage. John Lee Montgomery worked for many years at Turner's.

In the present time, Eugene "Gene" Hoots sits each day on his front porch near his family's former store, surveying the increased traffic and reminiscing about the good old days in Edneyville.

BROWS OF THE BLUE RIDGE

Many have written that early settler William Mills put place names to natural landmarks in what became Henderson County—Bear Wallow, Sugar Loaf, Bald Top, Mills Gap and more. Long before Mills's arrival in the region, French explorers had already mapped Mills River as "Milles." An exception to places named by Mills would include Lamb Mountain.

In the shadows of Sugarloaf Mountain, Lamb Mountain takes its name from Confederate private Emsley Burgess Hunter Lamb (1843–1930), married to Charlotte Tealue Justice Lamb (1844–1921), daughter of John Hiram Justice (1816–1901) and Mary Jane King "Doctor Polly"

Peaks

Allen Hill, 2,620 feet
Bald Top, 3,570 feet
Bank, 3,698 feet
Barnwell, 2,700 feet
Bearwallow, 4,232 feet
Burney, 2,990 feet
Burntshirt, 3,540 feet
Butler, 2,700 feet
Chickasaw Knobs, 2,660 feet
Corbin, 3,025 feet
Evans, 2,820 feet
Fork, 2,980 feet
Grant, 3,291 feet
Grassy, 3,300 feet
Grassy Top, 3,268 feet
Hightop, 3,570 feet
Hogback, 3,140 feet
Lamb, 2,650 feet
Little Bearwallow, 3,980 feet
Little Fork, 2,500 feet
Little Pisgah, 5,300 feet
Little Rich, 3,220 feet
Pilot, 2,570 feet
Piney, 2,770 feet
The Pinnacle, 3,780 feet
Poplar, 3,244 feet
Raven Rock, 2,860 feet
Rich, 3,442 feet
Stone, 3,660 feet
Stony Bald, 4,563 feet
Sugarloaf, 3,965 feet
Whiteside, 2,620 feet

Justice (1819–1904). The Lambs farmed in Edneyville on their namesake mountain, rising to 2,650 feet between Lewis Creek and Mills Gap, and are buried at the Jones Cemetery near the junction of Lamb Mountain Road and Marshall Road. Burgess's tombstone reads: "Burgess Lamb Co., I 22 N.C. Inf. C.S.A."

Named for Thomas Littleton "Ton" (also "Tunn") Lemuel Gilliam Sr. (1822–1865), Gilliam Mountain Road climbs Lamb Mountain in the vicinity of Bald Rock, Point Lookout and Jones Knob between the former post offices of Ottanola and Horace in Edneyville. Gilliam, born in McDowell County, North Carolina, married Roseanne (or Roseana) "Matilda" Young (circa 1830–circa 1920) and died from illness in Virginia while serving in the Confederate army. The Gilliams and many of their descendants, including Thomas Littleton Gilliam Jr. (1852–1930) and his wife, Mary Ann Jones Gilliam (1855–1901), are buried at Mount Moriah Baptist Church Cemetery.

Mount Moriah Baptist Church

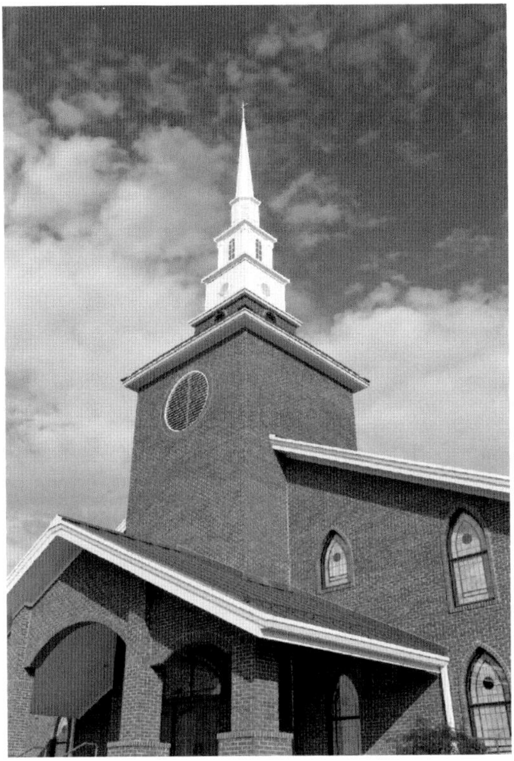

Mount Moriah Baptist Church.

In 1839, fourteen charter members, including Gabriel Jackson (1798–1883), John H. Justice (1816–1901), John Hill (1788–1875), Allen C. Stepp (1831–1895), Benjamin King Sr. (1777–1841) and John Lyon (1812–1875), organized Mount Moriah Baptist Church, the first Baptist church established in Edneyville. For one dollar, "Ton" Gilliam sold them the knoll on which, in 1851, they constructed a log meetinghouse chinked with mud and furnished with pews of split puncheon logs on peg legs. In 1885, Roseanne Gilliam and her children sold additional land to the congregation for the purpose of a cemetery. After the log structure burned, members constructed a weather-boarded frame church in 1886 on the same land, a building later veneered with red brick (1945) and appended with classrooms in the 1940s. Pews from a furniture manufacturer in Hickory replaced older ones in 1903. Until the installation of a furnace in 1941, woodstoves heated the facility, and before electricity came to the mountain, kerosene lanterns provided light. The DeWitt Post Office served this area from 1899 to 1906.

Reverend Ralph Allen Banning (1911–2007) became the first full-time pastor in 1954. In 1955, the acquisition of two more acres made room for a parsonage, a baptistery was added in the 1960s, a church library was started in 1970 and a steeple was erected in the 1980s. Other pastors have included Benjamin King Sr., Jacob Cantrell (circa 1780–1854), Homer Ortho Baker (1904–1992), W.H. Jones (1859–1948), John M. Walker (1920–1991), John Lynch Brookshire (1851–1926), Columbus Duren Cole (1874–1942),

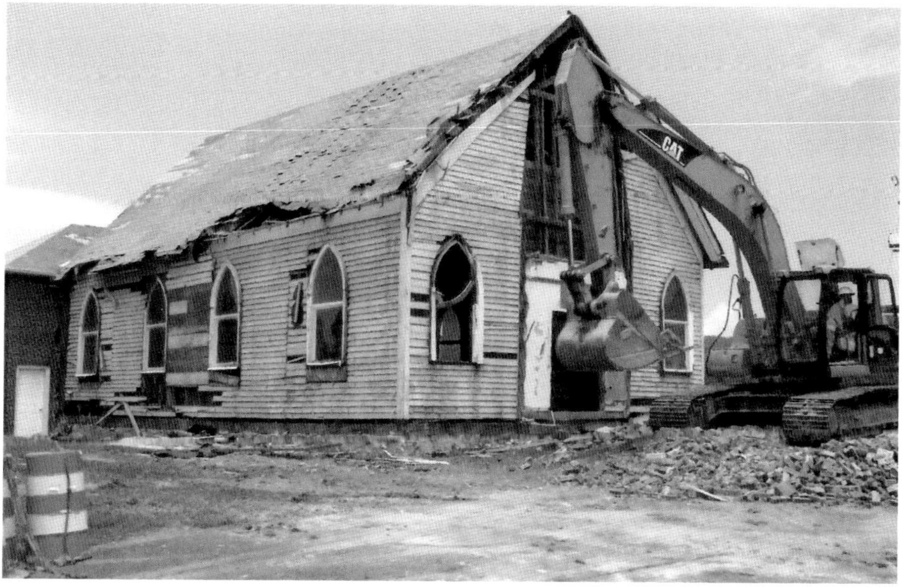

Demolition of the 1886 Mount Moriah Church in 2011 exposed its original weatherboarding. *Courtesy of Bill Barnwell.*

Thomas Alonzo Drake (1875–1948), Noah Abraham Melton (1881–1959), John B. Arledge (1854–1934), A.J. Nielson Sr. (1866–1950), R.P. Corn (1867–1944), Samuel F. Huntley (1864–1946), Sion Blythe Osborne McCall (1881–1961), W.A. Morris (1859–1941), M. Howard Drye (1892–1954), Arnold Edney (1900–1973), Wade W. Worley (1903–1982), Nathan Chapman (1900–1969), Lloyd Keith "Chick" Holbert (1915–1984), Ralph Marion Nix (1917–1986), Otto Parham (1903–1986), Herman F. Hicks (1937–), William W. Willingham (1929–2011) and Dean Elliott (1964–). Reverend Bryan Melton (1964–) has served as pastor since 1999.

Because the church stood on foundations of dry-stacked stones, officials deemed the entire structure unstable and razed it before construction of the current church, begun in 2011 and completed in 2012. Member William V. "Bill" Barnwell (1936–) reworked the old church's floor joists, doors and other woodwork to incorporate into the current structure. At the same time, craftsmen restored the stained-glass windows.

Boney A. Jackson (1875–1949), grandson of founding member Gabriel Jackson, worked for Frederick Law Olmsted (1822–1903) and Chauncey Delos Beadle (1866–1950) at George Vanderbilt's Biltmore estate. Beadle chose not to use one of the firs and one of the European copper beeches

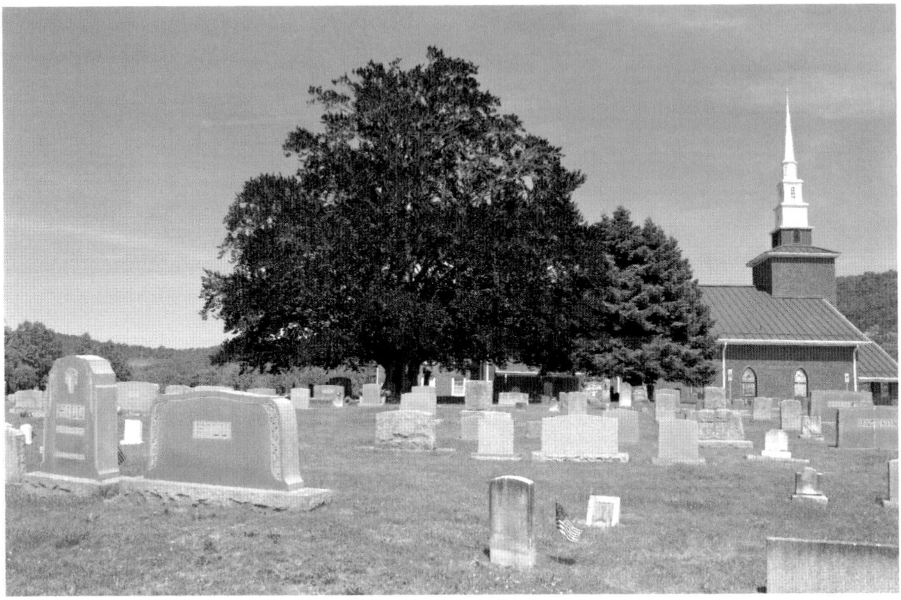

The mighty European beech planted as a sapling by Boney Jackson in the early 1900s in the Mount Moriah Baptist Church Cemetery.

(*Fagus sylvatica* "Atropunicea") Olmsted had planned for the landscaping and allowed Jackson to take the saplings, which Jackson planted in the churchyard at Mount Moriah Baptist Church. Nanneys, Jacksons and Browns now rest eternally beneath the shade of what have become trees of titanic proportions. The roots of the beech have encased part of the ornate, weather-etched monument of Edith Brown (1895–1898), daughter of Robert Jones Brown (1846–1918) and Mary Matilda Maxwell Brown (1853–1938). Boney Jackson is buried at Calvary Episcopal Church Cemetery in Fletcher.

From 14 founding members, the congregation grew to 129 in 1923 and to 410 by 1986. The membership of Mount Moriah Baptist Church currently stands at 350.

III

IN WITH THE INN CROWD

It is a provable fact that all conditions that tend to promote vigorous health are in and around this city. Unique hygienic conditions give Hendersonville the driest atmosphere, the purest air and water in the Appalachian Mountains.
—from an early twentieth-century brochure published by the Hendersonville Board of Trade

In addition to the Bee Hive Inn, visitors to Henderson County found scores of choices for lodging—those hospitable summer getaways proffering every convenience for the welfare of guests.

Vacationers from the lowlands thronged the vacation mecca of western North Carolina at the turn of the last century, when hospitality swelled the population of Henderson County during "the season." Situated in the midst of the "Land of the Sky," "Lake City" and the "Roof Garden of America," downtown Hendersonville boasted everything from modest to sumptuous accommodations: Ripley House, Globe, New Globe, Kentucky Home, Colonial (later the site of Hodgewell, Ames and Bowen), Mont-Clair (later renamed Wheeler, Carolina Terrace and then the Terrace before it burned), Whitehall (name changed to Marlborough), Gates (Imperial and St. John), the Blue Ridge Inn (later the Majestic), Aloah (later known as the Carson, Hendersonville Inn and Inn on Church), Ames, Oakley Florida Home (where Pardee Hospital would be built), Farm-City Home, Sunshine Lodge and the Skyland. Commercial boardinghouses included the Cedars, Gables, Ingleside (aka Dixie Inn and the Jefferson), Israel House, Fifth Avenue

Guesthouse (later called Elizabeth Leigh Inn), Carolina Home, Wilson Cottage, Waverly, Chewning House (Claddagh), the Orchards and a number of private homes that accepted guests. Hotels and inns near Hendersonville's Southern Railway station included Richelieu, Colorado, Mountain City Inn and Bruster's (known over the years by several different names, including Ford, Station, Exchange, Dewey and Caldwell). The slopes encompassing Laurel Park Estates sported Indian Cave Park Lodge, New Ames Hotel, Echo Mountain Inn, Poplar Lodge, Laurel Park Inn and a casino. Osceola had its Lake View Hotel (later called Copper Crest), casino and Lakeside Inn (later Camp Lakeside and Camp Mountain Lake for Jewish children), and East Flat Rock had its Wayside Inn. Sprinkled throughout the county stood hostelries now all but forgotten: Park Hill (once occupied by the Elks Club), Gray Gables, Inn Wood, the Recreation, Bonnie Bell, Bason Falls and the infamous Peacock Inn. Little has been written about Hillcrest, the home and one-time boardinghouse of Calvin Jones Edney (1853–1941) and his wife, Nancy Juno King Edney (1854–1931), grandparents of radio personality Kermit Edney (1924–2000).

Nationally acclaimed big bands performed in Hendersonville and Laurel Park, and farmers picked and grinned at square dances for rural vacationers. Speculators built the lakes Osceola, Kanuga, Rhododendron (Laurel Park Lake) and Rainbow for the ambiance of summer colonists, and soon campgrounds and religious retreats dotted the landscape as well. Lodges and guest cottages flourished alongside backcountry roads, and the Woodfield Inn (Henry Tudor Farmer's Hotel), plus accommodations at the Highland Lake Inn, wooed summer visitors to Flat Rock. As part of the backwash of the Florida land boom, eccentric Miami developer "Commodore" Jacob Perry Stoltz (1870–1945) visualized a world-class skyscraper atop Jump Off Mountain, and there he began to erect his ill-fated Fleetwood Hotel, which he patterned after his hotel by the same name in Miami Beach.

It wasn't until 1879, when the railroad at last reached Hendersonville, that word caught on and tourism boomed, concluding the region's former isolation, and enterprising locals capitalized on the summertime onrush of tourists. Livery services maintained a steady pace transporting guests between the Southern Railway stations and favorite mountain getaways. Seeking cooler temperatures, invigorating climate and rural bliss, many vacationers from the lowlands removed themselves from the in-town hubbub and the glitz and glamour of Asheville, favoring the asylum of Henderson's countrified, mountainous atmosphere in more rugged sectors of the county. Tuberculosis patients found restorative qualities in the mountains, where

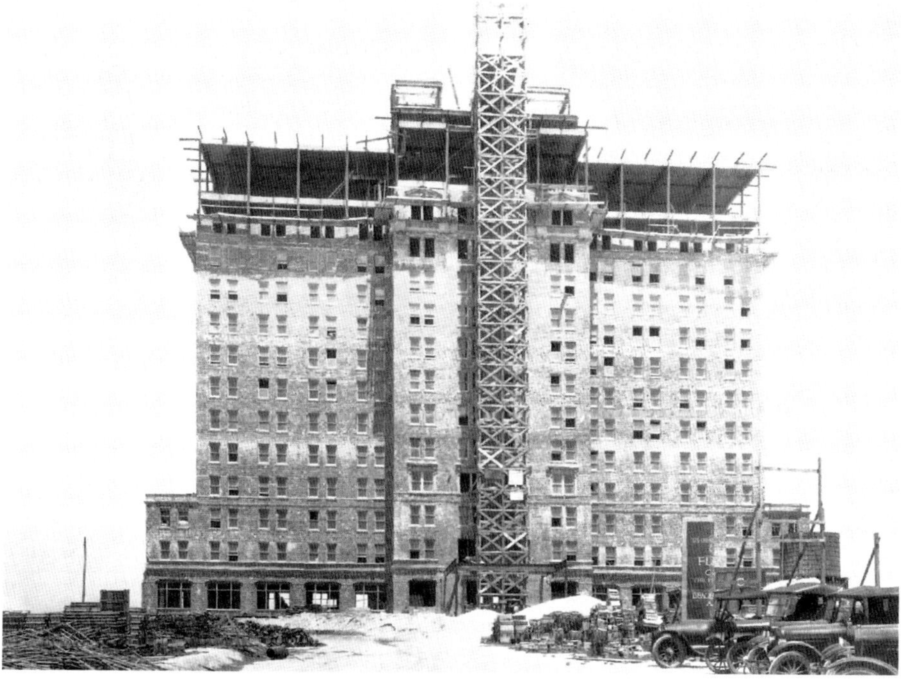

The Fleetwood Hotel at the summit of Jump Off Mountain. *Courtesy of James H. Toms.*

sanatoriums had opened for treatment of the dreaded disease. Moreover, Hendersonville was one of the few stations where tuberculosis patients were allowed to dismount the trains.

By railway, visitors could more readily reach western North Carolina's picturesque headlands, but more than the challenge of the precipitous climb by rail from Lowcountry locales, early carriageways proved at least as defiant in their winding steepness, their circumstance of either muddy or dust-choked surfaces and in the fording of streams devoid of bridges. Freshets scoured out sections of these crude thoroughfares, leaving in their wake roadbeds pockmarked with gullies and strewn with rocks and fallen trees and limbs, effecting bumpy excursions by hack line from the depot to, for instance, the slopes of Burney or Sugarloaf. These trips might last for nearly a day as passengers rumbled and bumped along the rocky two-rut roads. Once guests reached their destinations, the tumultuous excursions soon faded from their minds. By all accounts—and especially if one believed the embroidery printed in early promotional gloss and advertisements—Henderson County's accommodations afforded the milieu of Shangri La.

In 1905, Hendersonville experienced its best season to date, as reported in the *French Board Hustler*:

> *The Hendersonville Board of Trade has completed the census of visitors to the city this summer, ordered at a recent meeting and reports that 9,262 have registered at the various hotels and boardinghouses during the present season. Fully 5,000 were here on August 17, after the arrival of the excursion from the south. On that day more than 150 were compelled to seek accommodations elsewhere. Hendersonville was obliged to admit, for once, that she was full—very full. Many strangers within our gates had "not where to lay their heads" and boarded the first train for other points. More than twice the usual number of visitors was here this season. Nothing like it has ever before been experienced in the history of the town. Everything has been alive with glee and aglow with gaiety. We are delighted to have the tourists with us always.*

FLACK HOTEL

One seldom meets another vehicle on curvaceous St. Paul's Road, where all lingers still and calm, but back in the day one would have sensed the beating of hooves, the jingle of tack and the rumble of buckboards and buggies negotiating the bumpy, unpaved course. An occasional flivver might have raised a blur of dust and frightened a horse or two as seasonal guests headed to or from one of the summer getaways tucked into the coves of Edneyville.

Along the journey, weary travelers glimpsed young and old alike tending the fields and orchards. Smoky aromas of curing hams and bacon wafted on the salubrious air that had lured these tourists from their sultry lowland homes. Come twilight, they were delighted by a fleeting sparkle of fireflies and the dulcet resonance of string bands, dance callers and the cadence of heels clogging against hardwood.

In 1915, John Andrew Flack (1869–1920) of Rutherford County built a four-story, fifty-room hotel alongside St. Paul's Road, and he and his wife, Sallie Aletha Whiteside Flack (1870–1957), served as managers and hosts. The couple's hotel earned acclaim, not only for its hospitality but also for its recreational amenities, particularly its open-sided dancehall. The Pavilion, as they called it, stood in a ravine below the hotel, and on square dance nights, its bark-covered rafters pulsed with the reverberation of Flack's

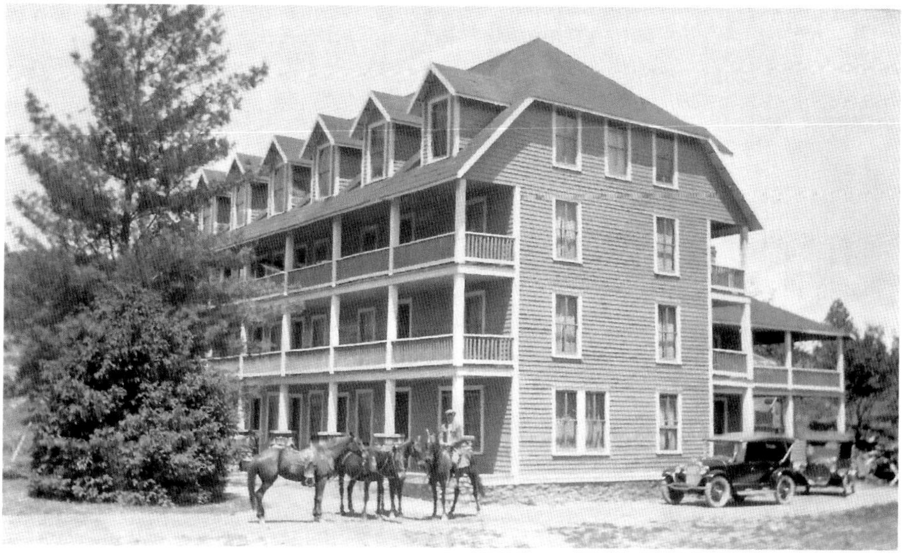

Flack Hotel. *Courtesy of Susan Flack Summerville.*

Orchestra, a group comprising brothers Alonzo Carmieal "Lon" Brookshire (1894–1960) on fiddle, William Jennings Bryant "Sleepy" Brookshire (1897–1982) on rhythm guitar, Dick Stepp on bass fiddle and Dick Rand on piano. Clarence Butler served as caller for dance moves. (Rand and Butler hailed from Cliffside.) Dances on Friday and Saturday evenings at the Flack drew, besides its own guests, local folks during its earlier years. Lon Brookshire organized Hendersonville's first street dance in 1924, with the idea of roping off a block of Main Street for the purpose of entertainment.

Flack descendants described the pavilion's pillars and beams as having had intact bark. The interior featured bleacher-style seating against its walls, a bandstand and concession stand and, of course, a wooden floor. Strung overhead, a network of colorful lights bestowed a festive glow on the dancers' revelry. On alternative nights of the week, square dancers found venues at other area inns, in Laurel Park and in downtown Hendersonville.

The Flack Hotel sported a clay tennis court, playground swings and slides and "turkey and ham shoots," where target practice winners selected a turkey or a ham for their prize. Early ads for the hotel boasted of acetylene lights, hot and cold baths and rates of five to six dollars per week.

On-site orchards and gardens, a herd of cattle, free-range poultry and a smokehouse ensured homegrown, homespun meals of fried chicken, ham, corn on the cob, fruit pies and buttermilk—all served family-style on long

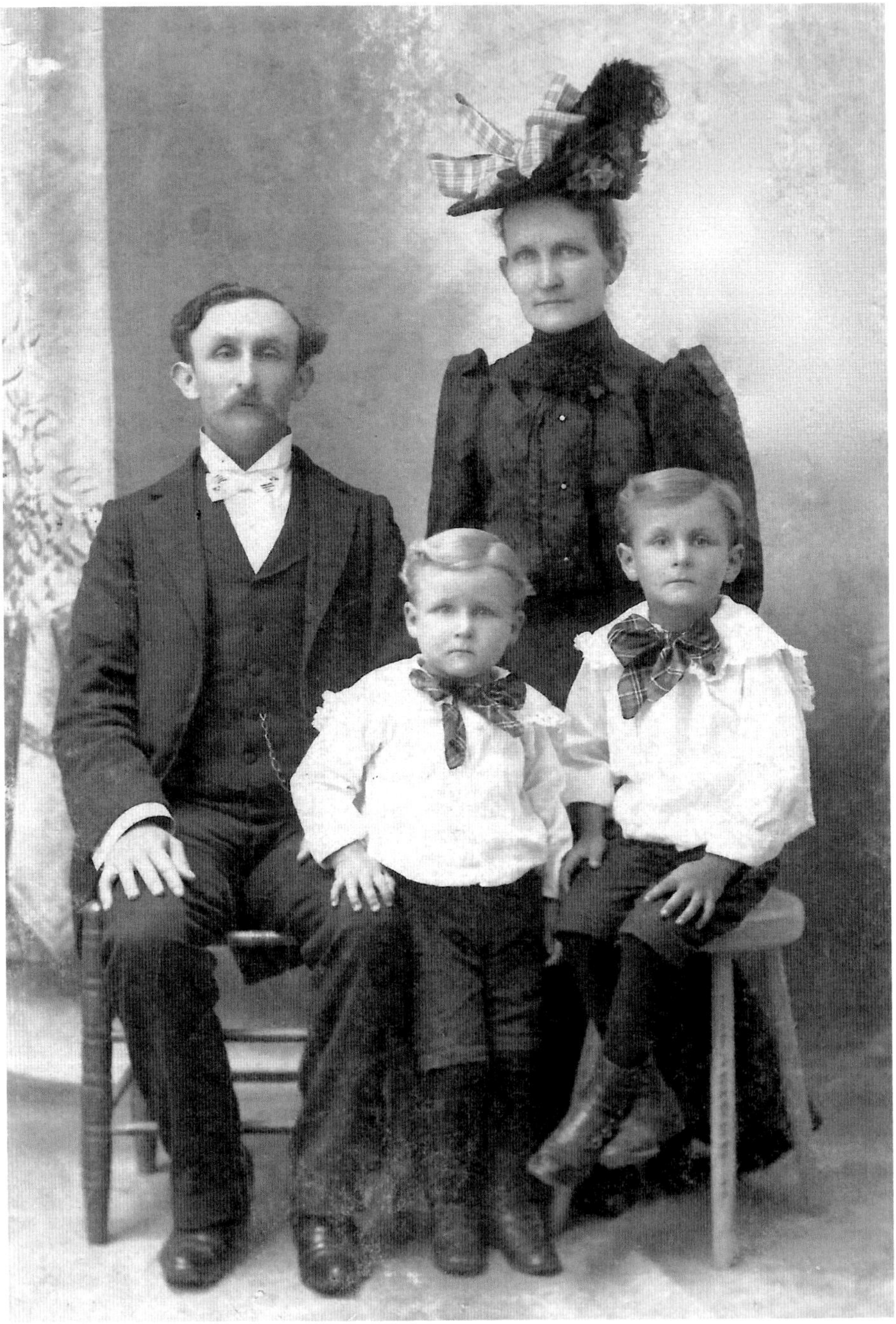

John and Sallie Flack with sons John Hoke Flack (left) and Horace Milner Flack (right). *Courtesy of Susan Flack Summerville.*

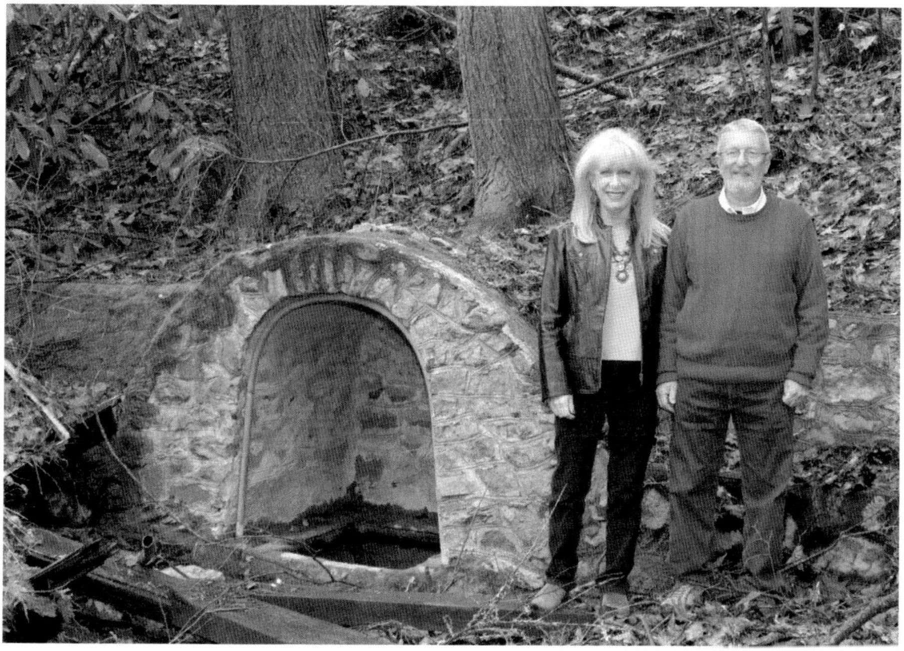

John and Sallie Flack's grandchildren, siblings Susan Flack Summerville and Greg Flack, at the former Flack Hotel's spring.

tables overlaid with white linen. The Flacks built their smokehouse on the foundations of the springhouse, in which they stored dressed chickens and dairy products, and Mrs. Flack always churned her own butter.

In addition to playing host to out-of-town guests, John Andrew Flack served as a rural postal carrier for Route 1, Edneyville, from 1906 to 1920, followed by his son John Hoke Flack (1895–1956) from 1920 to 1932. Ellen B. Heydock (Haydock) said of Mr. Flack:

> *Mr. Flack was a post office on wheels. He sold stamps and postcards, mailed registered letters, insured packages, delivered the letters and newspapers to the large mailboxes in front of Edney's Inn and beyond. Never has there been a kinder man.*

Celebrity guests of the Flack Hotel included movie director and screenwriter Hal Kanter (1918–2011) and radio personality/comedienne/actress/singer Judy Canova (1913–1983) and her siblings Anna and Zeke.

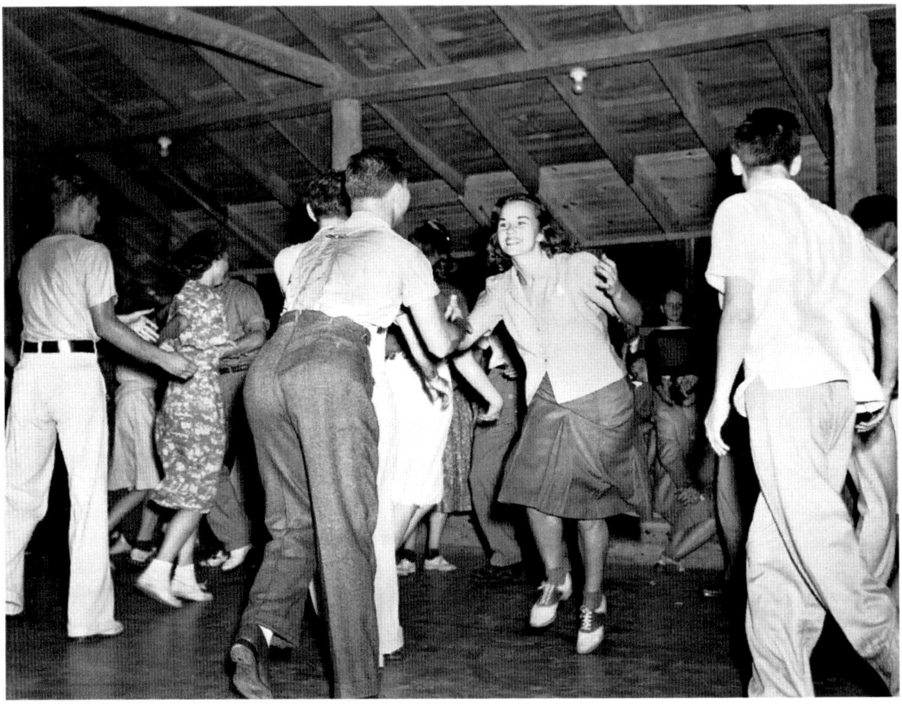

Square dancing at the Flack Hotel's open pavilion. *Courtesy of Teresa Flack Padgett.*

After occasional episodes of liquor being secreted onto the premises in the 1940s, the Flacks put a halt to musical festivities for outsiders. After Sallie's death, her son Horace Milner Flack (1893–1962) and his wife, Florida Edney Williams Flack (1903–1989), operated the inn, but only until 1959, when they shut it down rather than shoulder the gratuitous burden of updating the facilities under federal regulations. The hotel sat vacant until 1971, when it burned to the ground due to suspected arson. The pavilion later caved in from age and neglect.

CHICKASAW/BLUE RIDGE HOTEL

Before 1900, Jacob Manly Lyda (1849–1916) built a rambling, three-story summer resort he named Chickasaw on the south-facing slope of the East Chickasaw Knob. Ada Lyda (1891–1988), wife of W. Singleton Lyda (1887–1950), later ran the establishment. After Jacob's death, the inn and its associated twenty-eight acres went up for auction on the courthouse steps in 1917. Minnie Lee Waters Edney (1894–1978)—the highest bidder—bought the property at $1,000 and sold it in 1918 to S.S. and Annie Creesman and B.H. and Lessie Ledbetter, who in turn sold to Marguarett Schoppell and Mrs. E.E. Hautsch of Charleston in 1919. Schoppell sold her interest to Hautsch, who renamed the establishment the Blue Ridge Hotel and sold to Nell Yelton in 1928. J.H. and Nell Yelton sold to B.B. and Ida V. Jones of Buncombe County in 1931, the year it burned. Since that time, the property changed ownership from the B.B. Joneses to O.O. Smith of Greenville, South Carolina, and from Smith to C.E. and Maude Sims, also of Greenville. Successive owners included A. and N.M. Reaban, Eliza C. Dunn, R.F. and Tyma Hill, Cora Corak, Margaret Louise Ballard, Samuel Earl Ballard and Harriet M. Ballard. The home of Clyde Ballard currently stands near the site of the hotel.

The Recreation

The value of historical documentation becomes even more apparent when, dig as we may, researchers unearth little or nothing of a once-momentous, albeit short-lived, establishment. Such would be the case with the Recreation at Edneyville. Described as three stories tall and situated within reach of the Roosevelt Post Office in Edneyville, this hotel surely vied with neighboring Bee Hive Inn, the Chickasaw and the Flack Hotel for its share of summer guests in the nooks and slopes off St. Paul's Road, which cuts a conduit between the East and West Chickasaw Knobs—a course that remains restful and picturesque today. Purportedly built around 1920 by James Kennedy "Jake" Livingston (1881–1937) of Charleston, the inn's brief history disappeared or lies hidden, forgotten in scrapbooks or attic corners.*

Robert Livingston reported that his grandfather J.K. Livingston built the spacious hotel that burned to the ground about one year after its completion. The Livingston family, who lived at the hotel, boarded for a stretch after the fire at the neighboring Bee Hive Inn before removing to Hendersonville. Besides the inn, J.K. Livingston also owned Cinderella Boot Shoppe and the Bandbox, the latter a teen hangout on Hendersonville's Fourth Avenue.

* *Henderson County Deed Book* 109: 233, recorded a transaction for 107.5 acres of land in Edneyville for which J.K. Livingston paid T.A.W. Lyda $4,000 on December 20, 1920.

Cyril Earl "Buster" Livingston (1904–1992), son of Jake Livingston and Maude Victoire Soubeyroux Livingston (1883–1963), was a teenager when he lived with his parents at the Recreation and Bee Hive Inn. Buster went on to have an illustrious career and married Emma Alice Lyne (1908–2011). In the footprints of his father, Buster promoted big-name bands and brought them to Hendersonville, some of them including Hal Kemp, Jan Garber, Guy Lombardo, the Royal Canadians, the Dorsey Brothers and Cab Calloway and his Cotton Club Orchestra. Ever the entrepreneur, Buster also owned JK's Swimming Pool, Livingston's Promotions, the Union Bus Terminal (in the Ames Hotel building on Church Street) and Tracy's Place lunchroom, operated by Tracy H. Oelkers (1911–1964) at 701 North Main Street.

SALOLA INN/CLOW'S DUDE RANCH

At the turn of the last century, the Speculation Land Company sold land on Sugarloaf Mountain to ex–Hendersonville mayor and Henderson County sheriff Jonathan L. Williams (1847–1911), who built a large inn he named Salola* near the summit, intending to operate the facility as a health resort for tuberculosis and yellow fever patients. Williams married Lillie Lee Shipman (1870–1942) in 1893.

During several years of construction, Williams also built on the property a thirty-five-foot observation tower, claiming that four states could be seen from its deck: North and South Carolina, Georgia and Tennessee. A 1906 ad in the *Western North Carolina Times* listed R.M. Ivins as proprietor. The fare at the inn, in 1910, was "$2 per day; $8 to $10 per week including meals." In addition to the post offices of Ottanola and Horace at the foot of Sugarloaf, the inn also hosted a post office. An early twentieth-century brochure for Hendersonville by the Hackney & Moale Co. reads:

> *No pen can do justice to the number of views from Salola, or Sugar Loaf, a favorite mountain excursion, reached by a daily hack line to and from its well-kept inn...Bearwallow is reached by a drive absorbing in its picturesque loveliness and wild grandeur, along the ascent of which*

* According to Cherokee linguist Garfield Long, *saloli* translates as "squirrel" in the local Cherokee dialect. Salola would apply to the Oklahoma dialect.

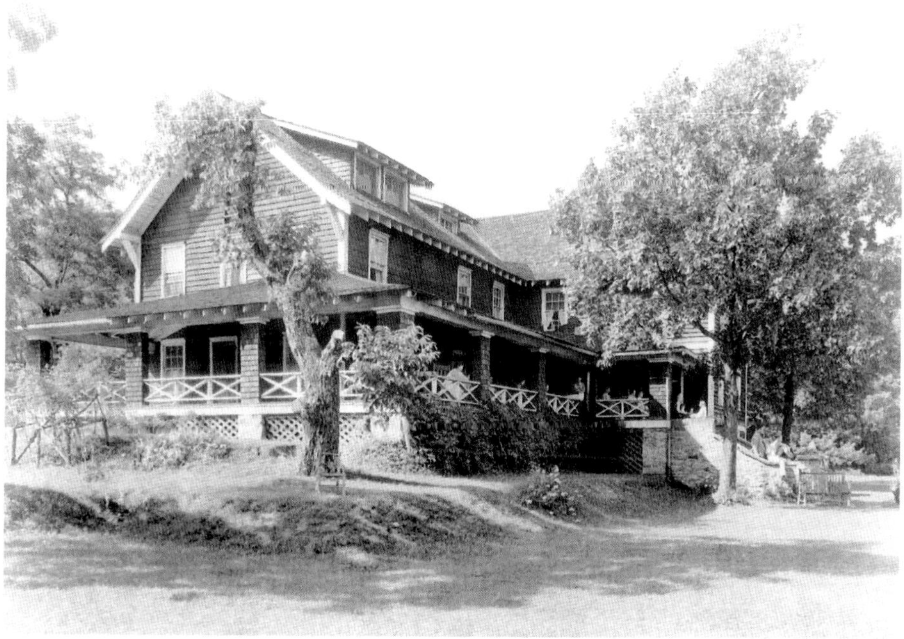

The Salola Inn. *Courtesy of Henderson County Genealogical and Historical Society, Inc.*

> *is found the far-famed rhododendron. From this lofty peak one might almost say they had seen the kingdoms of earth.*

In 1911, Williams sold the inn to Dr. W.M. Stinson, F.W. King and Stockton Brown, investors from Jacksonville, Florida, and New Orleans, Louisiana, who bought an additional 133 acres on the mountain. They had plans to build the "Jacksonville Club," including a golf course and guest cottages, from elaborate plans drawn by architect Burnett B. Carter. Neither the club nor the sanatorium ever materialized, in spite of Ben Merrell having completed the three-mile-long road up the mountain begun by W.A. Smith. John Augustus "Gus" Hooks (1887–1970) and Ethel N. Brundage Hooks (1893–1975) of Florida bought the property in 1920.

An illustrated brochure produced by the Hookses in the early 1920s flowed like treacle with hyperbole touting the "Land of the Sky," setting the stage for an idyllic summer country retreat. "Premier in every way…service the keystone of satisfied guests…comfort rather than luxury, refinement more than elegance," the Hookses wrote. The copy even alleged "ocean views," disclaiming this phrase by challenging the imagination to envision the sea in clouds waving over the valley far below. The lawn was "shady," the porches "spacious," the athletic courts "excellent," the cuisine "superb" and the breezes "life-giving." Vegetables and fruits were of "superior quality to the products of the lowlands," almost a given when considering the inn's "most fertile of gardens." Best of all, the inn's proprietors' claims of "electrically lighted" and "running water"—if one did not mind the latter being "down the hall." An article in the *Western North Carolina Times* made the following claim: "Almost equaling in its variety the Yosemite Valley."

The Hookses, farmers from Homestead, Florida, operated the Salola from 1923 to the early 1930s, each June 1 to October 31. The inn's athletic facilities consisted of clay and grass tennis courts, a horseshoe court and a croquet lawn with a promise of "a golf course in the near future." In addition to "unexcelled panoramas of land and sky," many sightseeing adventures awaited: "nature's freaks" and Williams's observation tower, all "within walking distance of the inn."

The freaks of nature included Castle Rock, Cloven Cliff, Sunset Rock, the Pinnacles, a natural oddity known as the Windows, Bear Pen Cliff, Ship Rock, Squirrel Rock, Bottomless Pools, Lake Lure, Chimney Rock, Hickory Nut Falls and "enchanting views of Hickory Nut Gap."

Husband and wife Johnson Orval "Jonce" Clow (1893–1964) and Sarah Arvilla Withers Clow (1888–1983) of Miami, Florida, began lodging at the Salola in 1925. During the Great Depression, Jonce purchased not only the inn but also a good deal of the top of Sugarloaf Mountain in 1932 from Mr. and Mrs. Joseph William Bailey. The Clows renamed the inn Clow's Dude Ranch, offering equestrian facilities and three daily family-style meals, incorporating on-site products of vegetables, pork and chicken. Local farmers and orchardists supplied dairy products, beef and fruit. Andrew and Rosalie Brown—the Clows' servants from Florida—worked as cook and chauffeur, with Andrew transporting guests between Hendersonville and Sugarloaf Mountain in Jonce Clow's woody station wagon. Mazie Nix Devore (1925–1994) and her husband, James Edward Devore (1924–1998), counted among local employees of the ranch, and according to an account written by William A. Thue, "Mazie's father worked as caretaker."

Gabriel "Gabe" Laughter (1870–1942) and his wife, Annie Melissa Ruff Laughter (1886–1950), farmed on a southern slope of Sugarloaf. Annie, a granny woman, turned chairs on a foot-operated lathe and sold these furnishings and other handicrafts to the innkeepers at the Salola Inn and Clow's Dude Ranch. Gabe, a noted moonshiner, supplied the inn with farm goods and—according to some—potent potables. Residents of the mountain frequently saw Gabe toting gunnysacks of corn or cornmeal across his shoulder between his farmstead and a gristmill. Gabe also led hotel guests on excursions to local sites and carried mail from Edneyville to the Horace and Ottanola post offices, reportedly on foot—or barefoot. Some of Annie's handicrafts and other hotel furnishings still accouter a few of the homes at the top of Sugarloaf.

The old hotel register listed guests from several states during the 1920s to early 1940s, when the ranch offered poker games, nickel slot machines and bands that entertained on Saturday nights after suppertime. On warm afternoons and evenings, in the midst of grazing cattle and inestimable panoramas, clientele could enjoy forever views and fresh air from any number of rocking chairs that lined the porches, while sipping lemonade served by staff attired in uniforms with red caps. The Clows charged daily fares ("American Plan") of "$3.50 and up" for single accommodations and "$7.00 and up" for doubles, as well as weekly fares of "$18.75 and up" for single accommodations and "$37.50 and up" for doubles and $5.00 per day or $20.00 per week for horses.

Although a proposed golf course never came to be on the Salola/Clow's property, ads boasted of "golfing," mentioning also "hunting trips by appointment."

Jonce maintained a tollgate to defray the costs of road upkeep, later leasing the top of the mountain to the United States for a radio beacon. The federal government maintained the roads on the mountain as part of the agreement.

The Clows operated the dude ranch until 1943. The hotel sat vacant until, after World War II, a couple with the surname Pelcher reopened the restaurant—a short-lived enterprise of less than two years, after which workers razed the establishment. Its materials were given away, and the remainders were control-burned by the Edneyville Fire Department.

The inn no longer stands, but around the site, a cluster of thirteen private homes sprang up, each of them standing today. The oldest dwelling in the secluded enclave, named the Nutshell, housed workers who helped construct the Salola Inn. Members of the Dearing family of Jacksonville and Tallahassee have owned the Nutshell since 1915. The other homes were built between 1940 and the 1970s. Carpenter Sidney Henderson (1889–1984) designed and built six of these houses for part-time residents from Florida.

The second-oldest dwelling, faced mostly with black granite, dates from about 1900. The home, currently owned by Thomas G. and Marilyn Buist

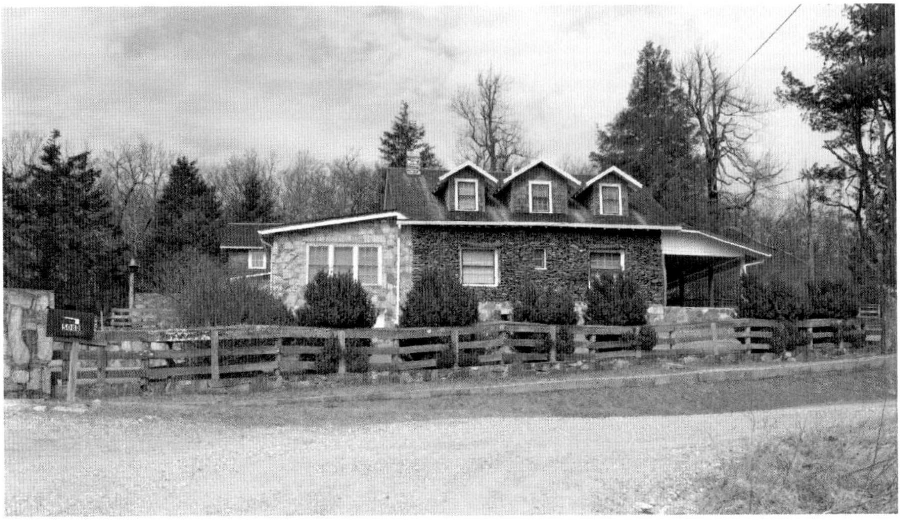

The Frink/Buist home near the top of Sugarloaf Mountain.

of Charleston, South Carolina, once belonged to Herbert Alexander Frink (1903–1962), the ex-mayor of Miami Beach (1945–1947), and his wife, Evelyn Patterson Frink (1914–1987), who purchased the property in 1936. After the ex-mayor died in his Sugarloaf home from a bullet wound, rumors buzzed—even after Henderson County officials determined the death to have been accidentally self-inflicted when Frink dropped his sixteen-gauge shotgun on his concrete patio and the gun discharged a shell into his abdomen. "Shot by His Own Gun," said the newspaper articles. Frink's death certificate stated, "Internal hemorrhages due to accidental gunshot wound to abdomen. Decedent fell on patio, shotgun discharged. May 8, 1962." The local rumor mill, however, suggested the mafia had something to do with Mr. Frink's demise.

Family names in the summer colony on the mountain appear frequently in the 1924–40 hotel register of the Salola and dude ranch—names including Withers, Crutchfield, Dearing and Clow. Mrs. Clow's brother Charles Elmer Withers (1895–1960) and his wife, Cassia, built a home on the mountain in 1932, owned currently by Jamie Withers Brown (1954–) and her husband.

Pictographs, arrowheads and chip stones in the hinterland of the Salola property signal prehistoric Native American activity on this mountaintop, which can be reached—even to this day—by a series of harrowing, unpaved switchbacks.

Lowrance Hotel

The Lowrance Hotel stood where David and Lola Coston's Coston Farm Apple House stands, at the corner of U.S. Highway 64 East and Pressley Road. Old-timers recall the long front porch and bygone days when the hotel housed one of the few telephones in the area, which local farmers would use in cases of emergency. Esley E. Lowrance (1869–1953) and his wife, Julia Peeler Lowrance (1876–1944), operated the hotel, and their daughter Julia Ella Lowrance Seymour (1896–1974) later took over and renamed it Oak Park Inn. Local resident Barbara Lyda Lackey recalled:

> *The Seymours lived in that little brick house on up behind where the inn sat. We always called the hotel the Oak Park Inn because it sat in a place with all those big oak trees around it. I can remember how pretty it looked at dinnertime when all the lights were on inside the dining room when guests were inside eating the evening meal. Goodness! Almost everyone had an inn back then.*

Edney Inn

Govan Perry Edney (1820–1906) built an inn on Bearwallow Mountain near Bat Cave in the mid-1800s. With his wife, Mourning Walker Freeman Edney (1831–1912), Govan operated the popular summer hostelry until his death, after which his son Marcus L. "Mark" Edney (1855–1929) and wife, Louisa Duvall Edney (1856–1929), took over in 1907. Wreathed by Fork and Little Fork Mountains, Raven's Cliff and the Pinnacles, this vacation lodge perched at the terminus of Little Creek Road off what is known now as Edney Inn Road. The inn, featuring thirty rooms, an expansive veranda and a ballroom, stood unattended after Mark's death in 1929, and on the Fourth of July in the mid-1930s, it burned to the ground, never to be rebuilt.

Local Ellen B. Heydock remembered the Edney Inn:

> *The outdoor facilities were not to be underestimated. Two large outhouses each had long seats provided with accommodations for several; clearly marked on each door were the words "For Men" and "For Women." Of course there was a catalogue in each building, a*

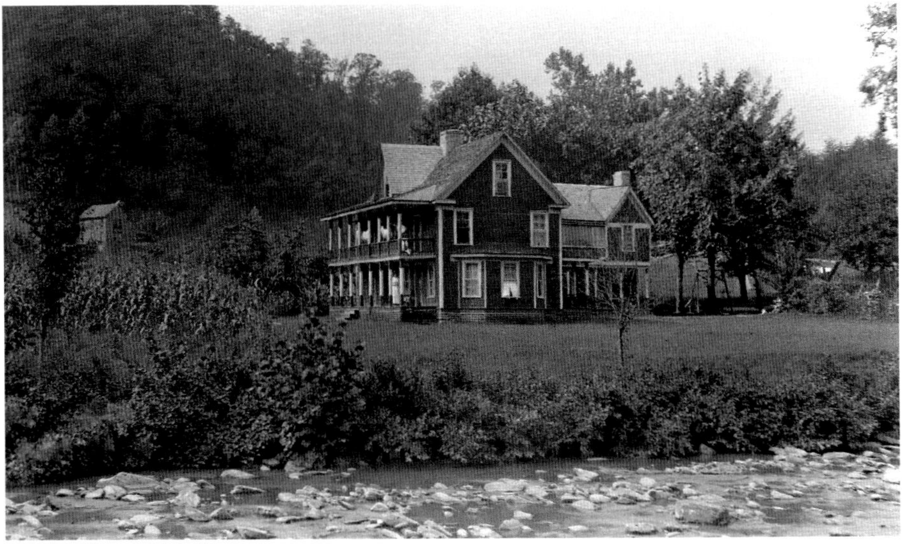

Edney Inn. *Courtesy of Baker-Barber Collection. Community Foundation of Henderson County. Henderson County Public Library.*

Sears Roebuck in the ladies'—and in each a wooden box of lime in the corner of the room holding a short-handled fire shovel with which to administer a cover-up.

SLICK ROCK INN

Before the turn of the twentieth century, Lum Dalton built a three-story Victorian-style inn and a few cottages above Chimney Rock Road near the waterfall of Reedy Patch Creek. Columbus Monroe "Lum" Dalton (1853–1919) married, first, Happy Sylvaney "Bunch" Hill (1855–1893) and second, Pearl Matilda Jackson (1872–1952). In the tradition of neighboring mountain hostelries, the Slick Rock featured double-seated yard swings, rocking chairs and a dance hall for the comfort and entertainment of its guests. Akin to many of the earlier inns, the Slick Rock operated without electricity, indoor plumbing or heating. It did, however, sport telephone service, rigged into the Fruitland party-line system by Lum Dalton, who also operated a general store on the property and served as postmaster of Fairbanks Post Office from 1904 to 1907.

Described by Daisy Barnwell Jones as "a beehive of activity in summer and a ghost town in winter," the enterprise provided jobs for locals during the season. Jones wrote of the property scattered with enormous boulders and walled in to the east by Big Fork Mountain, "looming straight up, threatening to let go of massive overhanging cliffs, clinging breathlessly to its forest-covered side, overlooking Reedy Patch Creek roaring past it all."

Hotel employees washed linens and guests' laundry on the shore of the creek in cast-iron wash pots over open fires—then line-dried and pressed the laundry by hand with flatirons. A big-horned Victrola—the only one for miles, according to Daisy Jones—supplied the musical background for dances in the hall. Lum Dalton, who suffered from diabetes and heart disease, hosted and cared for elderly relatives at his inn and, for the last five years of his life, continued operating the facility from his wheelchair.

ADDITIONAL HOSTELRIES IN the northeast sector of Henderson County and beyond included Sam Williamson's Beulah House near Ottanola, the Bat Cave boardinghouse operated by Mrs. B.F. Freeman and Mountain View Inn on Round Top Mountain at Chimney Rock. George P. Horton opened the latter, which James Mills Flack (1854–1943) purchased in 1898, adding to it until it reached the grand size of forty-four rooms and a dining room with a seating capacity of 120. The Mountain View Inn, described as "majestic" and "distinguished" in early ads and magazine articles, suffered damage during the flood of 1916. K.J. Kindley and his wife purchased and remodeled the legendary hostelry in 1947. A fire in 1956 destroyed the building.

PEACOCK INN

In the early twentieth century, Rosa Honor Lyda (1875–1933) and Mamie Mary Lyda (1878–1941)—spinster sisters of Andrew Lyda of the Bee Hive Inn—operated a small hostelry named the Peacock, which stood on the airport road, north of Fletcher, near Mills Gap and Cane Creek Roads in Hoopers Creek. Probably due to its exotic furnishings, including kitschy beaded curtains, posh accoutrements and the exotic McCaw parrots that dwelled there, rumors buzzed that the innkeepers ran a bawdy house. Locals also whispered gossip of illicit drinking,

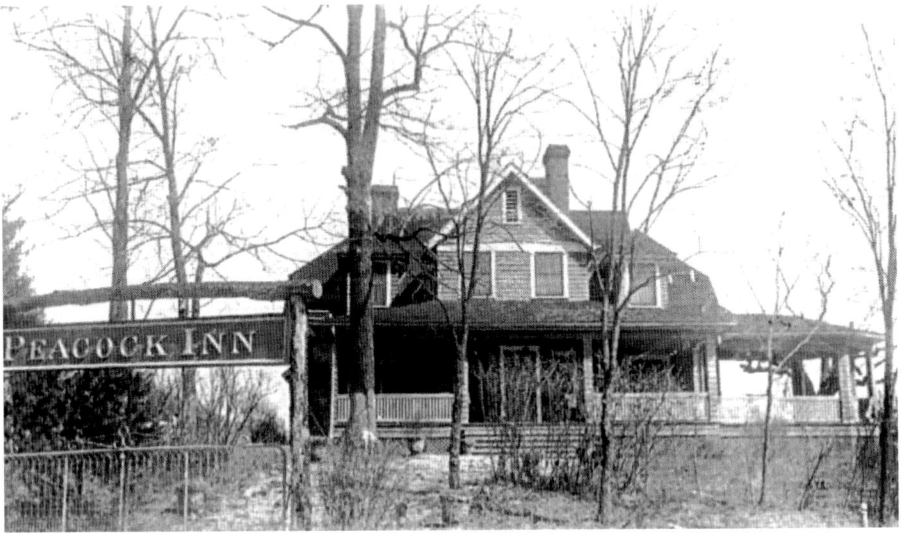

Peacock Inn. *Courtesy of Henderson County Genealogical and Historical Society, Inc.*

whereas, more likely, the Episcopalian spinster innkeepers enjoyed a sip of sherry at twilight.

On Thursday, January 7, 1943, the *Times-News* informed its readers, "Recently she [Mrs. W.W. Sims] had been convicted of driving an automobile while under the influence of liquor and her driver's license was suspended for twelve months."

Perhaps the Peacock earned its dark reputation following the Lyda sisters' tenure—when their younger cousin Ira Lyda Sims (1887–1944) operated the inn. Sims purportedly hosted gambling parties, during which, early in the morning of January 6, 1943, a heated argument led to one male guest killing another. Henderson County census records from 1940 list female residents of the small Peacock Inn as "servants."

Old-timers in Hoopers Creek recall the case when Ira Sims was tried for the death of Loyd Copeland Langston Jr. (1914–1943) of Royal Pines, Buncombe County. Mrs. Sims confessed to authorities and signed a statement that she shot Langston in self-defense, an appeal that ultimately effected no sentence for the murderer.

Ira Lyda Sims, married to William Winfield Sims (1885–1959) of Georgia, was daughter of William Washington Lyda (1845–1922) and Elizabeth Newman Lyda (1855–1910). Langston worked at his father's mop-manufacturing facility, L.C. Langston & Sons Manufacturing Company, in Arden.

Hendersonville *Times-News* articles in January and February 1943 described Sims's inn as the "Peacock Tavern" and reported that Mrs. Sims was held in the Henderson County jail but soon released on $6,500 bond. Brothers Arthur J. and Monroe Minor Redden represented Sims during her trial. News articles also described evidence found at the Peacock Inn: "A number of blood-soaked articles in a downstairs bedroom…a rug, curtain, pillow, sheet and towel, which…came from the lower floor of the Peacock Tavern." Sims had confessed that she shot Langford upstairs, through her bedroom door, during the alleged home invasion. A *Times-News* article on January 13, 1943, reported that the victim's wife told of having helped her husband count the money on his person on the night of January 5, immediately before retiring, at which time he had $150 in cash in addition to a number of checks. When she and Mr. Langston's mother counted his money at the hospital, he had only $28, she said.

According to a *Times-News* reporter, "During the entire hearing, Mrs. Sims, with her husband seated slightly behind her, sat in the courtroom, apparently unperturbed as the attorneys argued her guilt or innocence. Dressed in a fur coat and wearing numerous diamonds, she showed no emotion upon hearing the jury's verdict." Judge Zebulon V. Nettles (1893–1976) presided over the case.

Court minutes from the case *State v. Mrs. W.W. Sims* on October 14, 1943, read:

> *The jury heretofore empanelled in this case return into Court and take their seat in the jury box. At the conclusion of the State's evidence the Court allows motion for judgment as of non-suit and a directed verdict of not guilty. The pistols in connection with the case ordered delivered to the Sheriff to be destroyed.*

Which raises the question: had the murderer blackmailed Mrs. Sims, forcing her to cover for him?

On October 14, 1943, the *Times-News* reported, "Case Against Mrs. Sims Is Non-Suit."

Seven months later, on May 15, 1944, Ira Sims died at Mountain Sanitarium in Fletcher of a cerebral hemorrhage, according to her death certificate.*

---

* #185, Hoopers Creek, 1944.

Bason Falls Inn

Before and just after the turn of the twentieth century, beekeeper Washington Patterson "Washburn" Garren (1851–1928) and his wife, Mary Jane Tow Garren (1853–1923), operated an inn on a ridge of Bearwallow Mountain above the cascade known as Bason in Hoopers Creek. The Garrens had nine children, including Suemma Elizabeth Garren Gilbert (1887–1965), married to General Mace Gilbert (1887–1961), whose son Arnold Mace Gilbert (1932–) was born at the inn. The Gilberts sold the property to W.P. and Mary Jane Garren's grandson Hoover Tinley Connor (1903–1962). Today, not a trace remains of the establishment, not even its neatly dry-stacked retaining wall of stone.

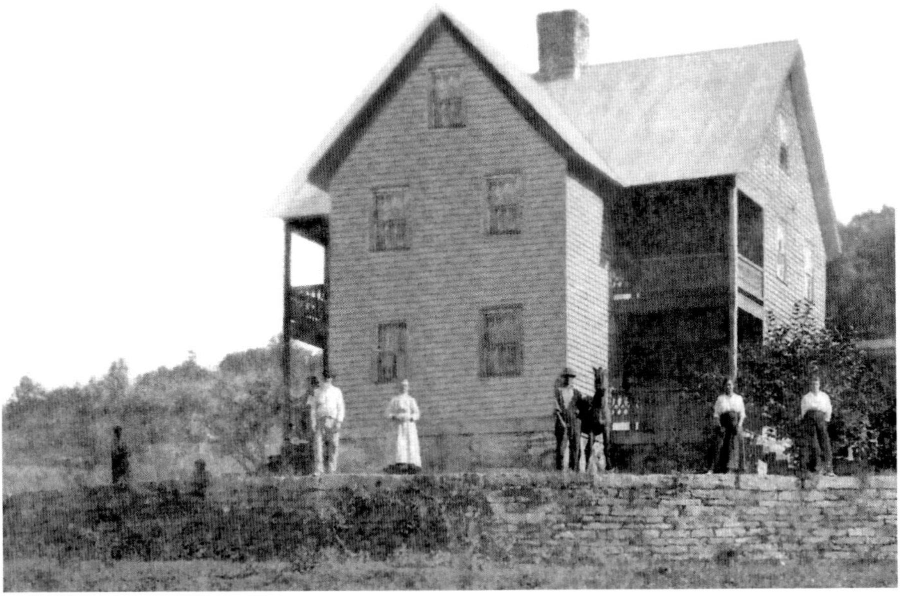

Bason Falls Inn, with members of the Garren and Gilbert families. *Courtesy of William Penn "Penny" Garren.*

IV

ESOTERIC HOOPERS CREEK

Venturing northbound on the Asheville Highway/U.S. Highway 25/ Hendersonville Road with the skyline of Hendersonville waning in the rear-view mirror, one passes by historic districts and sites, including Hyman Heights, Druid Hills, Balfour, Hillgirt (Mountain Home) and Naples, before reaching the city of Fletcher, home to historic stone mansions the Meadows and Rugby Grange and to Calvary Episcopal Church, "Mountain San" (Mountain Sanitarium, next called Fletcher Hospital and then Park Ridge Hospital since 1985) and the site of the former Moland-Drysdale brickyard in Brickton. Not far away, the abandoned Brickton Baptist Church, founded in 1955, molders alongside its wee cemetery. Veering right from the highway and onto Cane Creek Road, the voyager passes Fletcher First Baptist Church and Veritas Christian Academy (formerly the Fletcher School) on the way to Mills Gap Road. Having crossed over the creek called Cane and then gliding between business and industrial parks (former site of the Asheville-Hendersonville Airport) and by Hoopers Creek Grocery and Café and Hoopers Creek Quarry, the landscape suddenly brims over with master-planned subdivisions jampacked with look-alike homes until, near Hoopers Creek Baptist Church and Cemetery, time stops a few steps. From here the road follows the contours between pastures spreading like undulating quilts of green and gold, punctuated with venerable oaks and the occasional barn against a scrim of mountains hazed in gray-green and lavender. And should one choose to probe beyond its contemporary

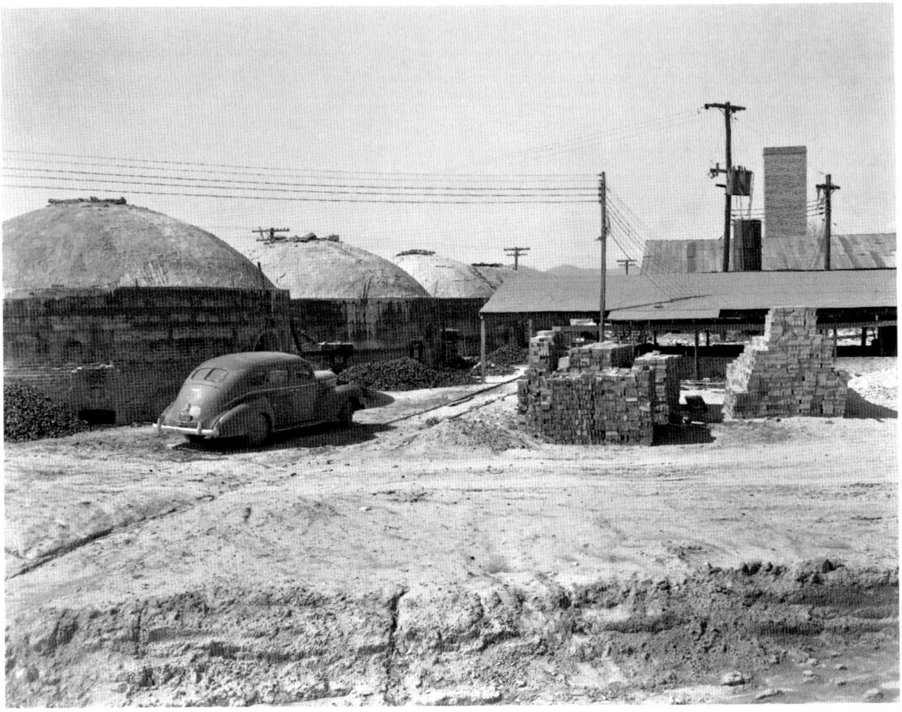

Moland-Drysdale brickyard. *Photo by Lucile Stepp Ray, courtesy of Henderson County Genealogical and Historical Society, Inc.*

surface, one finds here reminders of personalities and institutions that influenced and shaped this north-central sector of the county.

One of Henderson County's electoral townships, with the incorporated municipality of Fletcher within it, Hoopers Creek appears on the Fruitland U.S. Geological Survey Map at latitude 35.439 and longitude -82.4668. Lightly populated and for the most part rural, Hoopers Creek comprises 6.97 square miles, a speck on the map rising from 2,159 feet in the valley once served by the Goodluck store and post office to nearly 4,000 feet on the brawny slopes of Bearwallow Mountain. On his "Rhodes Family" website in 2010, Larry Rhodes (1937–) described Hoopers Creek:

> *A stream, a road and a place...a township along the northern edge of the county; a community known from the early days of Buncombe County. Henderson County was formed out of Buncombe in 1838, but Hoopers Creek remained in Buncombe until legislative action in 1851. That can cause confusion for the researcher when all of those*

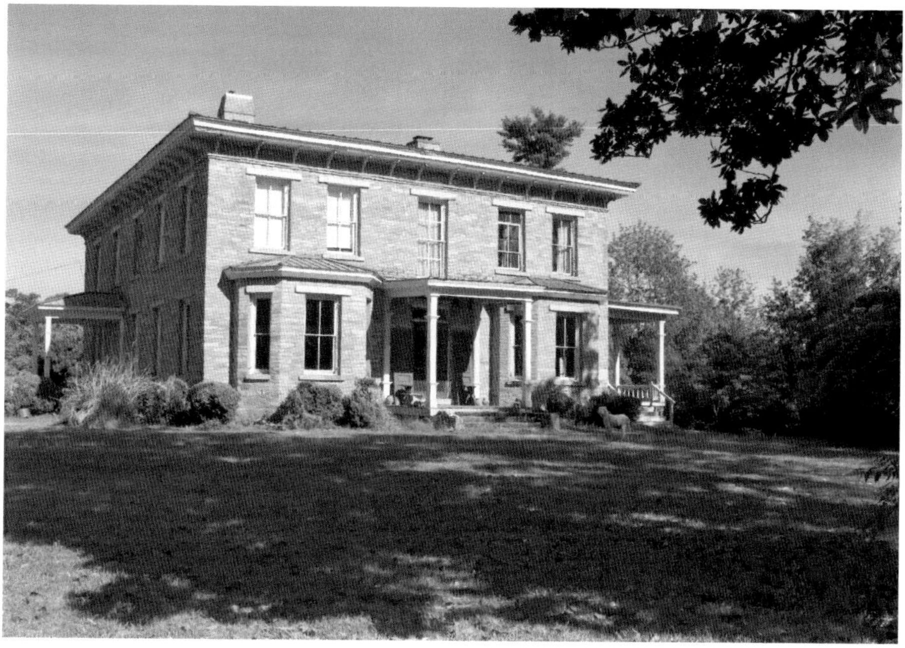

The Meadows/Blake House. *Photographed with permission.*

> *families found in Henderson County in 1860 are absent in 1850, only to be found in Buncombe County. Why did they all move? The question looms until it is learned that the only thing that moved was a line from one ridge-top to another. That's one of the curve balls that genealogical research can throw at you.*

First called Murraysville after innkeeper and postmaster William Murray (1783–1857) and then Limestone (for its quarry and a post office by this name), the population center was also named Shufordsville after postmaster and innkeeper Marcus Lafayette Shuford (1837–1917) and, finally, Fletcher after physician/innkeeper/farmer/merchant Dr. George Washington Fletcher (1829–1901). Statistics in 2012 disclosed a population of 7,290 for the city of Fletcher, which incorporated in 1989.

The headwaters of Hoopers Creek rise in Henderson County, flowing west into Cane Creek. Hoopers Creek resident, with a heritage reaching back seven generations in North Carolina, Jimmy P. Garren (1942–) explained, "Several branches form Hoopers Creek, one out of Burrell Holler, which feeds off Bearwallow near the Grand Highlands development, and others from Jimmy's

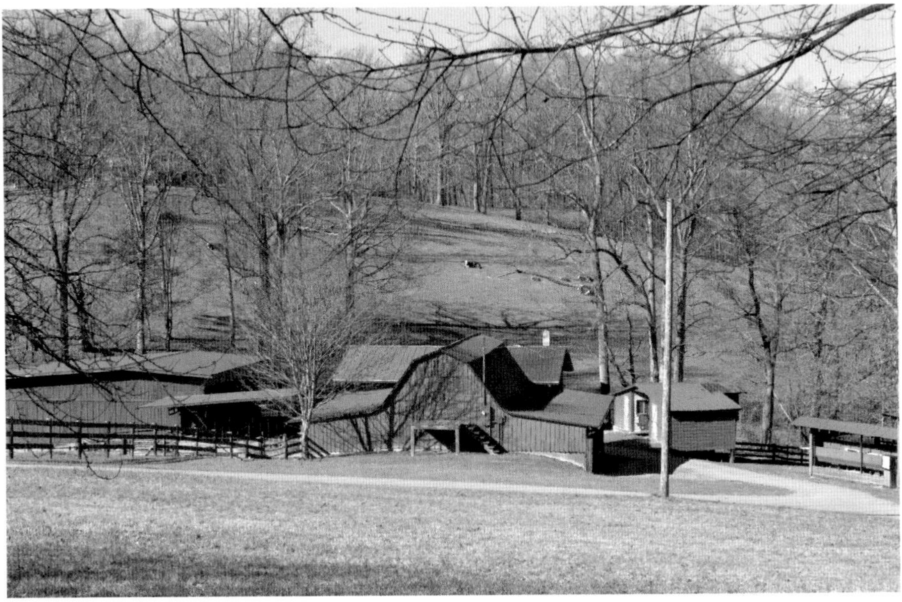

One of the picture-perfect farms of Hoopers Creek, this one belonging to George N. Fowler. *Photographed with permission.*

Cove with tributaries out of Terry's Gap and Young's Gap and off Hightop. The branches converge near Albert Gentry's property and near Goodluck and flow again as one large creek near the old Lanning and Lindsey mill site." Jimmy Garren, married to Cheryl Chambers Garren (1944–), descends from Garrens, who settled in Rowan County and removed to Fairview, Buncombe County, North Carolina.

The core of this remote ward of Henderson County once hosted summer vacationers at turn-of-the-twentieth-century inns known as the Peacock, Inn Wood and Bonnie Bell—none of them extant today. Along the loopy road, Jimmy Garren pointed out level plats where these summer hotels once stood, including a collapsed rock pillar marking the former entrance of the Bonnie Bell Hotel on Bearwallow Mountain. George Washington Connor (1873–1957) built the hotel before the turn of the twentieth century and named it for his niece. Connor, a machinist and inventor, applied for patents for a newfangled washing machine, a street sweeper and other inventions. He also served as postmaster at Bear Wallow. Connor married Augusta "Gussie" Wilson (1882–1966). Old-timers in the region speak of a feud between Connor and a neighbor, the latter accused of having set fire to the Bonnie Bell Hotel on three

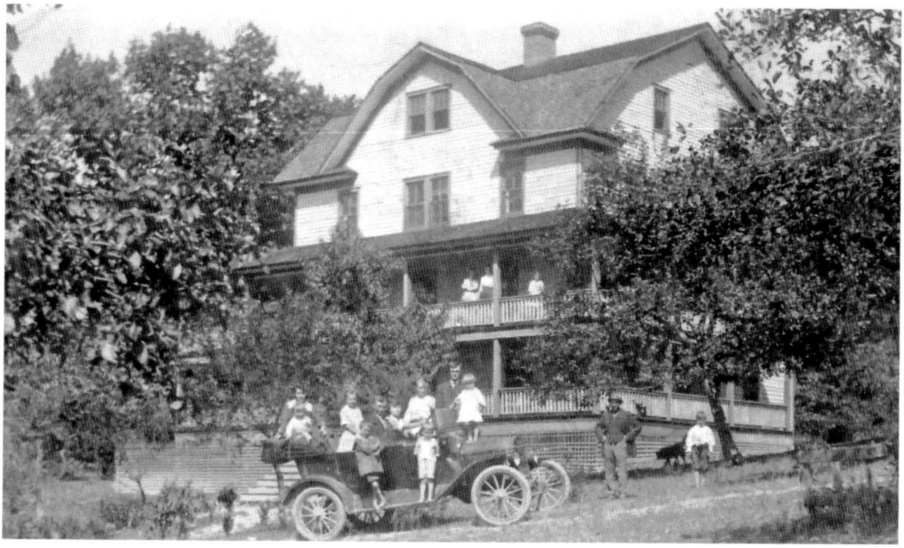

Inn Wood. *Courtesy of Henderson County Genealogical and Historical Society, Inc.*

different occasions. The third fire took the building to the ground. Connor picked up and removed to Marietta, South Carolina, believing his life was in jeopardy.

Another of Henderson County's early lodging facilities, Inn Wood, owned and operated by John M. Trantham (1844–1916) and his family, stood across Young's Gap on "Trantham Mountain," part of the heavily wooded Burney Mountain chain.

Vanished as well, tiny Mount Zion Baptist Church once perched on a small ledge of Bearwallow, now part of a gated private property. Mother Nature prevails here, reclaiming the chunk of land once dotted with dwellings, hostelries and mills, the 1916 flood having washed away many of the tangible traces of human history in this isolated sector of Henderson County. Today, few houses mar the wild and rugged beauty of the mountainside.

After the flood destroyed the Lanning family's dam and milling operations, the Lindseys rebuilt the site, but this enterprise, too, all but disappeared. In the midst of ruins, rushing water and tucked-away waterfalls course between laurel thickets, rhododendrons and pines—and boulder-studded silt swathes former pastureland and agricultural fields as cues that natural history continues its sometimes brutal itinerary through this rugged terrain.

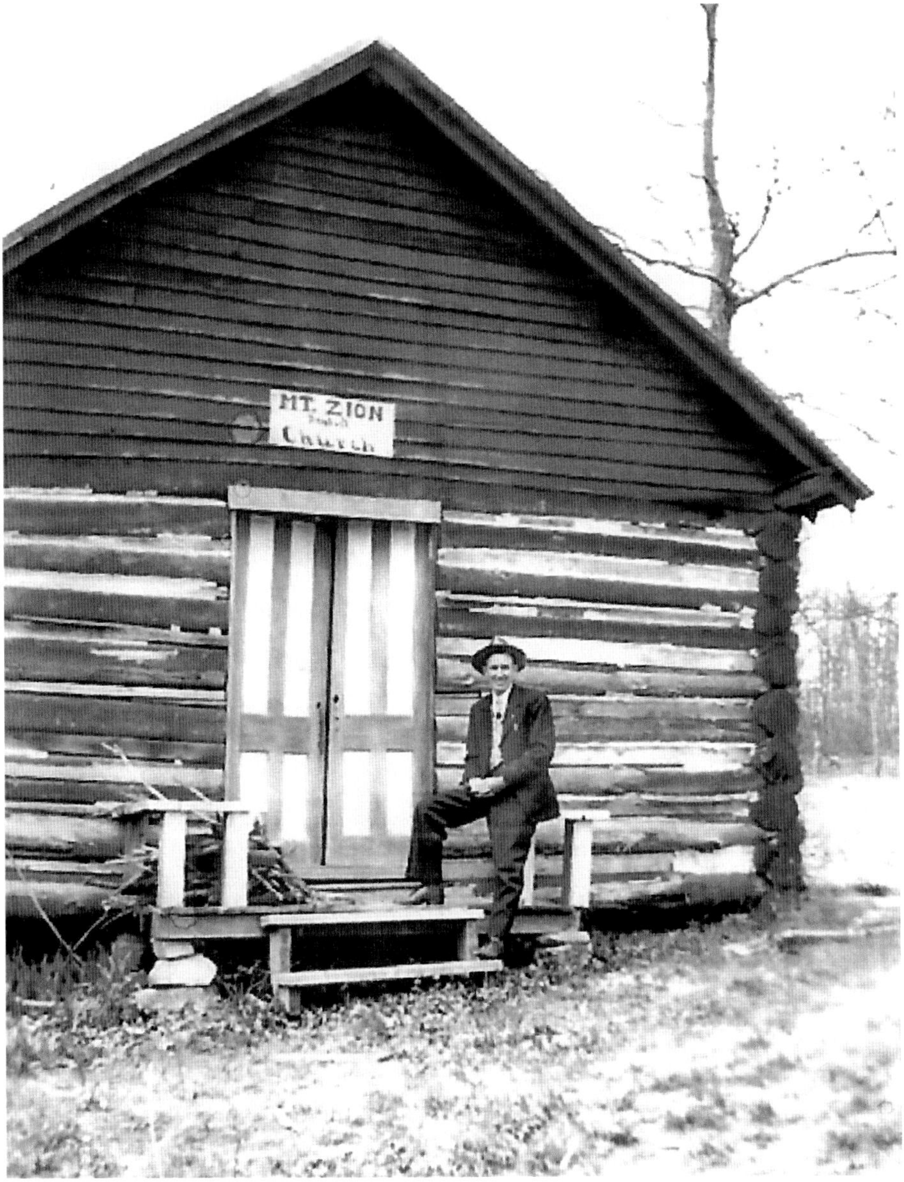

Hubert Collins poses at Mount Zion Baptist Church on Bearwallow Mountain in the early twentieth century. Reverend Harold McKinnish served as one of its preachers. *Courtesy of V. Leon Pace.*

The Lannings

Known as "the Pioneer," John Lanning (1757–1839), born in New Jersey, settled in Fairview, Buncombe County, North Carolina. He married Sarah Whitaker (1767–1848) of Rowan County, and the couple had fourteen children. Sarah was a daughter of Joshua Whitaker Sr. (1735–1798) and Mary Reed Whitaker (1748–1832). John Lanning, a "private in the American Revolution, served in [General Griffith] Rutherford's expedition [known as the Rutherford Trace] against the Cherokee [in 1776], in Lincoln's campaign against the British in South Carolina, in the Battle of Stono near Charleston, and in frequent skirmishes of this campaign, 1831," according to his tombstone inscription at Fairview. For his service, he earned an annual pension of $31.33, which, after his death, his wife, Sarah, continued to receive.

John and Sarah Lanning owned farmland in Fairview and Hoopers Creek. In 1805, John bought 298 acres on Hoopers Creek from Russell Twitty (circa 1766–1834)* and added to it until his holdings there included 419 acres. On Hoopers Creek, near present-day Lanning Mill Road, he operated a gristmill, which his descendants continued to run, including a sawmill on the property, until the 1916 flood ruined the site, together with its pond and dam. The Lindseys rebuilt the operation, which became known as the Lindsey Mills. James Joseph "Jim" Lindsey (1876–1957) operated the gristmill, and his brother Dock O. Lindsey (1873–1959) ran the sawmill. Dock, married to Loney Towe Lindsey (1874–1940), and Jim, married to Naomi Elizabeth "Omi" Lanning (1911–2011), were sons of George Bate Lindsey (1850–1913)† and Martha M. Frady Lindsey (1832–1928). Naomi outlived two more husbands after Jim Lindsey. Her parents were Joshua Elisha Lanning (1868–1947) and Lillie Bertha Rhodes Lanning (1884–1981).

---

* Russell Twitty married Mary "Polly" Mills (1773–circa 1830), daughter of Ambrose Mills and Anna Brown.

† George Bate Lindsey of Henderson County was the son of William Battie Lindsey (1823–1862), grandson of William Lindzey (1794–1880) of Mecklenburg and Buncombe Counties and great-grandson of Walter Lindzey (1764–1837) of Pennsylvania.

THE YOUNGBLOODS AND A PLACE CALLED GOODLUCK

On September 7, 1900, Jasper Newton Youngblood (1842–1918) became postmaster at an office named Goodluck in the tiny settlement on Hoopers Creek, which he operated with his wife, Mary Manervia "Miniver" Garren Youngblood (1848–1904), from their general store. The post office closed on April 18, 1905, when Rural Free Delivery out of Fletcher replaced it. Descendants of Jasper and Miniver continued to live on the land behind the store, which today stands on its original foundations as a replica. Successive owners of the farm have included Jasper and Mary's son Benjamin H. Youngblood (1887–1964) and his wife, Ella E. Lee Youngblood (1883–1953), who, in 1916–17, built the home we see today. Ben and Ella's son and daughter-in-law Conley Benjamin Youngblood (1918–1986) and Nellie Merrell Youngblood (1935–) next owned the family land currently owned by their son Danny Youngblood (1956–) and his wife, Mary Rhodes Youngblood (1958–), parents of Reverend Phillip Youngblood (1979–), pastor of Hoopers Creek Baptist Church and grandson of Reverend Lawrence Regial Rhodes (1924–2012).

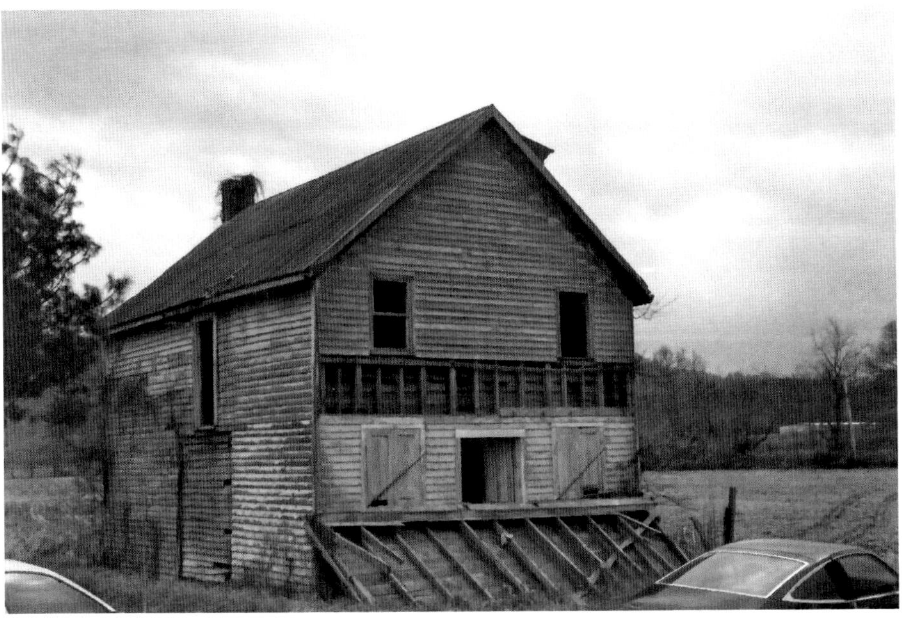

The Goodluck store and post office. *Courtesy of Danny and Mary Rhodes Youngblood.*

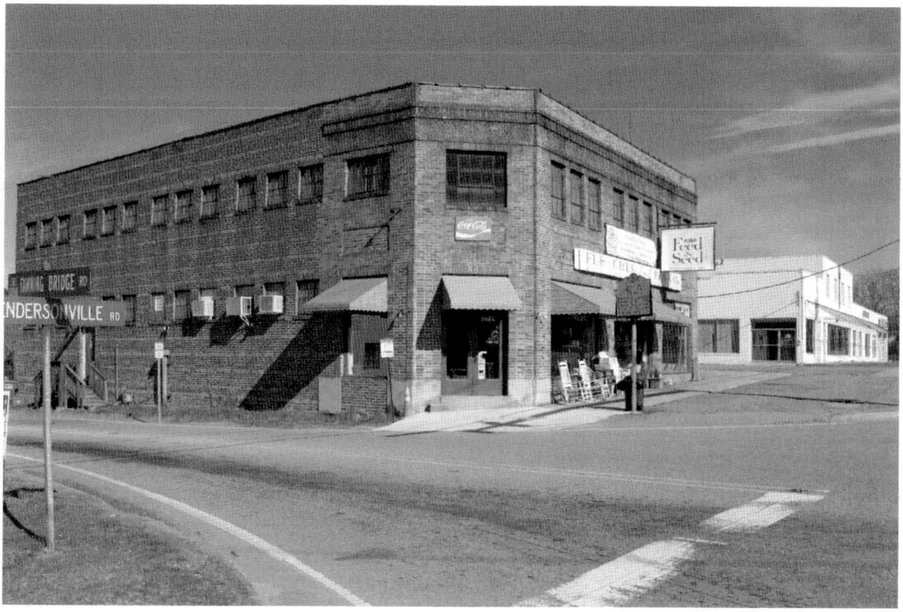

Benjamin H. Youngblood's Fletcher Supply Store.

Enterprising Benjamin H. Youngblood owned a sawmill in Fletcher, which became Midway Lumber & Supply Company, Inc. In 1919, he built the Fletcher Supply Store (Fletcher Seed & Feed) as a general store and butcher shop with a feed mill on its back lot. His drying kiln and lumber-plane operation stood near the Fletcher side of the railroad tracks. He also owned dairy farms, one of them evolving into one of the top dairies in western North Carolina—Dannydale Farm, operated by Ben's son Conley and grandson Danny.

Old-timers in Hoopers Creek enjoy retelling the story of Ella Youngblood having kept her butter, eggs and dressed chickens in a springhouse at a fork in the road near the family store when it was known as the Youngblood general store and Goodluck Post Office. Mischievous boys would filch the products and then endeavor to sell them back to Mrs. Youngblood. As local legend whispers, the market earned its namesake from folks who sat on the porch of the Youngbloods' store, wishing others "good luck" as they crossed Hoopers Creek by foot or on horseback or in wagons or buggies—all within eyeshot of the store's front porch. Across the road and creek, Marion Souther (1883–1955) ran a blacksmith shop, while his wife, French Eliza Garren Souther (1904–1974), kept their home and tended the gardens.

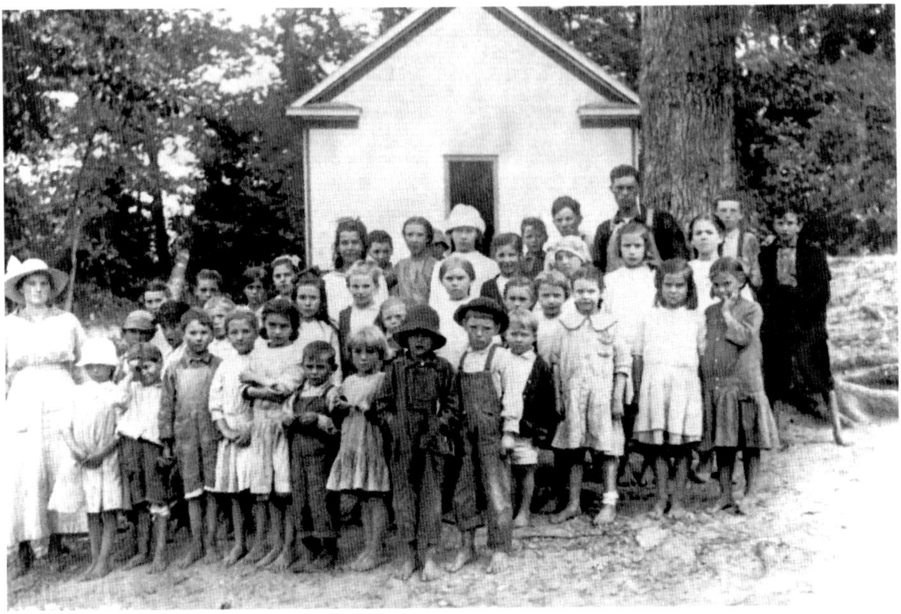

Hoopers Creek School stands today converted into a home. *Courtesy of Virginia Youngblood Brown.*

Around the turn of the twentieth century, John Baxter Middleton (1864–1939) donated property for the Goodluck schoolhouse on what is known as "Middleton Hill." Other schools in the area included the Hoopers Creek schoolhouse, Oak Forest (where a Baptist church by the same name stands today) and another on Bearwallow Mountain.

Who Were the Hoopers?

Given the earlier overlap of the counties Rutherford, Buncombe and Henderson, the origins of the namesake Hoopers in the region of Hoopers Creek proves most challenging. Early Buncombe deed records list a Thomas Hooper/Hopper married to Hannah Alexander Hooper/Hopper (1780–1871). Thomas and Hannah are buried in the Antioch Cemetery at Democrat/Barnardsville. Other western North Carolina Hoopers included William (1806–1893) and Nancy Bryson Hooper (1811–1877) of Jackson County, whose daughter Sarah (1830–1912) married Harvey Gillespie (1820–1877); Scudder Johnson, who married Ella Hooper; Dr. John Orville Hooper; and Catherine Evans (daughter of Reverend Joseph Evans, 1770–1869), who married a Hooper and moved to Jackson County.

Or—considering the term "hooper" as an obscure synonym for "cooper," was the creek perhaps named for a pioneer barrel-maker who lived and worked in the vicinity?

Mary Etta Pentecostal Holiness Church

After a profusion of leaves let loose their moorings each autumn, a ghostly structure looms apparent atop a bank of Hoopers Creek Road—a moldering minster of faith, its silent steeple penetrating the woods that now encase it. Adjacent to the cantilevered apse, a four-hole privy bows under years of decay. Shy of a miracle, a colossal oak crashed mere inches from the church's weather-boarded façade, barricading its front steps, yet shattered windowpanes proffer glimpses into the solemn interior, of a mute piano that heaved its wiry guts to the floor, rotting ceiling boards and a floor sagging, stippled with guano and strewn with shards of glass. What exactly was this hallowed edifice that bears no plaque or monument or references in the books on local history? And why would some uncaring soul plunder its bell?

Situated a stone's throw from Hoopers Creek Baptist Church and Cemetery, one might consider this ruin a predecessor of the neighboring sanctuary of brick—an erroneous assumption. Hendersonville *Times-News* editor Mead Parce (1929–2001) referred to its mode as "Henderson County Gothic" in a poster he designed but with no definitive information about the church's provenance. So who founded this old weather-boarded church, and who were its preachers? One persistent query led to another, and at long last, its back story unraveled in the parlor of George Newton Fowler (1926–).

"Holy rollers, they called them," said Mr. Fowler about the desolate church's former congregation. "A hand-me-down version. The group did not comply with Baptist convention and broke off from Hoopers Creek Church around 1912. [William Anderson] 'Billy' Lanning [1847–1932] sold them the land with a provision that it be used for a church."

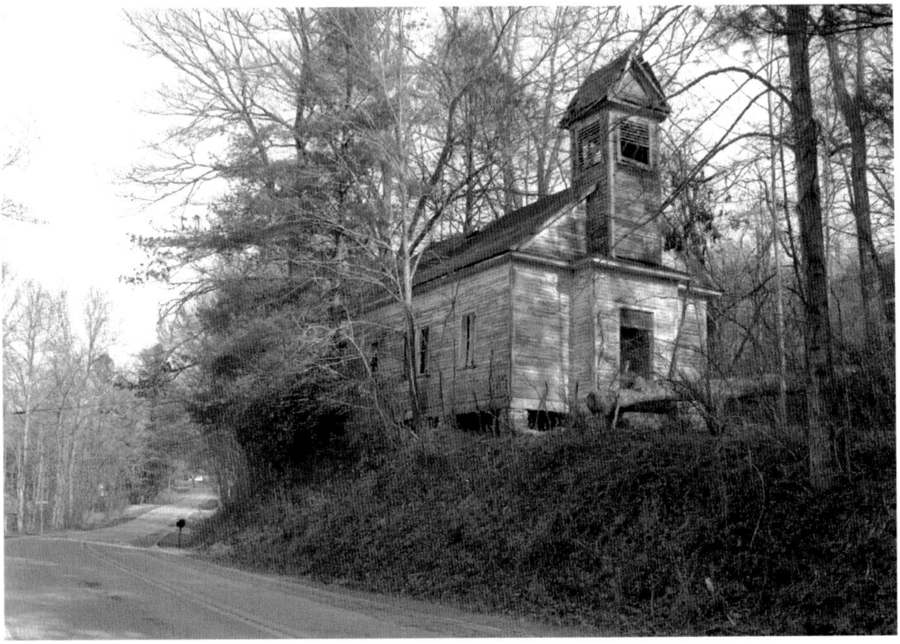

The entrancing Mary Etta Pentecostal Holiness Church.

According to George Fowler, the renegade cadre pulled out of Hoopers Creek Baptist Church after being told it could no longer hold meetings on the grounds with furniture it hauled out onto the church property. Together with fellow members who did not comply with conventional doctrine, the charismatic preacher Thomas Carl Pack (1895–1939) seceded to form a new church.

Early members of the fledgling congregation, known as Mary Etta Pentecostal Holiness Church, included Wesley Jasper Youngblood (1873–1953) and his wife, Mary Etta (also "Mae Etta" and "Maetter"); Ballenger Youngblood (1877–1913); James David "Jimmy" Garren (1863–1926); James Zebulon Souther (1880–1948); Reverend William S. "Billy" Huntley; and William Jasper Souther (1857–1939). Bert Williams (1884–1979) and Jenny Lois Maxwell Williams (1888–1925), Ella Mae Barnwell Williams (1904–1982), Baxter Buckner (1905–1971) and Bertha Ballenger Buckner (1910–1995), Johnnie Claude Laughter (1906–1995) and Ruth Williams Laughter (1909–2010), Hester Maxwell Lewis (1888–1947), Frank Biddix (1913–2008) and Dovie Geneva Lewis Biddix (1909–1971) also counted among the membership.

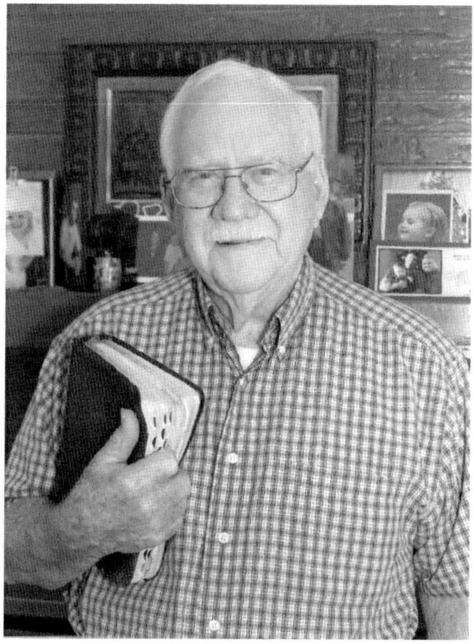

George Newton Fowler.

"Lumber for the church came from thc old Lanning Mill," George Fowler reported. "The Lannings ran grist- and sawmills on their property until the 1916 flood ruined the site. The Lannings owned about six hundred acres here and held slaves. I live on the land of their slaves."

Fowler's parents were Joseph Vernon "Verny"/"Red" Fowler (1886–1981) and Mary Elizabeth "Tina" Hyder Fowler (1896–1955). Verny taught shape-note singing* at the Mary Etta Church in the 1940s. George Fowler's wife, Edna Carney "Queenie" Fowler (1924–2013), was a daughter of Ovid Lamar Carney Jr. (1900–1969) and Elsie Jane Lanning Carney (1903–1996) and great-granddaughter of William Anderson Lanning.

According to George Fowler and Carroll Biddix (1938–), preachers at Mary Etta Church included Thomas Carl Pack; Billy Huntley; William Joseph "Joe" Souther (1904–1962); Arthur Lee Hill (1895–1988); Eli Jerome "Rome" Laughter (1874–1946) of McDowell County and Bat Cave, North Carolina, and later, Hoopers Creek; and John Davidson Rockerfellow "Boy" Overcash (1906–1970) of Elberton, Georgia. Evangelist Frank Biddix preached there in the early 1950s. Membership had dwindled by the late 1940s and dissolved in the 1960s. "Some

* A musical tradition of social singing from music books based on sight-reading, printed in distinctively shaped notes—a variant system of Western musical notation with the note heads printed in distinct shapes to indicate their scale degree and solemnization syllable *(do, re, mi, fa, so, la, ti, do)*. Since 1801, shaped notes have been associated with American sacred music, specifically with singing schools, musical conventions and all-day gatherings known as "singings." The simplified methodology has persisted in the rural South, where it continues to form the basis of strong traditions of church and community singing.

members returned to Hoopers Creek Baptist Church," Fowler said, "and others went elsewhere."

Claude A. Buckner (1927–2013), a caretaker for the old church, helped to get the property returned to the Lanning family. A film production crew for Bob Jones University included the abandoned site in one of the scenes in its 1977 movie *Sheffey*, about the nineteenth-century Methodist evangelist and circuit-riding preacher Robert Sayers Sheffey (1820–1902) of Virginia. Another of the movie scenes memorialized a view of Glenroy—former home of Dr. Mitchell Campbell King (1815–1901) and now the Kenmure clubhouse—in Flat Rock, North Carolina.

A *Henderson County Deed Book* lists W.A. Lanning as grantor, with grantee/trustees listed as W.J. Youngblood, J.Z. Souther, J.D. Garren and W.J. Sother [*sic*]. This deed, written on September 6, 1913, was recorded in 1921. The trustees paid the "sum of 10" for what was described as a "tract, Hoopers Creek," for the purpose of "Hoopers creek Holinest [*sic*] church"; signed by General G.W. Lyda (1879–1918).*

THE PENTECOSTAL HOLINESS MOVEMENT IN NORTH CAROLINA

The International Pentecostal Holiness Church (IPHC), a Pentecostal charismatic Christian denomination founded 1911 with the merger of two older denominations, derived its theological roots from John Wesley's teachings on sanctification. Reflecting its Methodist heritage, IPHC governs under the principles of connectional-ism, a mixed system of Episcopal and congregational polity. The oldest group of the Pentecostal Holiness Church (PHC) foundation originated in Olmitz, Iowa, 1895, as the Fire-Baptized Holiness Association. The first congregation to carry the name Pentecostal Holiness Church was formed in Goldsboro, North Carolina, in 1898, with "Pentecostal" being a common name for Holiness believers at the time. The first convention of the Holiness movement took place in Fayetteville, North Carolina, in 1900. The Fire-Baptized Holiness Association embraced Pentecostalism around the same time, taking the line that baptism in the Holy Spirit was the "baptism of fire"

* *Henderson County Deed Book* 113: 46.

that it had been seeking. Given the similarities in doctrine and geographic reach with PHC, the two groups began talks of a merger. The assemblage united on January 30, 1911, at the Falcon Tabernacle in Falcon, North Carolina, and the new denomination took the name of the smaller of the two: Pentecostal Holiness Church.

Early Pentecostals believed in trusting God for healing without turning to earthly means, such as traditional medical care, emphasizing divine healing. Congregational prayer and the laying on of hands counted among the healing techniques. Today, PHC teaches that Christians *should* believe in divine healing but likewise teaches that medical knowledge comes to humanity through the grace of God. In 2010, the IPHC reported 258,370 members in the United States and 1,390,347 members globally.

THE LIGHTHOUSE ON THE HILL

Typical of its time, Hoopers Creek Baptist Church began as a log meetinghouse organized by a small cluster of the faithful in a rural farming sector near Shufordsville in 1840, when early members constructed such a house of worship—with logs sawn at the Lanning Mill—on the grounds now occupied by Hoopers Creek Baptist Church Cemetery. William "Billy" (also spelled "Billie") Garren (1796–1874), husband of Sarah Lanning Garren (1792–1868), gave the land. Scarce records designate Elder William Mintz (and Mince or Minty, circa 1805–1882) as one of the church's first pastors, followed by William Job Wilkie (1830–1892), William S. "Billy" Huntley (1847–1922), Martin Luther Kirstein (1898–1980), Ernest Robert "Ed" Vaughn (1886–1952), Jesse Erwin "Irving" Whitaker (1886–1957), William Columbus "Buck" Huntley (1911–1988), Odell James Sevier Barnwell (1911–2001), Howard Cabe (1927–)—the first paid pastor—and Dr. Lawrence Regial Rhodes. Since Reverend Rhodes's death, Phillip Youngblood, who had served as interim pastor, was voted full-time pastor of Hoopers Creek Baptist Church. Supply pastors have included James O. Wall (1860–1953) of Gerton, Wade Franklin Sinclair (1883–1965) of Fruitland, Rufus Morgan (1885–1983) of Macon County and William Brycie Morgan (1900–1984) of Tuxedo. Rufus Morgan, a roving Episcopal minister known as "Moses of the Mountains" and "the Modern Moses," served Hoopers Creek Baptist Church as a supply pastor in 1918.

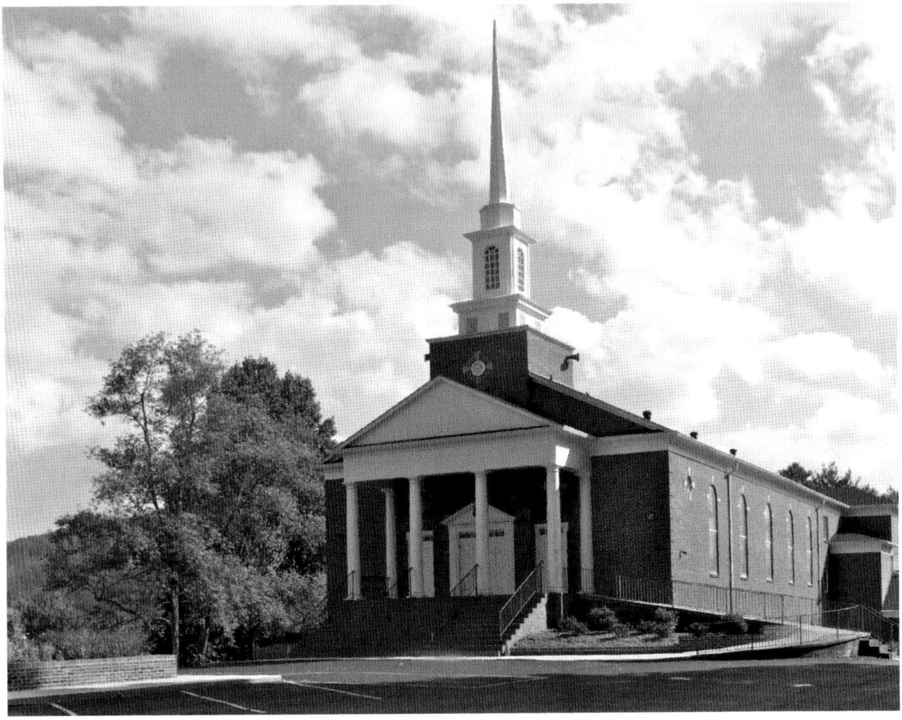

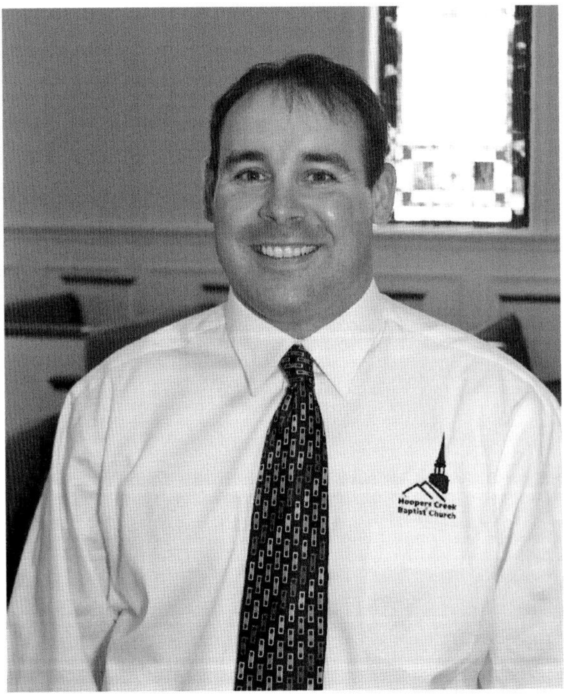

Above: Hoopers Creek Baptist Church.

Left: Reverend Phillip Youngblood.

Brief Baptist Biographies, 1707–1982, Vol. II, described Elder Mintz as

> *a man of little academic training but he is a man of faithfulness and perseverance. His name appears on the rolls of the Salem Associate Minutes for many years as an ordained minister...a good-looking black-haired man of medium size in stature...He lived in "house number 3 in Hoopers Creek Township"...by word of mouth according to some octogenarians, his body along with that of his wife lies in an "unmarked grave" in the Hoopers Creek Church Cemetery.*

Mintz married Arena (alternatively spelled Arrenny and Arreny, circa 1815 ?), and according to available census records, the couple had one female child and no male children.

William Mintz counted among the ministers involved in the organization of the Salem Baptist Association when it was formed "at Blake's Meeting House near Fletcher" on September 14–15, 1838. Mintz preached at Ebenezer Baptist Church in Hendersonville and Liberty Baptist Church in Clear Creek before his preaching term at Hoopers Creek. He preached also at Mud Creek (1846–47), Antioch (predecessor of Pleasant Hill Baptist Church, 1858–59), Old Salem (in Fletcher), Union (1866–68) and Hoopers Creek (1856–57).

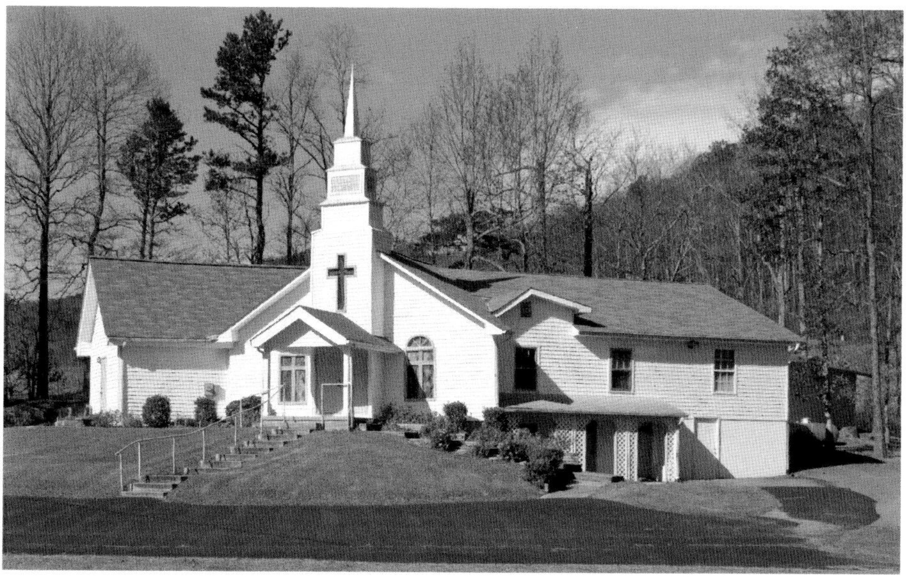

Liberty Baptist Church.

Brief Baptist Biographies said of Reverend Mintz:

> *Long and laborious research has revealed but scanty information concerning this faithful servant of the Lord who spent almost half a century in the Christian ministry. He was licensed before the year 1834, ordained by Beulah Church on July 6, 1834, and remained in the ministry until his death April __, 1882.*

On May 19, 1855, Liberty Baptist Church granted an arm to Hoopers Creek, and according to the Liberty Minutes, "Brother Mince [Mintz] joined by letter" on June 1, 1856. Mintz's wife, Sister Arena, joined on July 5, 1856. On September 1, 1855, David Garren (circa 1796–1865) and Nancy Lanning Garren (1795–1876) joined by letter. *Brief Baptist Biographies* continued:

> *1856—November 1st—After a sermon by Elder William Mince* [sic], *he inquired for the standing of the church—all in love. Received a request from the "Arm" for the following brethren to have a letter of recommendation that*

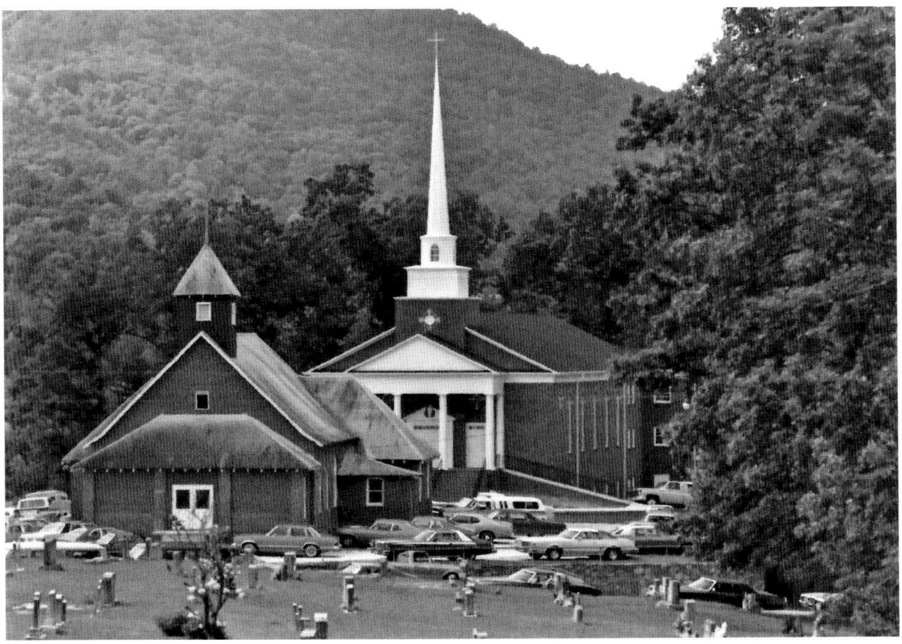

The 1895 Hoopers Creek Baptist Church as it stood in front of the newly constructed church in 1979, a short time before it was razed. *Courtesy of Danny and Mary Rhodes Youngblood.*

> *they might become a constituted church there (Hoopers Creek).* [A list of members follows, including Mintz, Garrens, Rymers, Rhoads [*sic*], Lanning, Mote and Piner/Pinner.]

Hoopers Creek Baptist Church was constituted on November 27, 1856. Wade Hampton "Ham" Souther (1875–1966) gave land for the second church, which he helped build in 1895. Reverend Billy Huntley served as its first elected pastor. This weather-boarded church went through many changes, including additions and a veneering of brick. Members installed the bell in 1912. Lightning struck the steeple in 1918, requiring a new one. The ministry serving Hoopers Creek Baptist Church included circuit-riding preachers in its early days. The pastors of Hoopers Creek baptized their flock in the Lanning millpond, and the church hosted several revivals in the 1930s and '40s.

Reverend Dr. Lawrence Regial Rhodes, ordained at Liberty Baptist Church in 1950, became pastor of Hoopers Creek Baptist Church in 1964, serving until his death. The beloved Dr. Rhodes served also at Little Ivey Baptist Church in Mars Hill, Jones Gap and Pleasant Hill Baptist Churches in Henderson County and fulfilled missionary work in Haiti.

The contemporary church, completed in 1979, the year of the current pastor's birth—and debt-free after only three years—currently serves a fellowship of five hundred. Members with pedigrees dating back to its founding include Barnwells, Garrens, Lannings, Maxwells, Russells, Southers, Townsends, Wilkies, Whitakers and Youngbloods.

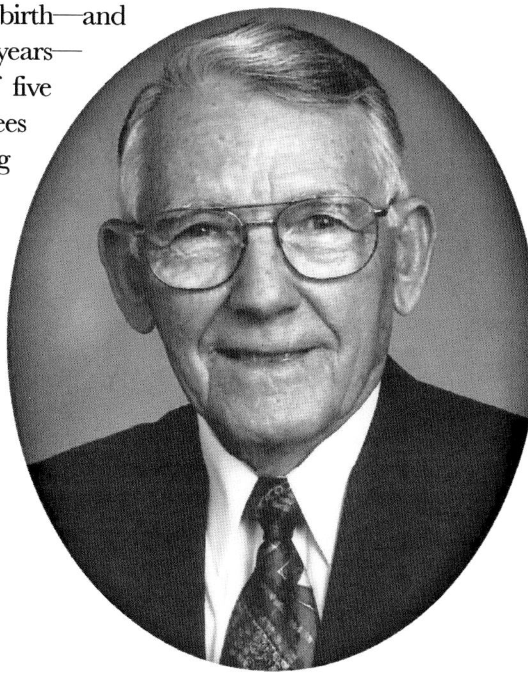

Reverend Lawrence Regial Rhodes. *Courtesy of Reverend Phillip Youngblood.*

Provenance of the Surname Garren

Variants of the Garren name include Garn, Garen, Garne, Garon, Garran, Garron and the Latin form Garanus. While some claim "Garren" comes from the German Garen and Garne, others suggest the French Garrant and still others, Gareau. The name Gareau was first found in Languedoc, a village in the Hautes-Pyrénées in the arrondissement of Bagnères in the southwest of France.

From Old Norman, *Garan* means "the dweller at the place where cranes gathered," while others cite "a descendant of Little Garo," meaning, "spear." The name, said to have arrived in England from France in the wake of the Norman Invasion of 1066, means "guardian," and a river in Herefordshire bears the latter name. A record of the name Richard Garran was recorded in Herefordshire in the year 1558.

V

SINISTER

Written histories frequently circumnavigate or entirely omit the grisliest of details—with war stories the possible exceptions. Small as it is, though, Henderson County has witnessed its share of catastrophes, including horrendous murders, aircraft disasters and unsolved mysteries.

The Mysterious Myrtle Hawkins

The corpse of a young woman floating facedown in Osceola Lake ended the search for a missing person. Or did it? Considered one of the "greatest mysteries of all time," a court case in Henderson County drew statewide and even national attention, creating media frenzy and kindling the imaginations of many. To the disappointment of those who followed the case, the mystery remained unsolved in spite of local residents having suggested that officials did *indeed* solve the case but kept their findings under wraps.

Myrtle Hawkins (1891–1911), a Flat Rock debutante who worked as a housekeeper for the Ellison Adger Smyth family of Connemara, went missing on September 7, 1911—before the eve of her wedding. Her parents, William Henry Hawkins (1851–1931) and Laura McFee Hawkins (1854–1944), delayed in contacting authorities about their missing daughter—for reasons having to do with Myrtle's alleged relationship and possible marriage

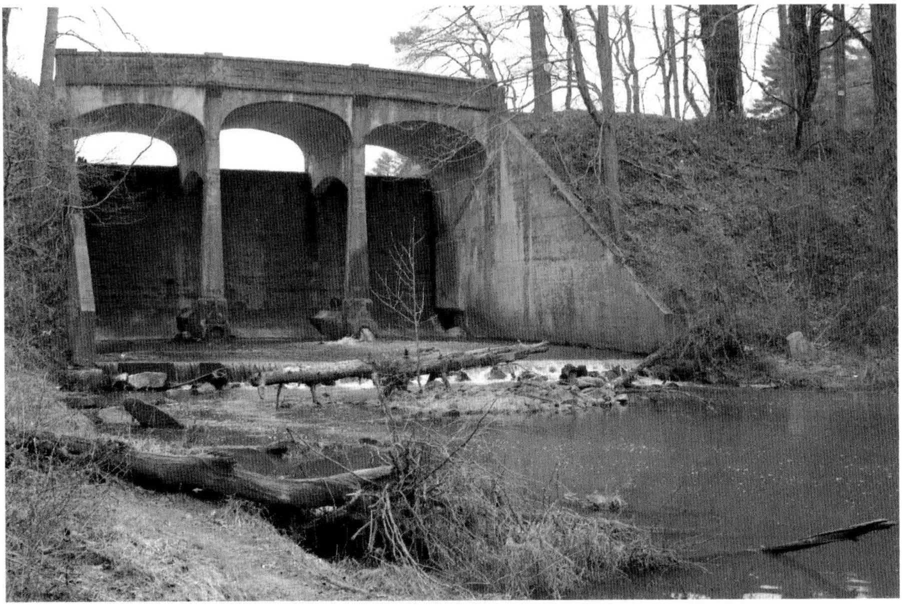

The bridge near the spillway at Osceola Lake.

plans with Hal Slater Cooper (1894–1943) of Johnson City, Tennessee. The parents suspected the youngsters had eloped, but the plot thickened when the court read the contents of a letter Myrtle left for her mother before her disappearance. In it, she wrote:

> *Daddy made me promise to write this to you because I could not have the face to tell you. I have been sick one and one half months, I think. I can't tell you the name of the second person in the affair, but this much I can tell you he was not to blame, only myself. He did everything he could for me and will continue to do so. Am getting away, for I could never stay here. I will have all I need and I can work. Please do not try to find out where I am. Sorry to have caused you so much trouble. Wish I could bear it by myself since I am the cause of it. Tell Carrie and Lou good-bye. They were all good to me. Tell them I have gone to Aida's. She is the best friend I have besides you. Good-bye.*

The "Lou" referred to in the letter was Lula Hawkins Thomas (1879–1948), Myrtle's sister, who testified in court that Myrtle had been "bilious" when visiting her earlier that week in Asheville. Family members believed that Myrtle was two and a half months pregnant.

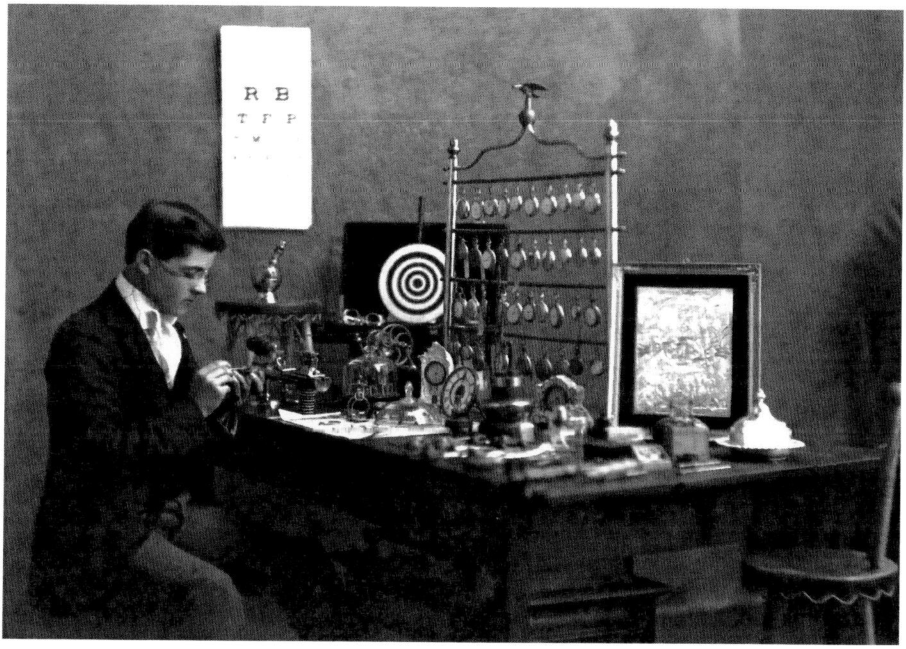

A. Homer Hawkins, W.H. Hawkins & Son, 413 North Main Street, Hendersonville, North Carolina, 1920. *Courtesy of Baker-Barber Collection. Community Foundation of Henderson County. Henderson County Public Library.*

William Henry Hawkins and his son A. Homer Hawkins (1879–1948) owned W.H. Hawkins & Son jewelers and optometry at 413 North Main Street, downtown Hendersonville. Hal Cooper, seventeen years old at the time of Myrtle's death, swore under oath that he had not been in Hendersonville and had not seen his fiancée, Myrtle, since June. Newspaper articles repeatedly listed Myrtle's age as seventeen, in spite of her correct age of twenty at the time of her death.

On September 10, 1911, two boys walking near the spillway at Osceola Lake spotted a corpse, later identified as the body of Myrtle Hawkins. Officers William Walker Staton (1859–1937) and Jesse "Det" Reese (1870–1916) fished the cadaver from three feet of water. During his investigation, Dr. William Redden Kirk (1870–1960), acting as county coroner, examined the remains and ordered an inquest. Kirk determined the death could not have been due to drowning and the body had likely been placed in the lake after death. Myrtle Hawkins, known as a "strong swimmer," had no water in her lungs or bruising on her flesh. Autopsy results did, however, point to chloroform—and to bloodstains on her underwear.

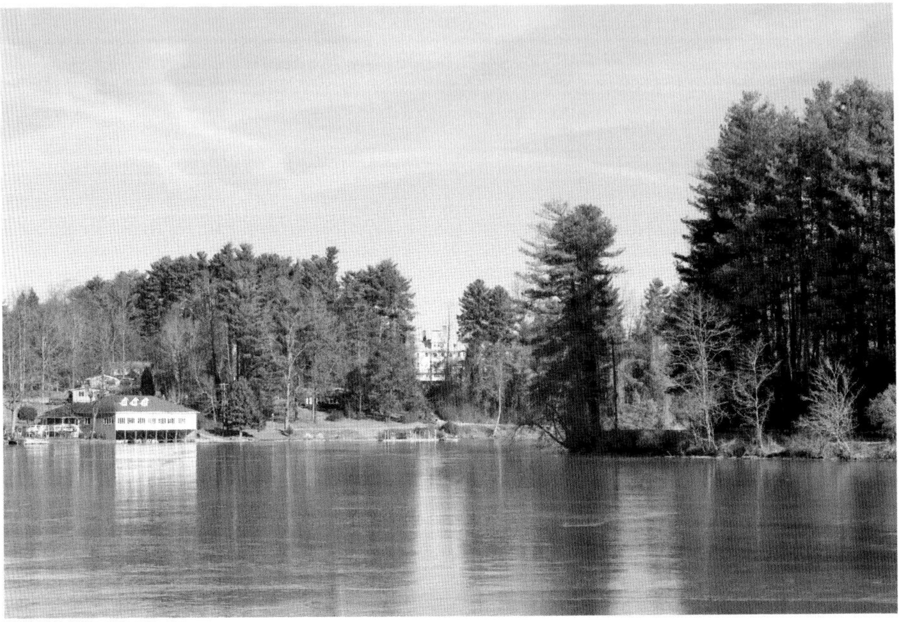

Osceola Lake, which did not exist before developers filled it in 1909, occupies approximately twelve acres with a maximum depth of about twenty feet. Findley, Perry and Tony's Creeks feed this lake, and Shepherd Creek drains it.

Dr. Kirk conducted his examinations in the undertaking establishment of J.M. Stepp, where Jeremiah Matthias "Jerry" Stepp (1865–1943) sold caskets from one end of the store and furniture from the other. In spite of the foul odor, several curiosity seekers, and others who might have confirmed the identity of the corpse, stepped into the undertaking parlor during the autopsy.

During the first inquest, suspects included Maggie Estelle Grant (1882–1976); Alfred Asberry McCall (1888–1959) and his wife, Beatrice McCall (1891–1939); Bessie Clark Guice (1897–1982); Nora Britt (1878–1960); and Elizabeth "Lizzie" Shaft (1850–1923), a midwife—resulting in no indictments. Testimonies ran the gamut, from details of a boardinghouse in Asheville—at times referred to as a "disorderly house" and having to do with defendants Shaft and Britt, "street walkers" and others who performed abortions—to the plausible misidentification of the woman found in the lake. Because of the victim's swollen state of decomposition, as well as a questionable growth behind one of her ears, some witnesses guessed the identity to be that of other missing women by the surnames of Huntley, Walker, Reeves or McCrary. A solicitor brought Mrs. Huntley to court as proof that she was still among the living.

After reading through the plethora of court transcripts, one might reckon that Mesdames Shaft and Britt brokered women—for domestic and "other" services. Mrs. Shaft seemingly had experience in methods of abortion, and portions of Mrs. Britt's testimony seemed to confirm this.

Legal proceedings began on September 11, 1911, but when examiners turned up no concrete evidence concerning foul play, Kirk opened an inquest on September 15 with a deeper probe into the case. This and still another inquest involved fifty witnesses—including some from Asheville, seventeen subpoenaed and eight examined and weeks of examination and testimony. The State of North Carolina and the Hawkins family offered rewards for the arrest and conviction of the guilty party. On September 19, after less than thirty minutes of deliberation, the jury returned a verdict that indicted murder—with the caveat, "Died as a result of a criminal operation." No arrests were made. Newspaper statements included: "Girl came to death from causes unknown to jurors" and "Death was at the hands of unknown parties."

On Wednesday, September 20, 1911, the *Charlotte News* reported:

> *Coroner's Jury Fails to Bring Indictment in Hawkins Case*
> *Thus ends the miserable affair—heartbreaking to the parents of the dead girl, revolting, in many respects, to the public. The little lake nestling in the shadows of great mountains keeps the secret.*

The next inquest, from March to May 1912, involved seven suspects: Alfred Asberry McCall, Beatrice McCall, Daniel Webster McCall (1863–1942), Lizzie Shaft, Nora Britt and brothers Boney Bradley (1879–1963) and George Bradley (1883–1976). Dan McCall was charged with accessory to the murder before the fact. McCall, together with George Bradley and his brother Boney and Nora Britt, was held in the Buncombe County jail, and Alfred and Beatrice McCall and Lizzie Shaft were held in the Henderson County jail.

The case encompassed an army of legal talent: Judge H.G. Ewart (1849–1919), Charles French Toms (1872–1937), Judge Orville Volney F. Blythe (1865–1931), Oscar K. Bennett (1882–1943), James Foy Justice (1886–1944), W.A. Smith (1858–1922), Joel Elbert Shipman (1873–1930), Robert Sevier McCall (1857–1923) and Thomas Settle (1872–

1956). Wiley C. Rector (1872–1926), Mayor Reuben Hilliard Staton, Jacob Francis Spainhour (1851–1917) and A. Hall Johnston (1882–1942) of Marion counted among the prosecutors. Between the two inquests, Judges Howard Alexander Foushee (1870–1916) and Columbus Mills Pace (1845–1925) presided over proceedings that drew large crowds.

Tom Hollingsworth, J.B. Arledge, A.W. Barnett, James Edney, Ted Justice, James Laughter, J.P. Israel and Ed Drake counted among the many witnesses who took the stand. Additional testimony revealed that the victim—brunette, pretty and about five feet tall—had been a bicycling enthusiast and was friendly with McCall family members who lived near Osceola Lake. A medical examiner took the stand and explained that someone about to go under the effects of chloroform would, in many cases, scream. Two black residents of the lake neighborhood—Reverend Frank Brown (1856–after 1920) and George Green (1894–?)—and Mrs. Reuben Wright (Anna Mae Hardin Wright, 1868–1953) heard a woman's cries of distress on Wednesday, September 6, at about 11:00 p.m., from the direction of the McCall property. The defense heard testimony about a Mr. Haynes, who owned an automobile that "screamed like a woman." Haynes was known to have driven this vehicle around the lake. Witnesses Wallace Reddin and Mary Granger allegedly saw George Bradley and the victim walking together at Osceola Lake the day before her disappearance, and later, Alfred Asberry McCall, Beatrice McCall and George Bradley had been observed near the lake. Other witnesses alluded to an affair between the recently married George Bradley (to Estelle Grant) and Myrtle Hawkins. "It was human nature," Bradley rebuffed. "I kissed her because I could."

Prosecutors produced witnesses suggesting the McCall barn had been used to perform an abortion that ended in Myrtle Hawkins's death. Feed sacks were spread out in the fashion of bedding on the floor of the mow, a missing plank possibly was used as a gurney to remove the body and a foul stench issued from the barn and later from the woods between the barn and the lake.

As examinations ensued, solicitors tilted with one another, and eyeballs rolled back as a general sense of ghoulishness and disrespect pervaded the courtroom's carnival atmosphere, at times eliciting ripples of laughter—for example, when Judge Columbus Mills Pace would nod off during lengthy arguments; when, for no apparent reason, Judge Foushee* fell out of his chair; and during inane statements from Cleophas R. Allen (1864 1926), a self-appointed "detective" on the case who worked full time as an umbrella salesman and repairer of umbrellas and was "not otherwise employed." Among those who testified, Atlanta swindler William Oscar Shellnutt (1858–1937) claimed to have espied Myrtle Hawkins—after her alleged death—on the streets of Jacksonville, Florida; claiming, too, that he could "produce her for the sum of three thousand dollars." More snickers erupted during far-fetched testimonials from other reward seekers, including those making claim to Myrtle Hawkins sightings in Key West, Florida, and as far away as Seattle, Washington.

In November 1914, the *French Broad Hustler* informed its readers:

> *CLEOPHAS ALLEN INSANE*
> *Cleophas Allen, who attracted considerable attention in Henderson County as a self-appointed detective in the Myrtle Hawkins case, has been adjudged insane by the Asheville Federal Court and will be returned to prison for violating the United States postal laws. Allen conducted his own defense in court after having been imprisoned for some time. Repairing umbrellas has been Allen's chief employment.*

Mayor R.H. Staton ultimately accused Shellnutt of being an "infamous liar" and "an imposter who came here to muddle the minds of the jury."

The county incurred considerable expense in its attempt to solve the baffling case, and as stated in the *French Broad Hustler*, weeks of proceedings and thirty-four hours of closing arguments in June 1912 resulted in

> *volumes and volumes of unprintable testimony and argument. The argument at times bordered on personalities. Both men and women and even children packed the courtroom with a craving, morbid appetite for the sensational and smutty things. They absorbed it wonderfully and sat with ears pricked and mouths wide open, unconscious of the outside world, in readiness to catch every dirty word that might slip from the tongue of some witness or attorney.*

* Biographical data on Superior Court judge Howard A. Foushee describes him as kind, fearless and dedicated, "a thorough North Carolinian" and "the purest of men." A poignant element would be the courtroom audience's derisive laughter following the judge's unfortunate tumble from his chair during the Hawkins trial. This mishap has been noted as the first of many such episodes, the forerunner of illness (pernicious anemia) that never left him. He nevertheless continued working rather than retiring from the bench, believing he owed a duty to the people who elected him.

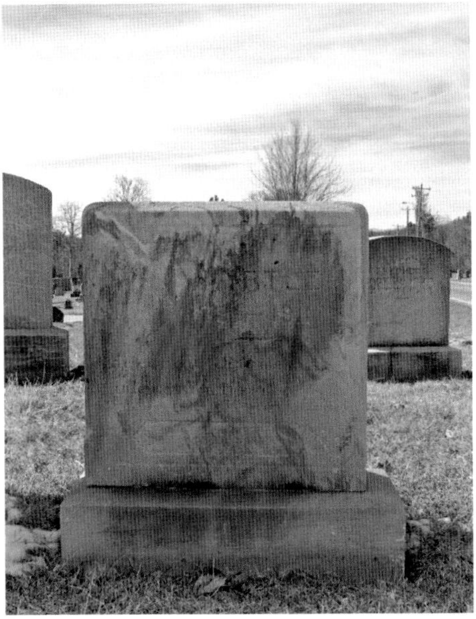

Myrtle Hawkins's grave at Oakdale Cemetery.

In his closing arguments, defense attorney James Foy Justice said, "The defendants had been made to suffer by reason of public sentiment and a newspaper humdrum."

The jury of farmers took several ballots before a verdict could be reached, some jurors holding out for murder in the second degree. Convinced that circumstantial evidence and testimony left reasonable doubt, and after only a brief deliberation, the jury gave a verdict of "not guilty," leaving the oft-repeated question: who killed Myrtle Hawkins?

Draw Your Own Conclusions

Did George Bradley impregnate Myrtle Hawkins? Could it have been Hal Cooper or Daniel Webster McCall? Did Myrtle die from an overdose of chloroform during a bungled abortion? Who performed the procedure? Was it Lizzie Shaft and Nora Britt from Asheville or…? And who dumped the body into Osceola Lake?

In the 1980s, the crime scene heated up in Henderson County, involving family members spitefully gunned down at a funeral, a multi-state pursuit of a Rambo-style survivalist possessed with the notion of slaughtering law officials and a schoolgirl snuffed out because she dared have a crush on her teacher.

A CASE OF PUPPY LOVE GONE AWRY

He was a sixty-four-year-old former Broadway star born in Indiana and she a golden-throated sixteen-year-old honor student from East Flat Rock—two divergent lives having crossed paths in rural Hendersonville and concluding in tragedy.

Wilton Werbe Clary (1916–1985) performed in the Broadway touring productions of *Desert Song* and *Guys and Dolls*, sang professionally in 1943 with the Civic Light Opera Company of Los Angeles and starred in *The Barrier* in 1950 and *Three Wishes* in 1952. In 1947, he played the male lead as Curley the singing cowboy in the original Broadway production *Oklahoma!* Clary's show business career also included supper club engagements in Puerto Rico, Florida and beyond.

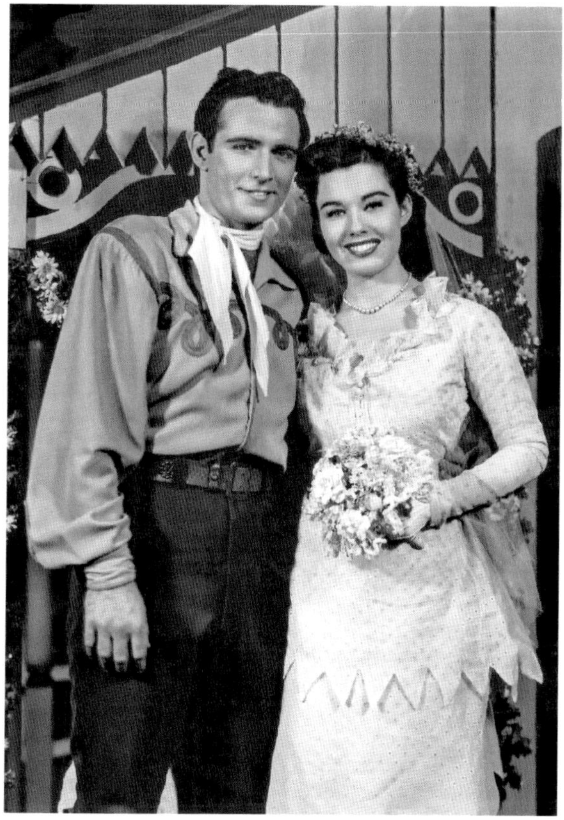

A press photo of Wilton Werbe Clary and Carolyn Tanner for the New York production of *Oklahoma!*, May 31, 1948. *Photograph by Vandamm from the collection of Terry Ruscin.*

Clary married Gene "Genie" Vacher Sexton, a woman dedicated to the humane treatment of animals. "She had the purse," said William Harley Stepp (1934–), a retired Hendersonville attorney. Others who knew Clary described him as an arrogant opportunist.

Genie Clary (1919–2012), born to Ralph Eugene Sexton (1885–1956) and Thyrza Vacher Sexton (1891–1978) in Pike's Peak, Colorado, grew up in the Panama Canal Zone, where her father ran Isthmian Airways. A civil engineer, Sexton also built bridges in Central and South America. Genie's maternal grandfather, Louis N. Vacher (1861–1916), had come from France to help build the Panama Canal.

Known as "Sweetheart of the Isthmus," Genie danced with Lucho Azcarraga (Luis Enrique Azcárraga Deliot, 1912–1996) and performed with his band and ranked as a champion swimmer, representing the Canal Zone in an international freestyle-swimming competition. An accomplished violinist, she participated in volunteer and performing arts activities to raise money for worthy causes in the Canal Zone, including her founding of a humane society.

In addition to Panama, Genie lived also in Puerto Rico, Los Angeles and Miami before moving to Hendersonville, North Carolina. She studied at the UCLA School of Music, Los Angeles, where director Henry King (1886–1982) of 20th Century Fox Studios offered her a job as an actress. She declined, having already devoted her life to rescuing animals. She later met Wilton Clary in Puerto Rico, where he performed in a nightclub, and thereafter accompanied him on road shows throughout Central and South America.

In August 1973, Wilton and Genie Clary moved from Miami to Hendersonville and purchased property from Charles Monroe Fisher Sr. (1936–2008) and his wife, Lorraine C. Fisher (1937–2015), at Price Road at Old Kanuga Road—across from Dawn Hill, the former estate of novelist and lyricist Edwin DuBose Heyward (1885–1940). The Fishers owned Fisher Auto Sales and Fisher Mazda and developed the Willow Place subdivision. The Clarys built a home with the address 702 Price Road, a house recently renovated by Robert Wallace (1969–). Genie soon became president of the Henderson County Humane Society, and Hendersonville entrepreneur Clifton Shipman (1923–2010) offered her rent-free space for her animal rescue efforts—a Humane Society thrift shop she named Woof 'n' Purr. Genie's husband, Wilton, assisted her in fundraising, animal care and rescue efforts. Working from his home studio, Wilton coached musical hopefuls in voice lessons and performed and emceed at local beauty pageants and musical shows. The Clarys had no offspring, considering their pets to be their children. But for their opulent beginnings, all appeared conventional concerning the couple once they'd settled into their rural Hendersonville digs.

Pamela Denise Durham (1964–1981), one of Wilton Clary's voice students, allegedly developed a crush on her teacher. "Infatuated with him," William Harley Stepp suggested. The unthinkable ensued after Genie Clary suspected an affair and asked her husband to break it off. The following headline appeared in the Hendersonville *Times-News* on Monday, February 9, 1981: "Two Charged in Slaying of Student."

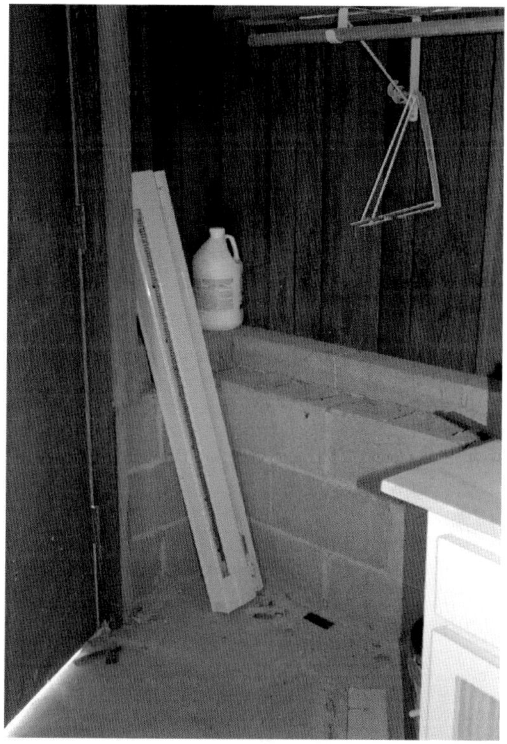

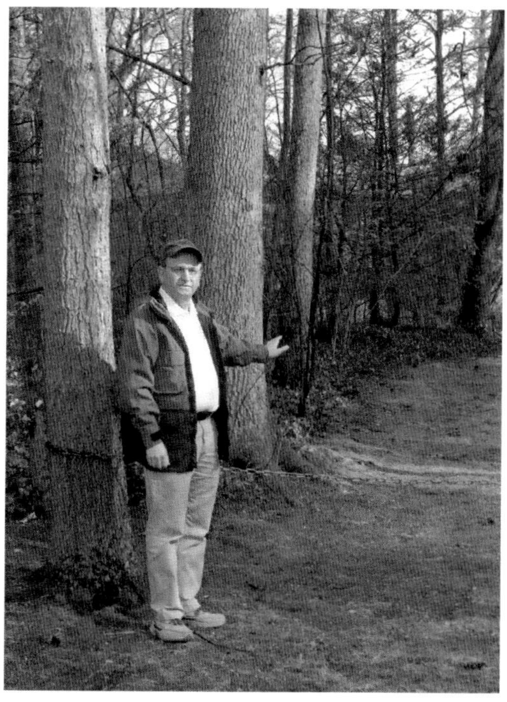

On February 7, 1981, Clary made a morning appointment to rendezvous with his student Denise Durham in the parking lot of Pardee Hospital in Hendersonville. Richard Edmond Amico (1942–1993) rode in Clary's van. Clary asked Amico to "duck down" so Denise would not see him, believing she would flee if she saw another man in the vehicle. Clary asked Denise to follow him, an appeal Denise resisted until Clary by some means convinced her to do so. Clary then drove to the Greenville Highway, with Denise trailing him, and turned onto Rutledge Drive, then pulled onto the semi-isolated track called Trenholm Road. Before they reached Little River Road, Clary stopped and exited his vehicle, walked up to Denise's car, shot her twice and made tracks. After dropping Amico at his home on Highland Lake

Top: The cinderblock foundation in a corner of the garage where Wilton Clary hid the gun and gloves he used in the murder of Denise Durham. *Photographed with permission.*

Right: Dwayne Durham standing at the site alongside Trenholm Road where he discovered his cousin's body.

Road, Clary returned to his home on Price Road, hid his .38-caliber revolver and a pair of gloves in a cinderblock in his garage and covered the evidence with earth. He then drove to the Woof 'n' Purr.

Henderson County EMS paramedic Dwayne "Doc" Durham (1955–) said the call came in at 10:43 a.m. from residents near the murder scene. Durham and his partner and longtime family friend Jerry Bishop (1959–) arrived first on the scene, where they found a girl's body facedown, respectfully concealed with a blanket, a few hundred feet from her vehicle with its engine still running. When Dwayne turned the corpse over, he discovered it to be his first cousin Denise.

When authorities questioned the victim's father, Robert Leroy Durham (1939–), about likely suspects, he cited Wilton Clary. Apparently, Clary and Denise had been corresponding, and Mr. Durham inferred that his daughter had grown fearful of Clary. Deputies apprehended Clary at the Woof 'n' Purr and took him to the sheriff's office for questioning. Henderson County sheriff Albert "Ab" Jackson (1917–2006) offered Clary a cup of coffee and then remained silent, glaring as Clary sipped from the cup. Upon finishing the last drop, Clary confessed to premeditated murder.

"He asked if I was Sheriff Jackson," Jackson said. "I told him I was, and he said, 'I might as well tell you, I shot the girl. She'd been bugging the hell out of me to leave my wife."

Clary had mailed letters to Miss Durham when she attended Governor's School of North Carolina at Raleigh, a summer residential program for intellectually gifted high school students. These letters, according to family members, contained Clary's attempt to dissuade the alleged infatuation.

Authorities arrested Clary and Amico on February 7, the afternoon of the homicide, charging Clary with first-degree murder and Amico with first-degree murder and being an accessory before and after the fact of first-degree murder. Defense attorneys deemed Clary's confession inadmissible as evidence, claiming that Clary had not been properly advised of his rights prior to talking with the sheriff.

Clary was released on February 9 on a $50,000 bond. After East Henderson High School students protested Clary's release in front of the courthouse and Robert L. Durham filed a $2 million civil suit charging wrongful death, Clary returned to prison with bail set at $500,000. A week later, Clary was again released. With death threats against him, Clary hired bodyguards. Co-defendant Amico was held without bond at the Henderson County jail. The *Times-News* ran the headline "Clary's Bond Revoked; Judge Orders Tests" on Friday, April 17, 1981.

North Carolina County Superior Court judge Ronald Wood Howell (1941–2005) at Marshall ordered Clary to be held without bail until trial and also ordered that he be dispatched to Dorothea Dix Hospital in Raleigh for psychiatric evaluation. At the time, Clary had been undergoing care at Mandela Psychiatric Hospital in Winston-Salem, North Carolina. Clary's trial was set for April 27, 1981, with a change of venue denied, Judge Howell having found the defendant competent to stand trial. Ronald G. Blanchard (1948–) and Boyd B. "Buddy" Massagee III (1954–) served as defense attorneys and district attorney Marion Leonard Lowe (1919–2009) as prosecutor. William Harley Stepp and Edwin R. Groce (1937–) represented the Durham family.

On Wednesday, April 18, 1981, the *Times-News* reported, "Clary in Hospital with Heart Condition."

After delays and rescheduled hearing dates, the trial commenced, with prosecutor Lowe seeking the death penalty. SBI agent David Jones supplied core testimony during the brief proceedings on April 27. "He told me he had made up his mind that morning to kill Pamela Denise Durham, that it was the only way out," Jones said. Ballistic tests had confirmed that a bullet

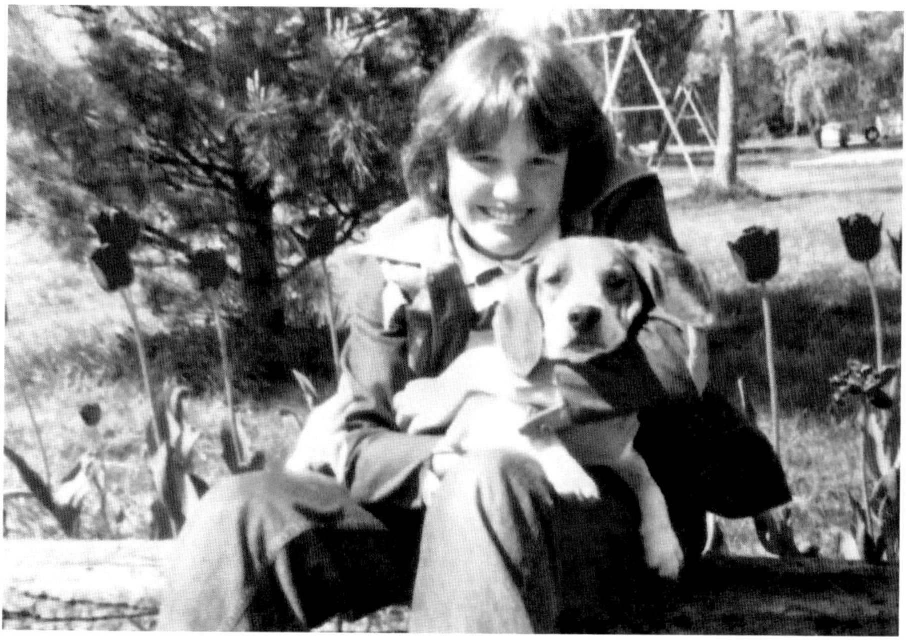

Pamela Denise Durham with her dog Alexander Spotswood, aka Spot, 1977. *Courtesy of Rená Durham Johnson.*

in the victim's body and another in her car-door panel came from Clary's revolver. Although never explicitly concluded, authorities determined the motive to have been a "romantic conflict."

"Wilton W. Clary Is Sentenced to Life in Prison," read a *Times-News* headline on Tuesday, April 28, 1981. Clary pleaded guilty to first-degree murder charges and was sentenced to life imprisonment. He'd told the court that he pleaded guilty to spare the victim's family the grief of a drawn-out trial. Described by reporters as "composed" and "unemotional" during the trial, Clary returned to his seat following the sentencing, turned to his wife, patted her knee and wept quietly for a moment.

During the Clary trial, a national crime tabloid picked up the story and grossly exaggerated its circumstances to the point that Sheriff Ab Jackson dispatched deputies to confiscate all copies from local outlets. Consequently, Hendersonville officials had all copies of the magazine removed from local newsstands.

On Monday, August 26, 1985, the *Times-News* reported, "Clary Dies in Craggy Prison." Clary, who had a history of heart-related issues, died of a heart attack after serving a mere four years of his sentence. Originally dispatched to Central Prison at Raleigh, Clary was moved to the Division of Prison's McCain correctional unit near Southern Pines and then to Craggy Correctional Center near Asheville.

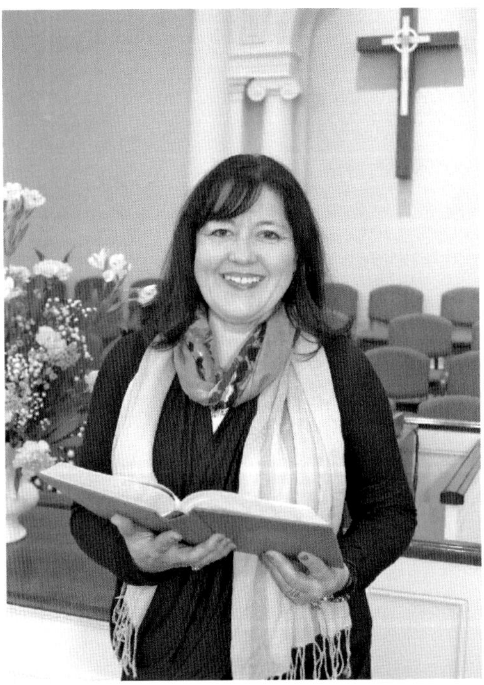

Rená Durham Johnson sang a tribute to her cousin and best childhood friend at First Presbyterian Church of Hendersonville in 2014.

Times-News staff reporter Joy Franklin quoted the victim's father, Robert L. Durham, as having said:

> *I hope he was able to make peace with God. That's my feelings concerning* [Clary's] *death. I know he never expressed any sincere regret to my family or to me for the tremendous sorrow he inflicted*

in our lives. I do feel some relief in that I will no longer have to keep track of his confinement and will no longer have to dread the day of his parole. He would probably have been paroled in a couple of years and that's no longer a dread for me. The murder of a dearly loved child is the most devastating of human tragedies. The second largest shock of my life was the state's lenient treatment of the man that murdered my child. Crime victim rights are long overdue.

Denise Durham's first cousin and close childhood friend Rená Durham Johnson (1960–) remembers Denise as fun loving and smart. The two had grown close. Upon hearing the news of Wilton Clary's death, Rená said she felt a sense of relief.

BORN IN NORTHAMPTON, PENNSYLVANIA, Richard E. Amico was a Vietnam War veteran and machinist and later described as Wilton Clary's manservant. Deemed indigent at the time of the Durham murder, court-appointed counsel Frank B. Jackson (1947–) represented him. Amico, who lied to investigators, later admitted that Clary had threatened to kill him if he told the authorities what had happened. Amico was sentenced to twenty years in prison beginning on September 9, 1981, and released on parole on September 9, 1983. Ten years later, he died in the Veterans Hospital in Asheville, North Carolina, at the age of fifty. He was buried at the Beulah Baptist Church Cemetery in Henderson County.

By all accounts a prodigy with multiple scholarly and artistic interests—honor student, high school band member, accomplished on the autoharp, choir member in her church and member of a group known as the Civil War Roundtable—one might wonder, after considering the facts, if Denise Durham truly posed a threat to the Clarys' marriage. Moreover, and according to family members, Denise had a boyfriend and was fearful of Wilton Clary at the time. About the real story, no one is certain, but theories abound.

RAMBO ON SUGARLOAF MOUNTAIN

What began as a simple misdemeanor pursuit around Thanksgiving time 1986 escalated into a massive manhunt on Sugarloaf Mountain. Five days later, a fugitive described as "Rambo" lay shot to death in a briar-choked ravine. This was back in the days when officers actually pulled litterbugs over and ticketed them or, at minimum, issued the offender a warning.

On a routine patrol of U.S. Highway 64 East on Saturday, November 22, 1986, Henderson County deputy James Franklin "Jimmy" Case (1962–) spotted a beer bottle being tossed from a brown Buick with Florida license tags. Case engaged his siren and blue light in an attempt to stop the offender near the Uno Grocery when someone in the Buick fired a shot at Case's patrol car, piercing the radiator and disabling the vehicle. Shortly thereafter, law enforcement agencies throughout the Southeast jumped into alert and set up roadblocks.

The driver of the Buick, Michael John Shornock (1965–1986), was a son of James J. Shornock Jr. (1942–1998) and Ann Elizabeth Raup Shornock (1943–). The Shornocks, originally of Carmel, Pennsylvania, moved in 1979 to Swansboro, North Carolina, and Michael later lived in Florida, where he worked as a carpenter. By the time Deputy Case encountered the beer bottle incident, Shornock had eluded law enforcement officials in Florida, Georgia and coastal North Carolina during a crime spree that spanned three months, involving a string of shootings and larcenies.

The Hendersonville *Times-News* reported on Monday, November 24, 1986, "Police Seek Suspect Tied to Edneyville Shootout."

In a quiet apple-farming sector of Henderson County, events heated up during the wee hours of Sunday, November 23, when SERT (Special Emergency Response Team) officers at a roadblock apprehended a white Plymouth Horizon riddled with bullet holes, which had been speeding east on U.S. Highway 64. Inside the car officers found twenty-two-year-old Edwin Pete Black Jr. (1964–) of Hendersonville, who was driving; thirty-one-year-old Myron Bale Pace of Tuxedo; Earl Chandler; Marie Bane; and twenty-five-year-old Ricky Charles Pack (1961–) of Green River. In the back seat, they discovered William Anthony Miller (1962–1986) with a fatal gunshot wound to his face. The passengers, together with Ricky Pack's brother, had piled into the car with Miller's body. Officers found one of the partygoers, Charles Dennis "Dennie" Pack (1949–1986), with a critical gunshot wound to his midsection lying in a ditch near the crime scene on Sugarloaf Mountain Road. Pack later died from his wound. The group in the car sped toward the Pardee hospital before officials pulled them over. Officers arrested Edwin Black and later charged Ricky Pack with murder in connection with the shooting death of Miller.

The confrontation began at a party in a home on Sugarloaf Mountain Road—of which Miller was a tenant—when a dispute arose, followed by a salvo of gunfire. Officers found Shornock's brown Buick—believed to have been stolen in Sarasota, Florida in an apple orchard on the Gilbert property, and Edwin Black matched Deputy Case's description of the passenger in the brown Buick. As far as anyone knew, Shornock was not involved in the murders that evening. (The DHS house has since burned.)

Edwin Pete Black Jr. surrendered for the murder of William Miller as 150 to 200 deputies combed the mountain in pursuit of Shornock, whose crime spree had begun in late September when authorities in Onslow County, Florida, spotted the suspect acting suspiciously near a Jacksonville used car lot. A man fitting Shornock's description stole a truck and fled, broke into a woman's home in Port Orange, shot her dog and forced her to make dinner for him. He absconded with her motorcycle and, by mid-October, had escaped into the Florida Everglades. He was also wanted in Jacksonville, North Carolina, for a pawnshop break-in and in Wrightsville Beach and Sunset Beach for armed robberies. Shornock's family and schoolmates knew him as a loner, a former honor roll student at Swansboro High School, a survivalist, an expert hunter and a hater of the law since his earlier imprisonment on charges of vehicle theft.

The previous Thursday, November 20, Shornock and Black, wearing ski masks, had robbed First Citizens Bank and Trust Company in Carteret on the coast of North Carolina. During their flight, Shornock shot at two police officers, wounding Sergeant Joe Willis and escaping with an estimated $1,400. Authorities had been trailing Shornock since September, having monitored his criminal activities for three years. Shornock had met Black in prison. Carteret County officials indicted Shornock and Black for armed robbery, two charges of attempted murder, two charges of discharging a firearm in occupied property, two charges of assault with a deadly weapon with intent to kill and inflicting injury and two charges of assault on a law enforcement officer with a firearm.

On record as the largest manhunt in Henderson County history, the chase involved perilous terrain, vexing weather conditions and an army of searchers equipped with bulletproof flack jackets scouring the region. Officers set up command posts at Mountain Home Baptist Church and the Edneyville Volunteer Fire Department. Law enforcement agencies from across the region joined in the search with units from Rutherford, Avery, Swain, Caldwell, Buncombe, Lincoln, Transylvania, Polk and Graham Counties and others from as far away as Kings Mountain. News reports stated that as many as four hundred law enforcement officers participated in the hunt as choppers thundered overhead and bloodhound teams from South Carolina and four local tracking dog teams joined in the pursuit. A *Times-News* headline read, "Search Expands for 'Survivalist' Shootout Suspect" on November 25, 1986.

On Monday evening, Shornock forced his way at gunpoint into the Little Creek home of Ivory Floy Marshall (1920–1997) and Ruby H. Watkins Marshall (1940–), stole their Jeep and later shot out the window of a state patrol car, slightly injuring trooper Ronald Keith Lovin. Police later found the Jeep abandoned near a field on Little Creek Road. The manhunt escalated on Gilliam Mountain Road later that night when officers equipped with searchlights and dog teams sealed off a ten- to fifteen-mile area with SWAT-type teams from five different agencies assisting with the search. Highway patrol officers ordered homes evacuated along Edney Inn Road, and helicopters from the highway patrol and National Guard patrolled overhead as agents continued combing the challenging terrain. Earlier that day, armed guards equipped with sidearms and shotguns rode school buses with one unmarked car following each bus as a measure of protecting students in the Gilliam Mountain Road area. Meanwhile, Griffin's Grocery on U.S. Highway 64 East had become a hub of activity for out-of-town officers and media representatives who flooded the area.

On November 25, 1986, the *New York Times* reported, "North Carolina Officers Search for Fugitive." Local resident Gayle Hamilton Stepp recalled:

> *It seemed a perfectly average fall day as I drove home from my job at church in my little yellow truck, but as I approached the intersection of Lamb Mountain and John Delk Roads, law enforcement officers signaled for me to stop. They informed me there had been a murder on the mountain the night before. After they inspected the cab of my truck I drove home and carefully locked the doors behind me. I later learned that a former East Henderson High School classmate, Dennie Pack, had been killed.*
>
> *The following four days unfolded like a television drama in my own neighborhood. The next morning when I left for work with a load of garbage in the back of my cab to take to the dump during lunchtime, law enforcement officers again checked to be sure I was not hiding someone in my cab. This happened each time I left home.*
>
> *After returning home from work in the evenings my husband and I sat on our high deck out back and watched patrol cars searching the roads on Sugarloaf Mountain. There seemed to be at least one hundred cars going up the mountain and then coming back down. Helicopters circled overhead. Officers visited the homes of folks who had gone home for Thanksgiving. Our neighbors, Morris and Ethel Young, had left for Indiana. Another*

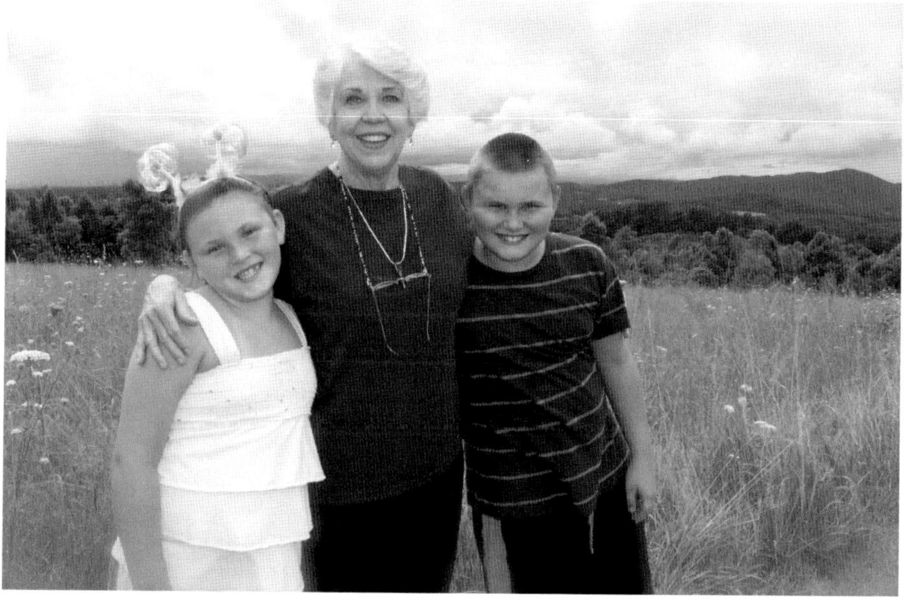

Gayle Hamilton Stepp at home with her grandchildren Luke and Natalie Stepp. The breathtaking panorama from the Stepps' property included helicopters and searchlights during Thanksgiving week 1986.

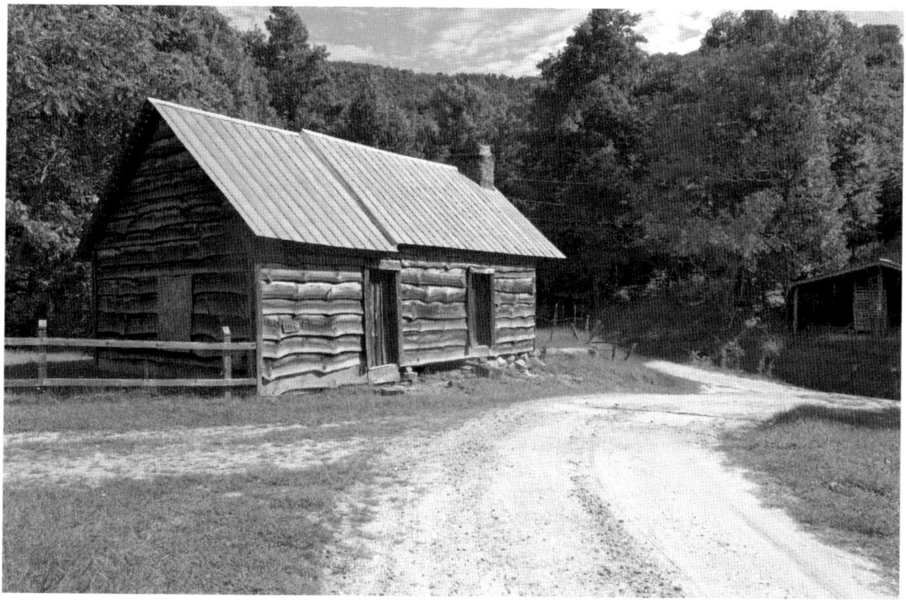

The Conner property on Little Creek Road includes a cabin built about 1891, with a kitchen and porch added in 1912.

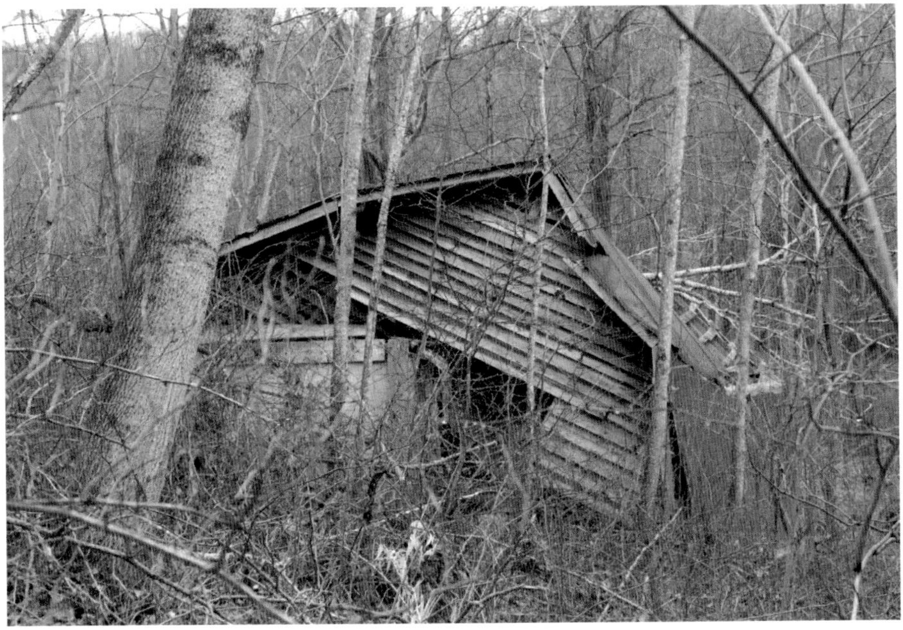

"Rambo's" last stand at Homer Conner's barn, where Michael John Shornock staged his final ambush. The now-collapsed building furnished shelter for Shornock as he hid out the night before a member of an Asheville tactical unit killed him.

neighbor called the authorities to report that they had seen someone in the Youngs' yard. Officers searched, but found no one.

Another neighbor, Virginia, had arrived ahead of her family who would join her for Thanksgiving. Her husband, Maurice, was to arrive by plane. Leaving to pick him up at the Asheville airport, Virginia believed she had closed and locked all the doors. Upon their return, however, they could see their front door standing open. They backed out of the driveway and dialed 911. Officers arrived and searched their home, the woods and our yard. Later, Virginia told me the officers had been cocking guns right in my front yard into the wee hours of the morning. Oblivious, I'd slept through that particular search knowing I had locked my doors and propped chairs in front of some of them before retiring for the evening.

While officers surrounded Shornock's stakeout on the mountain, girls drove up and down Highway 64 East holding homemade signs out of their windows, which read, "TWO HUNDRED TO ONE; AREN'T YOU PROUD?" These girls perceived Shornock to be a sort of "Rambo." Some young boys believed Shornock to be a survivalist who lived off the land while evading the authorities. Later, I learned that he was a scared young man who had not eaten for days as he ran from the law. Authorities contacted Shornock's mother as an attempt to get her son to surrender, but her efforts with a bullhorn proved unsuccessful.

On Tuesday, November 25, the fog-enshrouded landscape and torrential rain slowed down search efforts as thirty tactical team members maintained their positions, slowly sifting through the area they had narrowed to a five-mile radius. During the rain-soaked drama, officers announced over a public address system that if Shornock gave himself up peacefully, he would not be hurt. Instead of surrendering, Shornock shot at Sheriff's Sergeant Victor Burren Moss, wounding him under his left eye as he and three other officers explored a field above Little Creek Road. Highway patrol trooper David McMurray was also hit, but his ammunition clip deflected the bullet.

"He knows they're talking about big-time prison now," Shornock's mother said. "I don't know what he'll do for sure, but he said he would never go back to prison. I figure he's serious, and this all is just a form of suicide."

Captain Tom Hatchett of the Henderson County Sheriff's Department told reporters, "Apparently he lays in wait until an officer approaches, then fires and runs a further distance and waits again. [Officers are] very cautiously, very slowly pushing forward."

On November 26, 1986, a *Times-News* headline read, "Residents Near Search Area Nervous."

The weather broke, giving way to sunshine around noontime on Wednesday, November 26. Shortly after 1:15 p.m., SBI agents David Wooten of Ahoskie and Steve Meyers of Durham probed buildings on the secluded Little Creek Road farm of Homer Lee Conner (1921–1988) and Mae Barnwell Conner (1915–1975). As they opened a barn door, the officers found the suspect standing at the ready. Shornock opened fire, aiming at Wooten's head, then swung around, fired at Meyers, swung around again and shot Wooten, hitting Meyers in the arm and Wooten in the lower abdomen. As Shornock sprinted into a briar-choked ravine about fifty yards below the barn, an officer of a tactical unit from the Asheville Police Department took aim. One bullet sliced through Shornock's head, killing him instantly.

"I guess the old saying is true. If you live by the sword, you die by the sword, and that's what happened," Henderson County sheriff Ab Jackson said.

"Over the past few days, he shot at fifteen officers and wounded six," said SBI deputy director Charles Dunn of Asheville. During the hunt, Shornock was armed with a .30-caliber carbine and a .45-caliber handgun.

Homer Conner, an army veteran, retired apple grower and tomato farmer, said, "I can't remember anything like this happening around here before. It's the most excitement around here ever." Conner wasn't home when officers took down Shornock at his farm.

On Thursday, November 27, 1986, the *Times-News* reported, "Fugitive Dies on Mountain." Resident Kevin Haynes recalled:

> *I watched the news every night and saved all the newspaper clippings. Most memorable though were the first night and last day. The night it happened I was on my way with some friends—to a movie or something. Arby's was open twenty-four hours then, so afterwards we stopped for a bite before getting home by our 1:00 a.m. curfew. We overheard some people talking, saying Edneyville was on lockdown because of a shooting and a manhunt. Not having cellphones back then, we relied on Arby's phone for communication with our families. Around 1:30 or 2:00 a.m. we got word we could return home. On the way home, the first thing we saw was Deputy Jimmy Case's car at the Uno Grocery where it had been shot. Then just a couple miles down the road at Wilkie's Orchard we saw an abandoned white car off the road. It wasn't until the next morning at church that we heard more of the story and the details. Then on the last day—the day they got Shornock—my dad and I were out working in the yard. You can see Gilliam Mountain Road from our backyard, and we noticed seven or more law enforcement vehicles traveling pretty fast up the mountain. My dad said, "They caught him, and he is probably dead too." "How do you know?" I asked him. Dad used to be a deputy sheriff for Henderson County back in the late 1960s, and he said, "Because of the number of vehicles; if he were still alive they would have had their sirens on." I remember feeling sad for Shornock that he had*

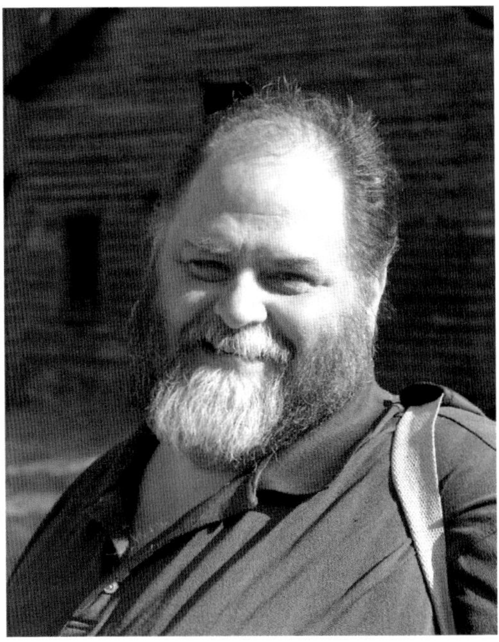

Edneyville native Kevin Haynes has appeared in locally filmed movies, including the 1996 production *My Fellow Americans*, starring Jack Lemmon, Lauren Bacall and Dan Aykroyd.

> *been killed because he was just a few years younger than I. I also felt bad for all the officers that had been hurt and involved in the whole ordeal.*

On Monday, December 1, 1986, a *Times-News* headline read, "Shornock Was Just Playing a Game He Lost, Mother Says." "It was just a game," Shornock's mother said. "On his terms."

Jeffery John Shornock (1966–), the deceased fugitive's brother, told reporters, "My brother was a hell-raiser, but he was a good guy until he went to prison."

On November 27, the *Times-News* assured its readers, "Calm Returns to Sugarloaf." Gayle Hamilton Stepp remembered:

> *During Shornock's rampage, the community lived in fear. Word spread that he had stolen Ivory Marshall's Jeep. He seemed to be everywhere at once, with each sighting reported and law-enforcement officials following up on each and every call. Television stations assigned cameramen and reporters to get the scoop, questioning patrolmen and officers from the Sherriff's Department, SBI and FBI. The two hundred officers were trying to catch a criminal and each reporter was trying to be the first to get the story live.*
>
> *I remember Shornock being apprehended and killed on the Wednesday before Thanksgiving. I was at work at Covenant Presbyterian Church. My mother heard on a television newscast that the fugitive had been shot, and she left that message with the church secretary. As tends to happen, opinions ran the gamut, some folks pitying the man who had died so young while others believed justice had been served. I was relieved that this time of fear was over.*
>
> *At a basketball game the following Friday, people spoke of the terrifying events of the previous week, but by the next Friday game, it was already long ago and we sat in the bleachers cheering, "Go Jackets!" After all, the byways had reverted back to quiet country roads; the skies were again clear and silent. No scuttle of patrol cars. No thunderous helicopters.*

EASTER MASSACRE

Louise Howe Bailey wrote in one of her "Along the Ridges" columns for the Hendersonville *Times-News*:

> *Church pews spill over as Christians around the world celebrate the greatest religious festival of the year. The music, the message and the hope that make*

> *today's services special will long be remembered. So will certain customs that are traditionally a part of the celebration…Just as the earth emerges from the grays and browns of winter to take on a fresh new look of spring, so do people set aside old garments for the proverbial Easter finery.*

Members of Edneyville's Mountain Home Baptist Church will no doubt long remember Easter 1988, but for unspeakable reasons. As mourners gathered to celebrate the life of Effie Collins Justice (1909–1988), a man described by friends and colleagues as "gentle, soft-spoken, friendly and kind" gunned down three members of a grieving family. The *Times-News* headline on Monday, April 4, 1988, read, "Gunman Kills Three at Funeral."

Psychological studies suggest that a person's snap into violence may come as a total surprise; in most cases, there's a psychological buildup to that point, the pathway to violence generally beginning with simple thoughts and then fantasizing about a scheme—a more explicit planning phase that goes unnoticed by the person's family and colleagues. "A person who has already decided to kill someone else may develop an eerie composure, firmly believing that the moment to turn back has passed," said Dr. Charles Raison, a psychiatrist and director of the Mind/Body Institute at Emory University.

This might well have been the case with Michael Leslie Rainey, who viciously murdered three members of his ex-in-laws and wounded three others.

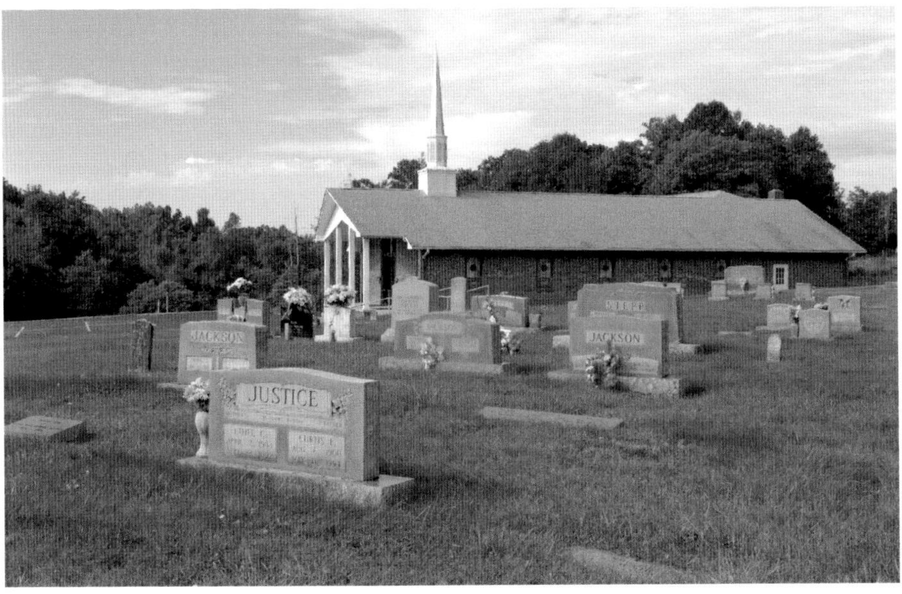

Mountain Home Baptist Church and Cemetery.

On the rainy Easter Sunday afternoon of April 3, 1988, as church members, family and friends viewed the body of Effie Justice and then took their places in the pews, violence erupted in the church's parking lot. Several shots rang out, and suddenly three lifeless bodies lay slumped on the asphalt as a yellow Ford Crown Victoria sped from the scene. The assassin then calmly walked a few hundred yards from the church to his home and dialed 911.

Forty-one-year-old Asheville native Michael Leslie Rainey, an installer for Southern Bell Telephone Company, had purchased nine acres from his wife's grandfather William T. Justice (1901–1985) in 1979. When Rainey and his wife built their home on this land on Sugarloaf Mountain, Justice had given permission to the Raineys to use an access road crossing his property to get to their own land from State Route 1707. Michael Leslie Rainey (1946–) and Andrea Owensby Rainey (1947–), who were married in 1970, lived in Kennesaw, Georgia, near Atlanta until 1979. They were divorced in 1985. The couple had two male children. In the divorce settlement, Michael kept possession of the Sugarloaf Mountain home, and Andrea, a critical care nurse, received a home the couple owned in Kennesaw. Andrea described the divorce as "amicable." At the time of the murders, Michael Rainey lived with his girlfriend, Carolyn Byrum of Candler, North Carolina.

"Land Dispute Ended with Shootings," read the *Times-News* on April 5, 1988.

In 1986, Rainey's ex-in-laws, Ponnelle Owensby (1928–1988) and Wilford Owensby (1926–1988), received land from Effie Justice—acreage abutting Rainey's property, which included a thirty-foot right of way, the sole means of entering his property. In 1987, the Owensbys installed locked gates with No Trespassing signs across the right of way. Rainey had previously asked his ex-in-laws to sell him fifteen feet of the access, which they refused to do. Meanwhile, the locked gates kept Rainey from reaching his property or removing his vehicles, so he filed a court suit against the Owensbys. Over time, friction ensued, and the dispute escalated to a point where, before Effie Justice's funeral, Andrea Rainey had asked her ex-husband to stay away from her grandmother's service. This might have been what pushed Rainey over the brink. Rainey, in spite of Andrea's admonition, went anyway, viewed the body and then left the church, marching, as one witness described, "Gestapo-style" into the parking lot. The hour was 3:00 p.m., the time scheduled for the funeral service. Rainey's ex-wife, Andrea; her sister; and both women's children had just arrived, whereupon Rainey goose-stepped to his vehicle, removed his .380 automatic pistol and twelve-gauge shotgun and shot through the windows of Andrea's Crown Victoria, wounding Andrea in the neck and her sister Sheila Owensby Johnston (1958–) of Fletcher in the spine and also shooting Johnston's eleven-year-old daughter, Wendy.

While Wilford and Ponnelle Owensby's nephew Russell Scott Bowles (1962–1988) hid behind the Owensbys' truck, Rainey's former brother-in-law William Johnston fired a shot at Rainey with a .25-caliber pistol, which Rainey forced away from Johnston and then shot Bowles multiple times. Rainey next opened fire on his ex-in-laws, Wilford and Ponnelle Owensby, at close range and continued shooting at and kicking their lifeless bodies. Coroner's results showed fifteen bullet wounds in Bowles, eighteen wounds in Ponnelle Owensby and at least six in the body of Wilford Owensby. After the shootings, Rainey placed his shotgun on the hood of the hearse and walked home.

Approximately thirty mourners remained in the church as Henderson County officers responded to Rainey's 911 call.

"People see things in movies, then the director says, 'Cut.' This is reality," said Reverend Ronald Dean Boone (1950–2014), pastor at Mountain Home Baptist Church.

Hendersonville police officers stopped Andrea's bullet-riddled car and called for ambulances to transport the victims to Pardee Hospital. Reports indicated that Michael Rainey surrendered calmly at about 3:30 p.m. Arraigned the next day, he was charged with three counts of first-degree murder and three counts of assault with a deadly weapon with intent to kill and held without bond in the Henderson County jail. Again, he appeared solemn. Within a few hours of the triple murders, Rainey, in a confessional statement, said, "Guilty is guilty; I'm not trying to get out of this." He also told officials that he had intended to kill Ponnelle Owensby if she continued to give him trouble.

Rainey was indicted on April 11, the day before his probable cause hearing. Seeking the death penalty, prosecutor Alan Leonard—who believed the triple murder to be premeditated because of the brutal manner of killing—portrayed Rainey as "a wolf in sheep's clothing." Leonard also described the crime as "brutal overkill." Rainey's trial began on Monday, August 22, 1988.

Rainey's defense attorneys, Ronald G. Blanchard (1939–) and Arthur "Skeeter" Redden (1935–), called to the stand character witnesses who testified about the good side of Michael Rainey, some speaking of the defendant's service during the Vietnam conflict and his volunteer service with Big Brother and Big Sister programs and Boy Scouts. Others vouched of their having been saved during white-water rafting disasters by Rainey, a former national champion whitewater canoer.

Prosecutor Alan Leonard argued, "He fired at those unarmed women and children in that car just like someone would fire at caged animals."

Rainey, who had pleaded "not guilty," delivered a tearful account of his rampage as he testified in his capital murder trial, mentioning during his ninety-minute testimony his ex-wife's having told him to not attend the funeral. On the day of the shootings, he thought his ex-wife had reached for a gun, that her hands were under her car seat before he opened fire. He also believed his ex-father-in-law was armed—his arm was folded behind his back. He shot Ponnelle Owensby as she hovered over her dead husband. "Her right hand was out of my view," Rainey added. He also spoke of the dispute concerning the right of way easement.

As Prosecutor Leonard said, "If everybody that builds a fence or blocks a driveway in Henderson County is to be shot, then blood is going to run in the streets."

Asheville psychologist Anthony Sciara (1946–) diagnosed Rainey as a paranoid-schizophrenic, basing part of his theory on a statement from Rainey: "When Mrs. Justice dies there will be nothing to stop them from killing me." Referring to his in-laws, he said, "They have nothing to lose." Sciara also explained Rainey's narcissistic tendencies, that he became enraged when someone dared challenge his idea of himself as a good person. "He was discharging emotions through firearms," Sciara concluded.

On August 26, 1988, a jury of nine women and three men, who deliberated for five hours, found Rainey guilty as charged. Rainey apologized for the murders, wiping away tears as he spoke the words, "I'm sorry to all the ones I've hurt. It's affected a lot of people and I'm going to accept the consequences, whatever they may be, without any hard feelings."

On Saturday, August 27, the *Times-News* reported, "Rainey Found Guilty."

Rainey sat calmly and seemingly unemotional as the judge read his sentence on August 31. Henderson County Superior Court judge James A. Beaty Jr. (1949–) ordered three first-degree murder sentences to be served consecutively for sixty years and sentenced him to an additional eighteen years in prison on three counts of felony assault.

Rainey's trial marked only the second time in the previous ten years that prosecutors had sought the death penalty in a Henderson County murder case. The first was the murder trial of Eldred Leon Hill (1956–), who was sentenced to death for the November 22, 1981 shooting of Hendersonville police officer Dennie Quay Enevold (1948–1981). The State Superior Court later reduced Hill's sentence to life in prison.

On August 31, a *Times-News* headline informed its readers, "Rainey Sentenced to Life."

The court later granted a civil judgment of more than $1 million to Owensby family members and the estates of the three people killed in the Easter massacre.

Hoover Engle, an Edneyville volunteer fireman, said of the brutal incident, "I hope I don't remember it. The best thing to do is try not to let it bother you. Just think another step forward. Don't look back and just hope it don't happen again."

Mountain Home Baptist Church

On March 19, 1892, thirty-one people met in the home of Samuel Williamson (1846–1924) to form Mountain Home Baptist Church of Christ at Point Lookout. J.H. Taylor (1855–1932) moderated and preached a sermon. Members nominated R.M. Gilbert (1847–1928) to be the first pastor and Williamson to the post of clerk and constituted the church on April 8.

Lacking for lumber and other supplies, the members determined on December 10, 1893, to delay until materials became more readily available. In the interim period, members scattered—some of them taking jobs in cotton mills and others attending services held by visiting preachers under an oak tree in the field of Benjamin F. Justice (1846–1917), where they hoped to eventually build their church. After a lapse of six years, members held their first meeting in a new church building on December 16, 1899, constructed on land purchased from Thomas Edward Justice (1863–1942). Emma Williamson (1877–1935), wife of Samuel, served as organist.

Members razed the church and sold its lumber in 1919 and built a larger sanctuary, which they dedicated on June 11, 1922. Classrooms were added in 1940. The church purchased two acres in 1922 from Valentine "Vol" Laughter (1875–1953) and Emma Nancy Jones Laughter (1880–1970) and built a parsonage. Membership grew, necessitating an even larger church, which was completed in 1974 with 215 in attendance at its first service. In 1990, the campus continued to grow with the addition of more classrooms, a fellowship hall and a pastor's study.

DISASTERS IN THE SKY

Identified by geologists as being among the oldest ranges on the planet, the Blue Ridge Mountains proffer breathtaking backdrops for Henderson County. White

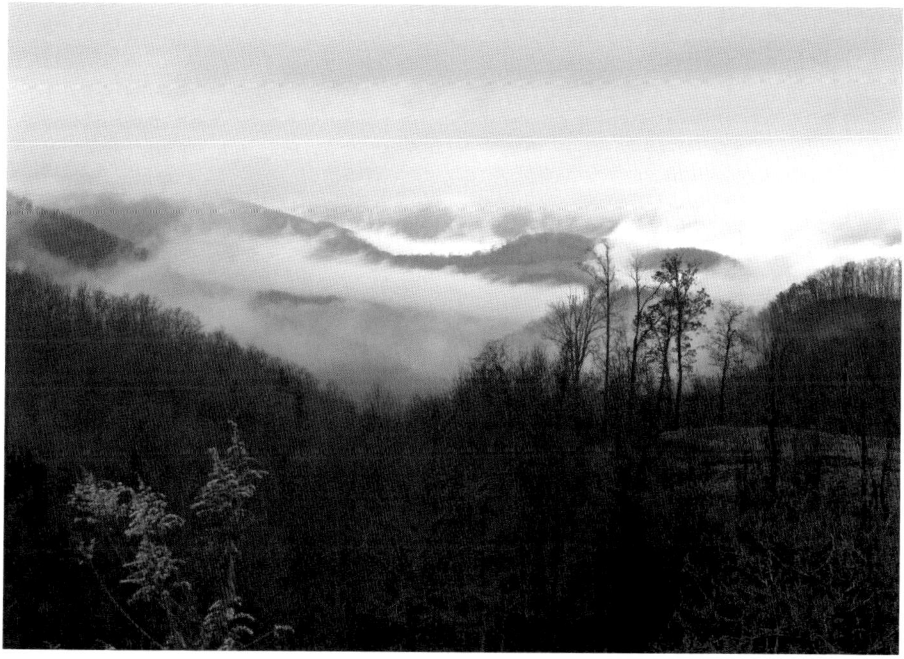

Mountains, fog and aircraft—a recipe for disaster.

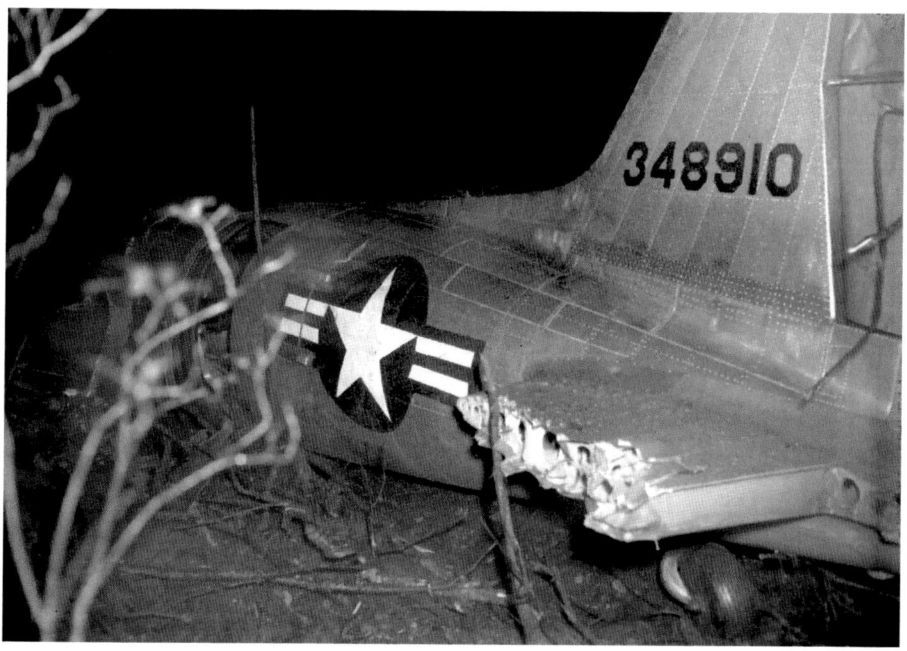

Courtesy of Baker-Barber Collection. Community Foundation of Henderson County. Henderson County Public Library.

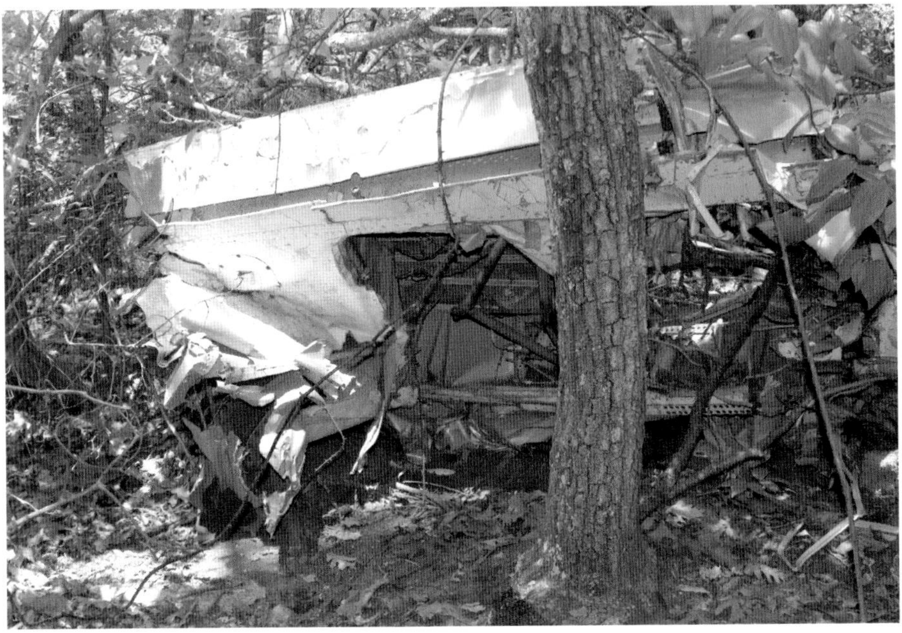

Although Boy Scout troops collected pieces in a scrap-metal drive on Sugarloaf, wreckage from the Oswolds' 1963 airplane crash remains on the mountainside.

water plunges over their cliffs and chasms, creeks and branches crisscross the vales between their time-eroded slopes, ice-cold springs course beneath their foundations of granite and hikers and birders find respite in their wooded, wild-flowered trails. Nevertheless, these ridges command respect from those venturing upon them—and through their perilous airspace.

Over the years, more than homicides and crime sprees have tarnished the splendor of Henderson County's otherwise idyllic milieu. Catastrophic weather conditions including fog and downdrafts, together with steep cliffs, pilots' unfamiliarity with the defiant terrain and the sheer height of the Blue Ridge, have brought down aircraft, claiming many lives. Pockmarked with crash sites, Henderson County's mountains have witnessed their share of air disasters.

Old-timers recall when a military craft collided with Mount Olivet near the end of the World War II years. This was on Saturday, July 21, 1945, when a B-25 medium bomber from the Army Air Base at Greenville, South Carolina, crashed and exploded near Tuxedo about 2:45 p.m. The pilot, Major Robert Belden Kuhn (1915–1986) of Canton, Ohio, endeavored to keep the bomber on an even keel after it developed a distressing shake. Unable to stabilize the craft, Kuhn ordered five crew members to abandon the ship. Kuhn and the copilot jumped just before the crash, which cut a furrow through the woods, scattering metal and trees across the road, halting traffic about one mile east of Mount Olivet Baptist Church and Cemetery. The seven men parachuted safely to the ground about three miles from the crash site.

Nearly two decades later—on October 23, 1963—August W. Oswold (1914–1963) and his wife, Mary Jane Oswold (1912–1963), were en route from Tulsa, Oklahoma, in a light, two-engine Beechcraft Baron to visit Mrs. Oswold's sister in Charlotte, North Carolina. Residents of Roslyn, New York, the Oswolds owned a taxi fleet in the Bronx. At about 2:30 p.m., Oswold flew his plane into a western slope of 3,500 feet at Sugarloaf Mountain. Investigators blamed fog. Early that evening, search teams discovered the impact had thrown Mrs. Oswold from the plane; her husband's body remained strapped into the cockpit.

Flight 22

The most tragic air disaster in North Carolina's history involved the collision of a private plane and a commercial airliner above the Dana area of Henderson County on Wednesday, July 19, 1967. Piedmont Flight 22, a Boeing 727 jetliner carrying seventy-four passengers and a crew of five, departed from Asheville Regional Airport's Runway 16 at 11:58 a.m., en route from Atlanta to Roanoke with a stop at Asheville and a scheduled termination at Washington, D.C. As it climbed above Hendersonville, a Cessna 310 charter flight, which had originated in Springfield, Missouri, tore into the jet's right underbelly near its front landing gear, claiming the lives of all eighty-two people aboard the two crafts. Before the impact, the Cessna had been traveling at 205 miles per hour and the jetliner climbing at a ground speed of about 275 miles per hour.

Local resident Charles Geffrey "Geff" Hoots recalled:

> *I was playing alone in the yard, underneath my grandfather's parked aluminum boat, when the two planes popped loudly in the sky above me. Just seconds later I heard a booming explosion, and the ground under my feet shook so strong that I fell down on my face.*

The red Cessna, piloted by John David "Dave" Addison (1919–1967) of Lebanon, Missouri, had taken off from Charlotte and was inbound to the Asheville airport. Some sources faulted Addison, a pilot of twenty-two years and

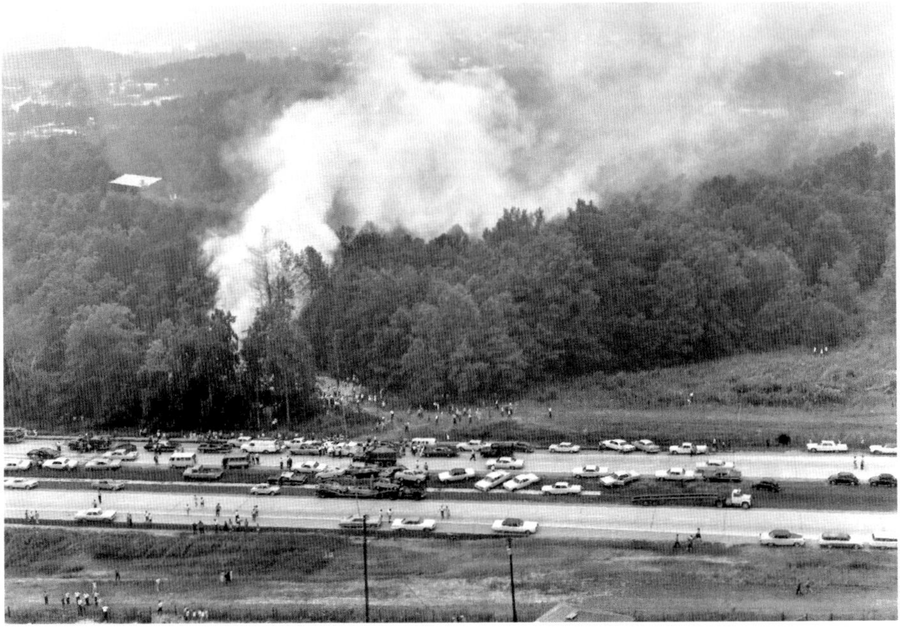

Crash site of Piedmont Flight 22, July 19, 1967. *Courtesy of Dwayne Durham and the Henderson County Rescue Squad.*

a World War II U.S. Army private, for not having radioed the tower at Asheville for landing clearance. Other sources blamed a confusing transmission message by the ATC and minimal control procedures utilized by the FAA in its handling of the Cessna. The Asheville tower did not have radar in those days but relied on VHF Omni-directional Range (VOR) using radio signals. Addison's deviation from his IFR (Instrument Flight Rules) clearance—approximately nine miles south and east of the glide pattern into Asheville—put him in a flight path allocated to the 727. According to the FAA, Addison's two-engine Cessna swept out of the pallor and flew directly into the 727. Weather conditions indicated a 2,500-foot ceiling with broken cloud cover and four miles of visibility in hazy conditions. Addison's passengers were Ralph Reynolds (1919–1967), vice-president of Lanseair, Inc. (an aviation insurance and development company) and owner of the craft, and Robert Eugene Anderson (1930–1967)—both from Springfield, Missouri.

Flight 22, the first jet in Piedmont's fleet and nicknamed the "Manhattan Pacemaker," had belonged to the Shah of Iran. Because fog had delayed flights that morning, Flight 22 was running thirty minutes behind schedule. The impact and explosion welded the Cessna into the jetliner's underbelly.

Passengers on Flight 22 included vacationing families, children returning home from camps, thirty-six food brokers from around the country en route to a Stokely–Van Camp convention in West Virginia and secretary of defense for international security affairs/secretary-designate of the U.S. Navy John T. McNaughton (1921–1967) and his wife and son. Georgiana "Jeorgina" Lopez Basurto (1945–1967), Grant E. Bubb (1905–1967) and Herbert Kiessling (1890–1967), each of Hendersonville, counted among the passengers on the commercial flight. Basurto's boyfriend, Kirby P. Rector (1943–1967) of Clyde, North Carolina, was also on board.

Officials believed the pilot of the commercial jet, Captain Raymond F. Schulte (1918–1967) of Norfolk, Virginia, had attempted to avoid the collision. Losing power quickly after the impact, Schulte made a right turn in what seemed to have been a maneuver to make it to nearby Interstate 26, where an emergency landing might have been possible. Investigations also revealed that the Cessna's pilot had likely been distracted while making dial changes to his radio settings.

Witnesses on the ground told news reporters that the smaller craft pulled up sharply and then exploded upon impact as the 727 briefly continued its progress forward at an altitude of 6,132 feet before suddenly nosing over, exploding into flames and breaking into two sections. Passengers, luggage and fuselage debris rained from the sky, and one human corpse crashed through the roof of a home. The body of a boy hung from the branches of a tree. Luggage, clothing and cocktail napkins drifted from above, snagging in the trees below. The calamity transpired above the airspace of the Holiday Inn motel and Martin Levine's Camp Pinewood,* where 145 children between the ages of six and fourteen years and a number of counselors took cover indoors and under canoes as wreckage and bodies plummeted to the ground. A profusion of the debris landed in and around the camp's dumpsite. Henderson County sheriff James F. Kilpatrick (1920–1976) dispatched every available piece of rescue equipment and each off-duty and reserve officer to the scene, and the North Carolina State Highway Patrol ordered its entire area force to report for duty.

Aviation investigators reassembled sections of the jet's fuselage in a field, which is now the site of McDonald's on Four Seasons Boulevard. In those days before fast-food restaurants, a muddle of signs and the Blue Ridge Mall

* Ulysses M. Orr's campground known as Orr's Camp, the namesake of the road, was predecessor of Camp Pinewood.

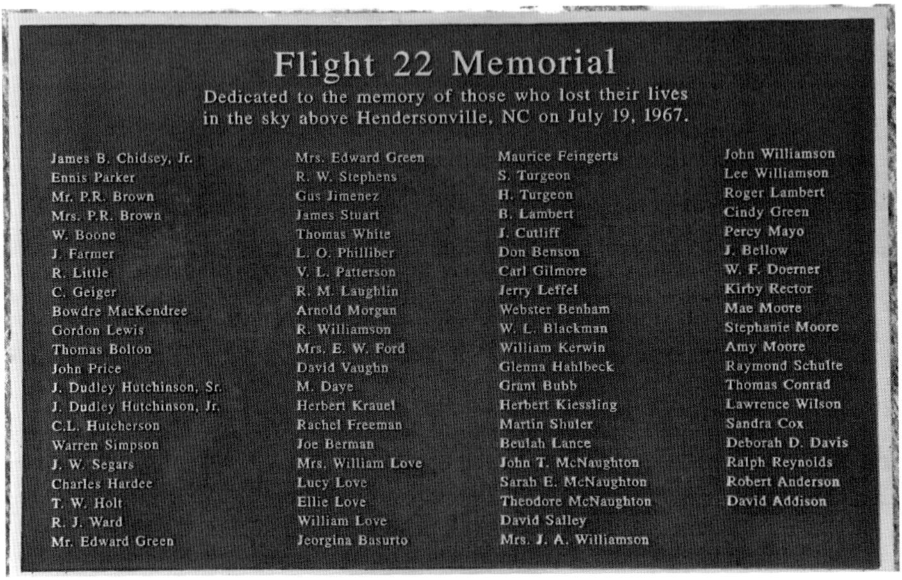

Paul Houle spearheaded efforts to erect a Flight 22 memorial. Mounted on a twelve-and-a-half-ton boulder, the bronze plaque documents the names of the victims. Officials dedicated the monument in July 2004.

cluttered the scenery, the area enfolding the crash sight was mostly rural greenways and the Blue Ridge Academy for Boys stood on the present site of the mall. Interstate 26 had not yet been completed.

In the aftermath of the tragedy—the first major accident investigated by the newly formed National Transportation Safety Board—officials worked to keep curiosity seekers and the media from the crash site as investigations proceeded. Hendersonville residents described the general atmosphere as solemn—for many days—as they attempted to persevere with their daily lives. Victims' families filed sixteen lawsuits seeking nearly $11 million in damages against Piedmont, Lanseair and others.

A memorial to the eighty-two victims stands one-quarter mile from the crash site at the intersection of Jack Street, Orr's Camp Road and Mitchelle Drive off Four Seasons Boulevard.

Copters Versus World's Edge

Sugarloaf Mountain claimed lives when a pair of CH-53 Sea Stallion helicopters on a routine flying mission—from the New River Marine Air Station

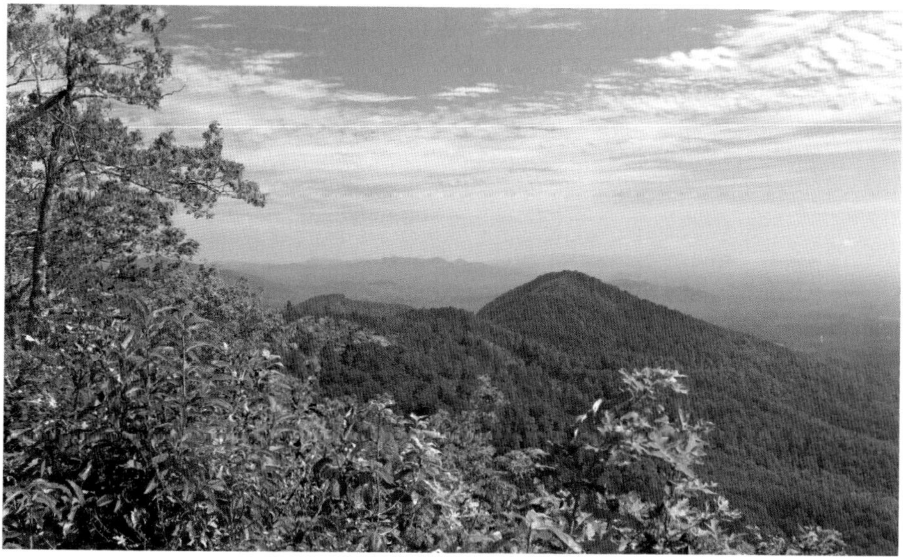

A view from World's Edge.

in Havelock, North Carolina, en route to Knoxville, Tennessee—crashed near World's Edge.

Planted at 3,930 feet on Sugarloaf Mountain, considered an "aviation crossroads," the Asheville VOR radio beacon tower serves as the chief signal for all aircraft traveling west through the area. Notwithstanding such an admonition, two choppers negotiating dense fog on March 11, 1977, crashed within moments of each other. Investigators speculated, besides the lack of visibility, that the copters had been flying too low. One of the CH-53s plowed directly into a cliff, bursting into flames and killing all four on board. Although seriously injured, the pilot of the second craft survived, as did two of his passengers, who were also injured. A wooded slope broke the fall of the second helicopter as it spun through the treetops, evidenced by sheered and toppled trees in its wake. In all, the mountain took five casualties that day.

Continued fog and rain hindered efforts as the Henderson County Rescue Squad, sheriff's deputies, EMS teams and a number of volunteers responded to the situation with ropes, bulldozers, chainsaws and the aid of generators to provide light. A newspaper article stated that there hadn't been so many people in the area since the great Indian battle at Point Lookout nearly two hundred years earlier.

Meanwhile, Sugarloaf awaits its next casualties.

Piper Versus Pinnacle

On August 23, 1985, a thunderous roar rattled the homes and nerves of residents on the sparsely populated slopes of the Pinnacle and Stone Mountain between the Green River and Crab Creek communities.

V. Leon Pace, resident of Sky Valley, Stone Mountain, recalled, "We were shaken from our sleep about 10:15 p.m., the noise so loud we thought the plane would hit our house. I ran to the back door to head outside when I noticed the door had been shaken open."

Other residents remembered the deafening growl of a low-flying craft as it sheered the tops of trees before plowing into a rock cliff face and then exploding into a ball of flames that lit up the night sky.

The point of impact, Stone Mountain, rises to 3,660 feet. Had the craft been flying only 75 feet higher, it would have continued its course without incident. Piloted by Hugh Van Pittman (1939–1985) of Dade City, Florida, the twin-engine turbo-prop Piper PA-31T slashed through treetops and flew into a cliff face approximately three hundred yards from the mountaintop on land owned by E.I. DuPont de Nemours and Company, Inc. The FFA later reported weather conditions as foggy and drizzly with visibility as low as two miles and that Pittman had not filed a flight plan. At about 8:00 p.m., the group had departed Louisville, Kentucky, where they had attended a cattlemen's convention. Pittman planned to land at Greer to drop off passenger James W. Carlisle (1949–1985) of Buffalo, South Carolina, and then continue to Florida with the rest of his passengers, Winnell Sanders (1952–1985), Robert Irvin Sanders Sr. (1937–1985) and Ruth Elizabeth Barthle (1966–1985), all of Dade City, Florida.

Rescue units from Valley Hill, Blue Ridge, Green River and Little River volunteer fire departments responded to the search effort. About 12:15 a.m., after cutting and bulldozing through dense laurel thickets and negotiating sheer rock cliffs and steep slopes, the rescuers—armed with flashlights—reached the mangled, smoking wreckage, which had been scattered around an area of four hundred to six hundred yards. Weather conditions and darkness necessitated the rescue units' calling it a night. Crews returned the following day and removed the bodies, but intrepid hikers can find wreckage on the mountainside to this day.

AFTERWORD

Time and nature conspire, extinguishing lives, eroding human monuments. This—plus unsustainable development and cryptic or mislaid records—goads the researcher to recapture the past before it altogether fades into oblivion.

Bygone places and personalities eventually let loose their secrets should dedicated inquisitors probe deeply enough, employing a combination of patience and perseverance, assembling a network of history-passionate people and crosschecking clues and hearsay against documents. At times, the course entails blood, sweat and tears. In pursuit of overgrown cemeteries and other sites, the researcher may likely be pricked and slashed while wading chest-deep through briar hells, stumbling and falling over woodland debris. I have hiked countless miles across gaps long since beaten through all manner of weather, scaling and rappelling treacherous slopes in the midst of predatory insects and venomous vipers, and have spent a small fortune on petrol between travels that crisscross what would seem every inch of Henderson County. And I have experienced moments of melancholy while poring through murder cases and air disasters, witnessing pent-up grief when interviewees fought back tears or broke down and openly wept.

Unsure of what drives all this, I nevertheless find the process stimulating, endeavoring as I do to bring times past to the fore—peering into yesteryear, documenting my conclusions through text and photography—in hopes of preserving yesteryear to enrich the future. Meanwhile, history continues to unfold.

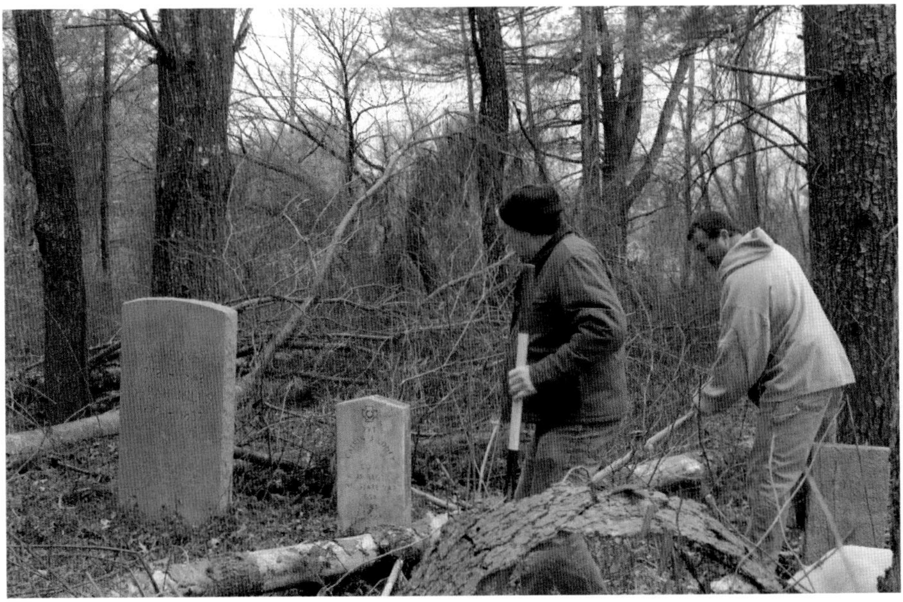

David Hill and Mark Splawn accommodating the author's research in the Asa Edney Family Cemetery.

To paraphrase Ellen Baldwin Heydock: This region is so different with the passing of time; so many who raised large families are no longer here, many of them departing for better employment or moving on to their heavenly rewards. Their homes have burned or rotted on the mountainsides, with new homes springing up on every available spot of land. Somebody please write the next chapters, lest some of the heritage be omitted and lost.

> *With his special gift for writing, together with the sharp eye of the professional photographer, Terry Ruscin is preserving much of our area's past and underscoring its promise of future enrichment.*
>
> —*Louise Howe Bailey, "Along the Ridges,"*
> *Hendersonville* Times-News, *2007*

BIBLIOGRAPHY

Addington, Omer C. "Methodism Comes to the Holston." *Historical Sketches of Southwest Virginia* 17 (1983).

Babb, Clara Capps. "Fruitland Institute: The Light That Has Not Failed." Unpublished paper. Henderson County, NC, 1965.

Bailey, Louise Howe, and Jody Barber. *Hendersonville and Henderson County: A Pictorial History*. Norfolk, VA: Donning Company Publishers, 1995.

Beddingfield, Octavia Freeman. *The Family History of Merideth Malone Freeman and His Descendants*. Henderson County, NC: self-published, 2006.

Bennett, Daniel K. *Chronology of North Carolina*. New York: James M. Edney, Publisher, 1858.

Bishir, Catherine W., Michael T. Southern and Jennifer F. Martin. *A Guide to the Historic Architecture of Western North Carolina*. Chapel Hill: University of North Carolina Press, 1999.

Bray, Mary, and Genon Hickerson Neblett. *Chosen Exile*. Nashville, TN: Rutledge Hill Press, 1980.

Durden, Robert F. *Electrifying the Piedmont Carolinas: The Duke Power Company, 1907–1997*. Durham, NC: Carolina Academic Press, 2001.

Fain, James T., Jr. *A Partial History of Henderson County*. New York: Arno Press, 1980.

FitzSimons, Frank L., Sr. *From the Banks of the Oklawaha*. 3 vols. Hendersonville, NC: Golden Glow Publishing Co., 1976–79.

Fruitland Institute: Catalogue and Annual of the Fruitland Institute. Asheville, NC: Inland Press, 1921.

Garren, Terrell T. *Measured in Blood: The Role of Henderson County, North Carolina, in the American Civil War*. Asheville, NC: Daniels Graphics, 2012.

Grissom, William Lee. *History of Methodism in North Carolina from 1772 to the Present Time*. Nashville, TN: Publishing House of the M.E. Church, South, 1905.

Hamby, Robert Palmer. *Brief Baptist Biographies, 1707–1982*. Vol. 2. Greenville, SC: A Press, Inc., 1982.

Hemphill, James Calvin. *Men of Mark in South Carolina; Ideals of American Life, A Collection of Biographies of Leading Men of the State*. Vol. 1. Washington, D.C.: Men of Mark Publishing Company, 1907.

Henderson County Genealogical and Historical Society. *Henderson County, North Carolina Cemeteries*. Spartanburg, SC: The Reprint Company, 1995.

Heydock, Ellen Baldwin. *Without the Master's Knowledge No Sparrow Falls*. Edneyville, NC: self-published, 1987.

Honeycutt, Frances F. *The Ones That Came Before: A Family History and Memoirs*. 2 vols. Baltimore, MD: Gateway Press Inc., 1989.

Hooks, John Augustus. *Salola Inn, Sugar Loaf Mountain, Hendersonville, North Carolina*. Brochure. Hendersonville, NC, 1921.

Howard Alexander Foushee: 1870–1916: A Collection of Newspaper Reports of His Life and Death and Editorial Comments Thereon. Pamphlet. Raleigh, NC: Sloan Foundation, North Carolina State Library, Digitized by the Internet Archive, 2012.

Huggins, Maloy A. *A History of North Carolina Baptists: 1727–1936*. Raleigh: General Board, Baptist State Convention of North Carolina, Edwards & Broughton Co., 1967.

Jenkins, Reverend Mark. *Calvary Episcopal Church: First 100 Years*. Fletcher, NC: Calvary Parish, 1959.

Jones, Daisy Barnwell. *My First Eighty Years*. Baltimore, MD: Gateway Press, 1986.

Jones, George Alexander, ThM, PhD, ed. *The Heritage of Henderson County, North Carolina*. 2 vols. Spartanburg, SC: The Reprint Company, 1988–2003.

Journal of the Executive Proceedings of the Senate of the United States of America. Vol. 8. Washington, D.C.: National Archives and Records Administration, 1848–52.

Kephart, Horace. *Our Southern Highlanders*. Alexander, NC: Land of the Sky Books, 1913.

Lininger, Jay L. "The First Commercial Use of Rare Earth Minerals: North Carolina's Monazite and Zircon Industry." *Matrix: A Journal of the History of Minerals* (Winter 2002–03).

Miller's Hendersonville, N.C. City Directories. Asheville, NC: Miller Press, Inc., 1915–65.

North Carolina State Board of Agriculture, Raleigh. *North Carolina and Its Resources Illustrated*. Winston, NC: M.I. & J.C. Stewart, Public Printers and Binders, 1896.

Patton, Sadie Smathers. *The Kingdom of the Happy Land.* Asheville, NC: Stephens Press, Inc., 1957.

Price, R.N. *Holston Methodism from Origin to Present.* Nashville, TN: Publishing House of the M.E. Church, South, 1904.

Ray, Lenoir. *Postmarks: A History of Henderson County, North Carolina, 1787–1968.* Chicago: Adams Press, 1970.

Sondley, Forster Alexander. *History of Buncombe County, Asheville, North Carolina.* 2 vols. Asheville, NC: Inland Press, 1930.

Styles, Marshall L. *My North Carolina Heritage: Descendants of Robert Edney and Anna A. Wrensher of North Carolina and Tennessee, 1660–1996.* Vol. 6. Simpsonville, SC: self-published, 1997.

———. *Western North Carolina's Revolutionary War Patriot Soldiers: A Collection of Their Records.* Vol. 8. John Lanning, Pension File W4711, Rowan & Buncombe Counties. Simpsonville, SC, 2010.

Sychra, Katherine Jones. *Levi Jones of Zirconia: Civil War Soldier, Country Doctor and Landowner.* Greenville, SC: self-published, 1980.

Taylor, Frederick Eugene. *A History of Tuxedo, North Carolina.* Tuxedo, NC: part I, self-published, 1967; part II, Friends of the Green River Library, 2005.

Thomson, Elizabeth Willcox. *Man of Vision: The Story of a Missionary-Priest, the Reverend Reginald Norton Willcox.* Edneyville, NC: Vision Enterprise, 1989.

Thue, William A. *Sugarloaf Stories.* Henderson County, NC: self-published, 2005.

Wilkie, Elizabeth Ann. "The Beginning of a Church." Unpublished paper, 1979.

Wood, Dorothy (Kelly) MacDowell. *Gleanings from the* French Broad Hustler, *Hendersonville, North Carolina.* 4 vols. Hendersonville, NC, 1991–96.

Zeigler, Wilbur G., and Ben S. Grosscup. *The Heart of the Alleghanies* [sic] *or Western North Carolina.* Raleigh, NC: Alfred Williams & Co., 1883.

Web Resources

ancestry.com
archives.ncdcr.gov
courtrecordfinder.com
duke-energy.com
findagrave.com

genforum.genealogy.com
hendersonheritage.com
joecowart.com
legacy.com
wikipedia.org
wikitree.com

INDEX

C

D

G

H

N

O

S

Y

ABOUT THE AUTHOR

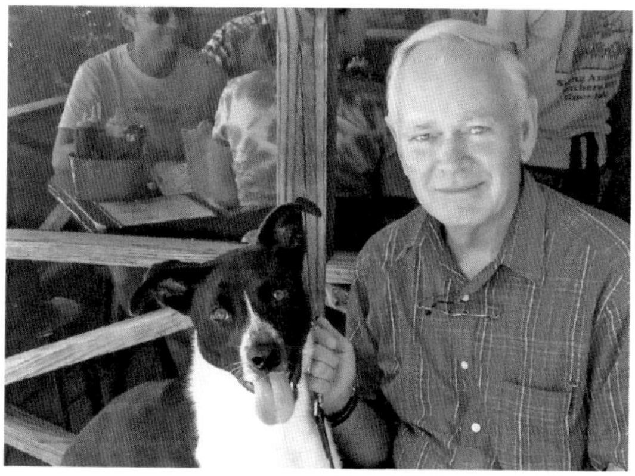

The author with his fur baby, Lucy Ann Barker. *Photograph by Charles A. Herrmann.*

Terry Ruscin, an author, photographer, researcher and retired advertising executive, is a member of the Henderson County Genealogical and Historical Society, Inc.; Historic Flat Rock, Inc.; and DRAC (Design Review Advisory Committee, overseeing the city's historic districts for the Hendersonville Historic Preservation Commission), as well as a commissioner with HRC (Henderson County Historic Resources Commission). Ruscin has served on the boards of the Henderson County Heritage Museum and the California Missions Foundation.

A graduate of Wayne State University in Detroit, Ruscin owned and served as creative director for Ruscin Advertising, Inc., in San Diego, California, before retiring to Hendersonville, North Carolina, in 2004. In addition to writing and research, Ruscin enjoys adventures with his dog, Lucy, and photographing architecture and the wonders of nature in western North Carolina.

Also by Terry Ruscin

Dining & Whining: Commiseration and Celebration for Gastro-Snobs

Hendersonville & Flat Rock: An Intimate Tour

Hidden History of Henderson County, North Carolina

Los Duendes: A Nostalgic Journey through Spain

Mission Memoirs: A Collection of Photographs, Illustrations, and Late Twentieth-Century Reflections on California's Past (Benjamin Franklin Award winner, 2000)

Taste for Travel: A Trilogy of Gastronomic Adventures: Great Britain, France, Italy

Terry Ruscin also collaborated on *An Uncommon Mission* with Father Jerome Tupa and coauthored and edited Louise Howe Bailey's last book, *Historic Henderson County: Tales from Along the Ridges.*